The **Pattern System**
for the **Bass Player**

Ariane Cap
with Wolf Wein

Sharpen Your Musical Mind
through Fretboard Proficiency,
Improvisation and Mental Practice

Editing by Steve Wilfong and Frederick J. Pucci

Cover Design by Carlo Dela Cruz

Photos by SN Jacobson and Aren Markousian

Book Design & Music Typesetting by Charylu Roberts

Skippy by Francesco Nardo

ISBN: 978-0-9967276-9-3 (spiral bound)

ISBN: 978-0-9967276-6-2 (perfect bound)

CapCat
— MUSIC MEDIA, INC. —

"The Pattern System and connection exercises will be a revelation for most bass players and should be an essential component of bass education. Ariane and Wolf present a beautifully comprehensive explanation of the pattern system with diagrams and assignments geared towards players with varying levels of experience. Furthermore, unlike most other music books, they actually address the fundamental process of practicing music. They show how to cultivate the proper emotional state for learning and present step-by-step instructions on how to learn using simple tricks like "cheater beats," "thinking ahead," "visualization" and "saying while playing." I would recommend this book to any bass player who wants to take their playing to the next level!

Josh Cohen
Bassist, Composer, Session Musician, Author and Music Educator

"I found The Pattern System to be a brilliant aid to master arpeggios and modes in all keys played from any position anywhere on the neck. Ari has managed to make the approach about as simple and logically compelling as it can be, providing a structural framework within which to practice and progress creatively."

Bill Speares, Student, UK

"The Pattern System is the path to electric bass fretboard enlightenment and it continues to provide benefits when you put down your electric and pick up your upright. Studious application of the concepts embodied in the Pattern System probably won't magically turn you into Jaco Pastorious but you will establish the ability to effortlessly locate the notes that you need wherever you are on the neck of your bass."

Carmie Hull, Student, USA

"Ari's Pattern System has completely opened up the fretboard for me in ways I never thought possible. There's no shortcut, but after 2 years with the Pattern System I can confidently find my way around in any key anywhere on the neck. What's more, I can explain it to help friends and fellow musicians while jamming and I've been able to apply it to learning the double bass. Thank you!!!"

Jeremy Sherman, Student, USA

"As a relative newcomer to the bass, The Pattern System has given me the ability to visualize the fretboard as series of interconnected shapes, discover shapes within those shapes, understand the theory behind them and how to apply them musically. They are also excellent for building technique, and there is no doubt that I will be practicing various elements of this system for the rest of my bass playing life."

Paul Bienick, Student, USA

"The Pattern System has been a great help in my improvising!"

David Sinclair, Student, USA

"Ari's Pattern System has opened up my bass playing. It's as if the fingerboard is talking to me as I play through songs, grooving, dropping in fills and improvising. Everything seems to light up in my mind… It's freeing and refreshing to now be able to navigate all areas of the bass."

Johnny Jones, Student, USA

"The Pattern System has started to unlock something I have been trying to open for decades."

Laurent, Student, UK

ACKNOWLEDGMENTS

We would like to thank **Dr. Howard Asher** for much appreciated psychological and business advice;

Frederick J. Pucci for valuable marketing support and additional edits, as well as for tireless help finalizing the videos;

Stephen Wilfong for editing the early versions;

Robert Bowlus and **Authentica Media** for help with the Indiegogo Campaign videos;

Heather Polley for thoughtful social media management;

Josh Cohen for enthusiastically playing through the exercises and diagram proofing;

Rob Smith for providing another expert check on the fretboard diagrams;

Andre Chen for drawing out the diagrams for the results section;

Carlo Dela Cruz for another awesome cover;

Charylu Roberts for beautiful book design;

and **Francesco Nardo** for expertly translating the teachings into pictures — **Skippy** is the star of this book and we bow to his beat with a smile!

CONTENTS

PRAISE FOR THE PATTERN SYSTEM FOR THE BASS PLAYER

"Ariane's The Pattern System for the Bass Player *is a landmark book! It presents a wealth of musical information with a thoughtful, systematic approach, designed to guide any student through the process of learning to create music with the bass. It is comprehensive and well organized, using a holistic learning paradigm aimed at developing the full constellation of skills involved in music making. I not only very highly recommend it, I'll be using it myself!"*

Michael Manring
Solo Bass Pioneer

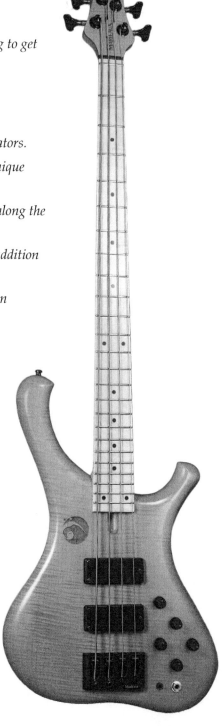

"Want to get comfortable with scales, phrases and the the entire fingerboard of you bass guitar!? Pick up this book. A compelling study for anyone looking to get vital insight in organizing and revealing harmonic knowledge."

Jimmy Haslip
Bassist, Co-Founder, Yellowjackets

"Over the years, Ariane Cap has quickly become one of my favorite bass educators.

Her new epic volume the Pattern System for the Bass Player *presents a unique all-round approach to the essential integration of rock solid basics.*

Her method comes embedded with a clever road-map skillfully nudging you along the often tricky road towards creative freedom.

While there are many excellent books available on the subject, Ari's work in addition stands out in its careful attention to the psychological aspects of practicing.

The delicate balance between the WHAT *and the* HOW *of practicing has been masterfully accomplished.*

In practical terms her approach will bring you much clarity and save you valuable time by uncovering hidden patterns, allowing you to discover the simplicity inside the world of often intimidating musical complexity. All of this comes wrapped in fun graphics and plenty of TLC.

Before you know it you'll find yourself skipping a movie night with this awesome book!"

Kai Eckhardt
Composer, Bassist

"Along with being a fine player, Ari has established herself as one of the top Electric Bass educators today. This publication is a wonderful addition to her catalogue and a great resource for any bassist."

Stuart Hamm
Bassist, Tapping Pioneer

"Anyone can show you a scale shape but it takes a master teacher like Ariane to help you unlock the true creative potential of scales and melodic patterns."

Rob Smith
Bassist, Educator

INTRODUCTION

What Is The Pattern System?

- Is this just moving shapes up and down the fretboard?
- Is it the seven-string bass method? Is it just another version of the CAGED concept?
- Is it the modes?
- Oh, I know those five patterns you mention! I don't need to read this book then, right?
- Is this just TAB?
- Are you saying if I study this, I don't need to know theory?
- Or that I don't need to learn how to read notation?
- Is this a magic bullet, so I don't have to practice?

None of the above!

The Pattern System is a comprehensive step-by-step method that — at a quick glance — trains you in the mastery of the fretboard by showing you a well-thought-out system based on five basic scale shapes.

While true, that just marks the starting point. At its core, *The Pattern System* teaches you how to think music and effortlessly translate it onto the bass. The scales, arpeggios, intervals, etc., are just the tools we use for this training. As you put this method into practice, you will gain deep confidence and previously elusive freedom:

- Your understanding of the instrument will reach a whole new dimension.
- As we explore patterns within patterns, you will train your musical mind to recognize and freely apply the patterns of music itself.
- Music theory shapes such as scales, arpeggios and common chord progressions will literally be at your fingertips:
  - In all keys
  - In all areas of the bass
  - Without looking at the fretboard or your hands
- Your technique will soar.
- Your new improvisation skills will surprise you.

The Pattern System teaches you to think ahead "in time." Think about the power and importance of that for a moment — being able to think ahead while the beat keeps going. This will make your timing much more solid, your improvisation more exciting, and your grooves and fills more creative. Rather than chasing the music, you are now on top of it. With that comes less stress, more relaxation, better accuracy and a more purposeful tone.

And because this system incorporates mental practice techniques, it trains you to practice with stunning efficiency.

- It will teach you how to listen to yourself.
- It will help the self-directed learner how to become his/her own coach.
- This method builds awareness, discipline, and determination.
- Some even say the study of this method builds character.

I have never seen a student whose playing was not vastly improved through the study of this method. You'll learn a very effective approach to practicing as well. Even if you do just a part of it, your playing and way of practicing will benefit.

You may think the claims above are exaggerated. Or you may think you don't need this book because you already know scales and arpeggios. All I ask is that you give it a serious try. Work with it for a few weeks, following the prescriptions precisely and allow yourself to be surprised by the results.

I want to caution you on one point with this method: it cannot be easily explained in a sentence or two. Rather, it needs to be experienced and worked with to appreciate its power and potential. If you give it a casual glance without actually working with it for at least a few weeks, you will at best vastly underestimate its power, and at worst, misunderstand and dismiss it.

NOTE: You will encounter a demonstration video of the method in a couple of pages. Look for this flag:

You can access all videos in this book by scanning this code with your smartphone or by simply visiting *ArisBassBlog.com/PatternSystem*

A free, one-time registration lets you access all the videos in this book.

What this book is:

- An introduction to *The Pattern System*
- A robust tool for the self-guided student and/or experienced learner, complete with a practice guide at the end of each chapter
- The most compelling and fastest way I know to get a true and thorough understanding of the fretboard
- A system to boost creativity and allow you to experience making music freely

What this book is not:

- A beginner's method
- All there is to this system (this book provides a solid foundation; for more resources and exercises, please see our course at *ArisBassBlog.com/PatternSystem*).
- A lazy shortcut (It is a shortcut alright, but one that puts you to work and covers the most important bases of the System.)

Keep in mind:

- Anyone can learn this. But if you are a complete beginner without a basic ability to produce notes on the bass and have no foundational theory knowledge, start with my book (and optional course) *Music Theory for the Bass Player* — then return here.
- This workbook uses some unconventional routines — keep an open mind.
- The method is suitable for academia. Professors, please peruse the teacher's resources at *ArisBassBlog.com/PatternSystem*.

TIP: This book can be used as a stand-alone method for the self-directed learner. But we also offer a variety of additional resources for those who want more guidance, including practice plans, courses with support, wall charts, practice groups, additional pattern paper for download, and resources for teachers. Find details or get in touch at *ArisBassBlog.com/PatternSystem*.

"The Pattern System"… Just Moving Some Patterns Around?

There are patterns involved alright, but let go of any preconceived notions you may have for the moment.

Before I practiced the system we are presenting you here, I could not in my wildest dreams imagine knowing the fretboard as well as I do now — and most importantly, conceptualize what this knowledge would enable me to do creatively!

When I mention patterns in the context of learning to play bass, most students think of the patterns formed on the fretboard by scales and arpeggios. Yes, you will learn those shapes, but these are just the beginning of the journey of connecting your mind, your music, your fingers, and your bass.

There are many kinds of patterns in music: scales, triads, pentatonics, intervals, but also melodies, sequences, and common chord progressions.

Yes, the book in your hand will address all these patterns and enable you to play them in any key anywhere on the fretboard, improvise freely according to their inherent structures, and understand and create basslines freely. And there is so much more — I will:

- Share **precisely how to practice** these shapes (with exact instructions on how to **embed them into your mind!**)
- Use some **unconventional methods** such as:
  - Practicing using visualization
  - Engaging internal hearing and targeted kinesthetic drills
  - Writing out shapes using pencil and paper
  - Forming creative associations to boost memory and recall
  - Doing exercises comprehensively all over the bass in a variety of combinations
  - Showing how to use these shapes in **creative contexts** (improvisation makes things stick!)
  - Demonstrating how understanding *shapes within shapes* will **guide** not only your **fingers** but also your **ears** and your **memorization** of tunes
  - Explaining how and when to incorporate the metronome

Most importantly, in this context, it will help you **think ahead**, which is one of the most powerful skills to have when looking to play with more freedom. In fact, this is so important that you get a little sidekick along for the journey. His name is Skippy. He is a metronome with an attitude. You will meet properly soon.

Watch this video

I want to show you an example of what this method will enable you to do if you practice as prescribed. Remember, this is but a few examples to show you where you are headed. We build up to that level step by step. Anyone can learn this.

The "Before" Test

If you want to test yourself, try improvising using only diatonic triads over this chord progression (a I – VImin – IImin – V progression in A, which then modulates to F):

$$\frac{4}{4}\|\!: A \quad | F\sharp min \quad | Bmin \quad | E \quad |$$
$$| F \quad | Dmin \quad | Gmin \quad | C \quad :\|$$

For the purpose of this evaluation, stay in *Area 3*, which in this case means you will be operating only between the **sixth and tenth frets.** Give it a go and see how well you are doing. Record yourself: this is your "Before" snapshot.

Then give our system a try and return to this exercise with much more ease and total command.

There is much more you will learn — your creativity will soar, and your technical abilities will improve dramatically. You will be able to express the basslines you hear in your head. You will have an easier time figuring out the music you hear.

Are you ready to take on the challenge?

Anyone can learn this, but it requires three ingredients (inspired by the teachings of Leadership Coach Marshal Goldsmith):

- **Discipline**. In this book, we show you exactly what and how to practice. Your part is to work on it regularly and consistently for the duration of these lessons. If you like, you can also join our cohorts and practice groups and use our many additional resources at *ArisBassBlog.com/PatternSystem*.

- **An open mind**. The mind is like a parachute — it works best when it's open. Some of the things we do are likely new to you. Be willing to give them a serious chance by working on them.

- **Courage**. Buckle up. You are about to enter unknown depths of musical joys and challenges. You got this!

HOW TO USE THIS BOOK

Consider it a Workbook!

Work through it:

- Bass in hand.
- Pencil in hand: answer the *Test Your Understanding* questions and fill in the diagrams. Don't use design applications on your tablet or computer. No copy/paste. No keyboards, mouse clicks and perfect circles. Rather, use a pencil and write directly into this book. (I will explain why we deem this absolutely essential soon!)
- Go in order, don't skip around.

Unconventional Methods

I invite you to have an open mind. I will introduce some learning techniques which may be new or curious to you, such as:

Visualizing

Throughout the book I give recommendations for effective practice. Heed them well because the mental processes that you learn in this system are even more important than learning scales and arpeggios all over the bass. They translate well to any other aspect of music (and life) that you will study.

Speaking out loud

From saying fingerings to scale degrees (great for ear training if done right!) to (gasp!) note names and pattern shapes — speaking out loud what you are doing makes it more real. This may be hard in the beginning, but a little goes a very long way and it gets easier quickly if you follow my instructions about getting into the *Zone of Learning*. The rewards are huge because speaking helps you acquire those very valuable *Thinking Ahead* skills.

Writing

See all these empty diagrams in the book? I was not trying to save on ink. As a matter of fact, you can find all the answers in the our Resources. But if you write out the assignments yourself, you will retain them much better. The finished diagrams will be personal to you and your mind will remember them more deeply than impersonal printed versions. I will give you precise guidance on how to fill them in! Think of these as puzzles — like fretboard sudokus. And in case you are wondering, doing these will count as practice time, very valuable practice time at that!

If you need additional pattern paper, you may download it from my website at *ArisBassBlog.com/PatternSystem*.

Appendix

The appendix contains valuable resources:

- **Definitions:** Find some important definitions ("pattern," "area," "tonic," etc.) there. Though I explain all this as you go through the book, there may be a moment where you need a quick refresher. Consult the *Appendix!*
- **Answers to the questions:** To check if you did the *Test Your Understanding* correctly, look in the answer key. Working them out yourself first empowers your learning process. And you will get faster with each study segment.
- **The diagrams:** Throughout the book you will fill in various patterns yourself. With some of them you can check your work in the back. In order to save on paper, we provide a complete listing of all diagrams via our online resources at *ArisBassBlog.com/PatternSystem*.
- **A brief history of this system**
- **Recommendations, authors' bios, how to connect**

Videos

As a reminder:

You can access all videos in this book, as well as a comprehensive listing of all patterns by scanning this code with your smartphone or by simply visiting *ArisBassBlog.com/PatternSystem*.

A free, one-time registration lets you access all videos in this book.

Make sure to watch Video 0!

Questions and FAQs

Questions will come up as you work your way through the book. Make a note of them; it is likely you will be able to answer them yourself as you continue through this method. Also check the many FAQs that are strategically placed throughout. If you can answer your own question, you are more likely to remember it. You are also welcome to join our monthly live Q & A sessions called "Ask Ari featuring Wolf" or the practice community we are building at *ArisBassBlog.com/ PatternSystem*.

A Note for Left-handed Players

All diagrams in this book show right-handed versions, so please reverse accordingly in your mind — or by taking a photo and mirroring the diagram in photoshop or a similar app.

Since you will write out most of the pattern shapes yourself, you may choose to stick with the right-handed pattern paper or download the left-handed version (download for free at *ArisBassBlog.com/PatternSystem*). Whatever you choose to do, I recommend staying consistent with that choice throughout your learning path.

Who should not work with this book (at least for now):

- If you are a complete beginner and have no knowledge of music theory basics, work through my *Music Theory for the Bass Player* book first. It starts from zero and moves swiftly to help you attain all the necessary prerequisite information. It also includes technique basics! Start there, or at least use it in parallel with this book.

- Those only wanting to learn songs, or are fine with just playing a bassline note-for-note using TAB or YouTube videos, and have no interest in knowing how to construct their own basslines, or how and why it fits into the overall arrangement — which is perfectly fine if that really fulfills you, it's just not what we are offering here.

- The casual player looking for a few quick tips to sound hip in certain situations. While you will sound plenty hip with the materials of this system, getting there is not a casual affair.

- Those believing that knowing the names of things takes the magic away. (Hint: it actually deepens the magic!)

- Those who want to focus exclusively on studying the style of their bass hero. While this system teaches you many materials that make such a study much more effective, this book does not analyze specific players.

Who this book is for:

- Bass players who long to express themselves freely on their instrument
- Those who want to play effortlessly in all keys
- Those who are open-minded and have a bit of discipline
- Those who believe that practicing and playing music can be satisfying and meditative (I will help you get there in this book.)
- Anyone who has an interest in acquiring a thorough knowledge of the notes on the fretboard
- Professionals, university students, or aspiring pros who want to be equally confident in any key, anywhere on the bass
- Hobbyists who want to improve
- Purely intuitive players who'd like to study applied music theory

The freedom that comes from knowing the fretboard that way cannot be overstated. It takes a bit of effort, but it is well worth it! What we teach here and how we teach it goes way beyond "moving some patterns up or down" — we give you a thorough grasp of the fretboard in a highly usable and creativity invoking way.

 How can I use this with my students?

I designed this program so teachers can use it in lessons effectively. It is also usable for an academic curriculum. We offer many resources for teachers, including lesson plans, tips for quizzing and assessments and more (info below).

If this method helps your students get a solid foundation, we are thrilled for them! It will also assist in allowing them to progress quicker in relation to your own ideas and special methods.

If you are an educator or advanced player experimenting with this method, we would love to hear from you! Get in touch with us at *ArisBassBlog.com/Contact*. If you simply would like to be in the know about teacher resources, please add your name to the teacher list here: *ArisBassBlog.com/PatternSystem*.

 I am an experienced player. I have my own way and style of playing. Is there something for me in this book?

Undoubtedly as an experienced player you have developed strong internal representations of the sounds of music and corresponding shapes on the fretboard. For some, this is a highly conscious process as they study (or create) a certain method. For others, it is a mostly unconscious process that likely developed over a long period of time.

View *The Pattern System* as we present it here like meditation practice. In meditation, one core practice is to focus on the breath and gradually let go of all other mental activity. Although you breathe all the time without thinking about it, there is great utility in placing your focus on each breath with attention, curiosity, and the intention to be more present. Similarly, this system and its many drills direct your attention to the "breath" of how you make music.

We offer a beautifully simple yet comprehensive and symmetric way of experiencing "the breath" and the patterns of music.

We invite you to give some of the later exercises in this book a go to understand the trajectory of the method and to experience their effect.

For example: try the *Connection Exercises* in the later chapters, the drills involving improvisation, *Shapes within Shapes*, or the exercises covering diatonic progressions. Make sure to follow the instructions precisely to get their full benefit. Then, if this seems intriguing, start from the beginning following the method. This is a step-by-step system that is best pursued from beginning to end as it builds on specific and well-thought-out processes.

In addition, we trust that you will pick up ideas on how to practice and apply them to your own routines — such as using improvisation with targeted precision, using sequences other than the cycle of fifths, perhaps using diatonic chord progressions for such improvisation drills and the like. Your tried and proven strategies and exercises may well fit into some of the elements we offer here, and we hope you take them as inspiration.

Experienced Musicians

I love having conversations with musicians (and composers) on questions such as:

- How did you come up with this amazing groove?
- You played this incredible solo — what happened for you in that moment? How did you know to do what you did?
- What did you think, feel, see, hear inside in those moments?

Most often these questions are first met with "I don't know. It just came to me." If I persist, some talk about internal representations: "I heard it and then played it!" "I saw the notes appear." "I closed my eyes and felt the fretboard." "My fingers moved without me thinking about it."

Others relate to a specific physical sensation: "Some feeling in my chest told me it was time to go into a different section." "I felt an arc building; I felt something lifting." "It seemed like I was somehow outside of my body." "I just closed my eyes and felt as one with the band."

Yet again others cite an external trigger: "The drummer played this little fill that took me to another place."

Most report a sense of "flow" and a complete absence of judging or otherwise interfering internal voices.

I have also seen some players get quite protective of that process and prefer not to talk about it, often out of concern that the magic might be destroyed or interrupted when looking too closely or analytically. Others experience the opposite, namely that it is possible through mindful practice to deepen the magic and the inspiration that flows from it.

I have forever been fascinated with this sacred and mystical space — the responses I get; the way I, in my own musical endeavors, aim to "chase" or prepare for these magical moments; and how I can help my students drink from that well. While the description of this space is quite elusive, it is also the sort of thing where "you know it when you found it" applies. *The Pattern System* and the approaches I describe in this book are the best vehicles I have found to succeed on this path.

This is because the type of practice we do in *The Pattern System* includes:

- Multitasking on high levels
- Sustained focus
- Internal work that directly translates to its physical application
- Promoting more relaxed playing through consistency and thinking ahead
- Knowing the fretboard inside and out
- Learning through improvisation

And the practice is quite specific. — I explain:

- The Levels of Learning ("Unconscious Competence")
- The channels of learning/representation (in this context, especially the ones I call "musicality" and "spirituality").
- Being your own coach, by listening to yourself and by applying constructive self-evaluation
- Attaining the ideal *Zone of Learning* when practicing
- And the section on self-talk is an important one in this context as well — interestingly, the negative voices seem to be completely silent in these moments of *Flow*.

If you can relate to this treasure hunt, you may be intrigued to use *The Pattern System* practice to decode music according to the various senses (visual, auditory, kinesthetic, conceptual, musical, spiritual).

Beginners*

Even complete beginners intuitively know that the magical space I described above exists — witnessing our heroes evokes it; it is often what draws all of us to try this in the first place.

I have never been satisfied with answers chalking musical abilities up to mere "talent," or to "you either have it, or you don't." No matter their predisposition, no matter their particular path to music, motivated students who are willing to put in the work can experience satisfying results and become one with the music.

In general, "talent" is often overrated, or at least not the most important aspect. Sure, some things such as a feel for rhythm, a naturally good ear, or having an easier time with reading, technique, or theory are highly individual. However, I have seen student after student — including those starting later in life — make big strides towards competency with the right guidance, even if they encounter big difficulties at first. I have yet to meet the person who really wanted to learn but just could not manage to improve. Talent will develop with the right ingredients: a sound attitude, reliable consistency, great (teaching) materials, and suitable feedback. This will beat so-called "raw talent" in the long run. And even "talented" people need to work on their craft.

Learning paths are also individual to some extent (and are rarely fast enough!), but after leading hundreds of students through *The Pattern System* (and my other programs), progress has become quite reliable and way more predictable than even I would have thought at first.

PREREQUISITES

I have been teaching this system for a long time and to a wide variety of playing levels. Interestingly, no matter the experience level of the player, the program is always the same. An advanced player will use more facility — especially in the improvisation exercises — than a more basic player; the process, however, is always the same. A student working through this book should grasp a few basic concepts and be able to play the following on the bass:

- Note names
- Intervals
- Triads
- Major scales and their modes
- Basic rhythms
- The "Diatonic Cycle"
- The Circle of Fifths

My book *Music Theory for the Bass Player* as well as the optional accompanying online course of the same name are the ideal preparation for *The Pattern System* because they describe the most important aspects of music theory that are relevant to a bass player. I demonstrate these aspects of music theory directly on the bass and provide a variety of creative exercises to help make these concepts your own. I created both the course, as well as the book with the 89 accompanying videos as an introduction to the book you are holding in your hands.

---

* I advise complete beginners to read and work through *Music Theory for the Bass Player* before working on "*The Pattern System*" because it provides a solid theory and technique foundation.

Also essential:

- A general command of the bass (basic skills absolutely suffice, you should be able to play notes on the bass.)
- A fundamental grasp of bass technique

I explain all the technique essentials in *Music Theory for the Bass Player* as well.)

HOW TO READ THE DIAGRAMS

We use pattern paper (or "fretboard paper") to write down the patterns. Pattern paper represents the fretboard.

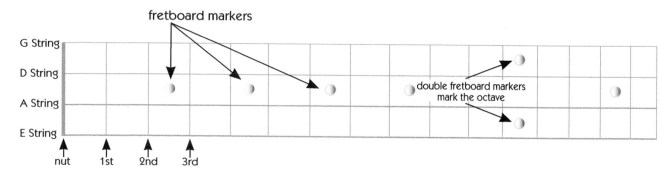

Fretboard markers are between frets on most basses.

Notice the thickness of the line — it corresponds with the gauge of the string. In essence, you will look at the diagram as if you are looking down on your bass — the E-string is closest to you and is represented by the thickest line. Imagine placing the diagram straight from the page under your bass. Do not reverse this (unless you are left-handed).

If you are left-handed, please reverse accordingly as you are going through the book.*

Here is a sample pattern to show how its contents are labeled (for demonstration purposes only):

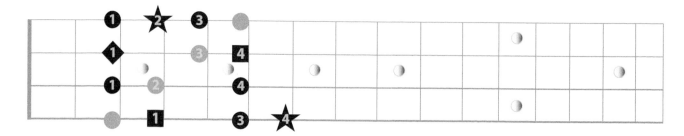

- A circle (or dot) signifies a note.
- Grey circles show the notes of the parent scale when we display *Shapes Within Shapes*.
- Squares mark the tonic of the major scale.
- A diamond marks the relative minor scale or other non-tonic root important in the context (later chapters).
- Stars mark blue notes in the blues scale.

---

* We have included left-handed pattern paper for download at *ArisBassBlog.com/PatternSystem* as well for your convenience.

- Grey numbers designate fingerings.
- White numbers signify scale degrees.

The diagram on the previous page shows the E blues scale (with fingerings inside the G major Pattern).

Notice that I place the dots close to the point where the fret and the string intersect. Ideally, you place your finger exactly where the dot shows — this will assure a buzz-free tone.

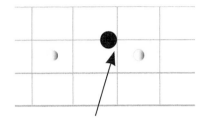

On the fretboard, this looks like this:

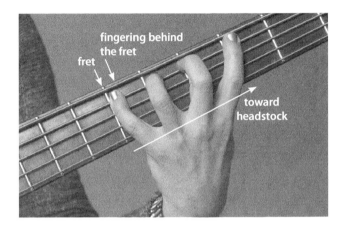

NOTE: I use the terms *patterns* and *shapes* interchangeably at this stage. We will go into much greater detail regarding this later in this book, but please consider these terms the same for now.

PROPER TOOLS

Any four-string electric bass will work. Stay away from fretless and short-scale for now (see below).

Do You Play a Five- or Six-String Bass?

All diagrams, videos, and explanations in this book feature a four-string bass. If you play a five- or six-string bass, that does not mean that you have to toss this book (or your bass).
Rather, you have two options to work with this method:

1) Work through the system in four-string fashion on your five- or six-string bass. Just use the E-, A-, D- and G-strings and skip the rest. Or,

2) Print extra pattern paper (see appendix) and write out five- or six-string versions of the patterns.

I highly recommend taking the first route until you have the hang of the system because:

- **The symmetry of the four string diagrams helps with the visualization exercises.**
- **It is simpler without any drawbacks for your learning.**
- **It allows you to stay in sync with the book without having to do additional work.**

The way to do this is to just ignore your low B- and/or high C-strings. You will see that once you have the patterns under your fingers, you can easily extend them to include all strings. Learn the shapes in the four-string version first and study all four-string diagrams. (Watch for an FAQ on that later!)

My advice differs for the *Open Area* which includes open strings:

- I recommend that you write out the *Open Area* for your number of strings. You will use this area a lot, and you want to be proficient when including the low B- or high C-string. You can download five-string or six-string pattern paper at *ArisBassBlog.com/PatternSystem*.

- As for all other areas on the bass, I usually recommend learning them four-string style at first and ignoring the extra strings. The reason for this has to do with proper fingerings and with getting the hang of the patterns. In addition, most find visualizing the patterns in their symmetric four-string forms much easier. If you'd rather not disregard some strings, then at least do it four-string fashion for *Chapter 2*. It will help you get the hang of fingerings.

What if You Play Short-Scale? Or How About Fretless?

I advise against a short-scale because it will likely not be your main bass in many of your band activities or recording life. *The Pattern System* provides you with excellent technique practice, and it would be a lost opportunity to do this on anything but a regular 34-inch (or longer if you prefer) scale bass.

As for fretless, your intonation will improve vastly if you work your way through *The Pattern System* on a fretted bass following my one-finger-per-fret prescriptions. To train your fingers for precise placement (= good intonation), I recommend you always place them as close to the frets as possible. Obviously, your orientation and fretboard knowledge will apply entirely, even if your bass has no lines. But the lack of frets makes transferring the visualization exercises to the fretboard more challenging because such a fretboard provides much less visual feedback or recognition.

As a somewhat extreme example, doing the practice on a short-scale bass and then playing fretless on the gig has a lot of potential to backfire badly — it will likely result in most notes being out of tune.

Instead, focus on learning *The Pattern System* on the 34-inch fretted bass, then reap the benefits on the fretless later on — it will be great for your intonation! Feel free to play other basses: short-scale, fretless, U•basses® in your other activities.

TIP: Throughout your *Pattern Practice*, stick with one particular bass to facilitate your kinesthetic and visual learning. This bass should be regular scale length, fretted and have fret markers on the fretboard, not just on the side of the neck. The diagram paper I use also shows these fret markers. They become a visual anchor helping you to get into *Pattern System* learning mode. You will start seeing that particular bass in your mind's eye when doing the visualization exercises.

 How do you determine the scale length?

Measure the distance between the two spots where the strings touch down on your bass — the bridge and the nut.

PLAYING WITH A METRONOME (PART I)

You could use a sidekick for this journey you are about to embark on. And I have the perfect one for you:

Meet your new buddy: Skippy MacBeat!

Skippy sometimes gets a bad rap. That he sounds — or makes you sound — mechanical or stiff, for example, or that he prevents you from developing your own internal sense of timing. Some even claim that he can hold you back from figuring out a passage that may still be too hard to play at the designated tempo.

I must defend him here: Don't blame user error on Skippy (he is sensitive, you know!)

If used correctly, the metronome will:

- Help your precision, technique and timing immensely (nothing new here)

- **Not** make you sound "stiff"! Rather, it's bad habits such as these that are responsible for a player sounding stiff:

    - Not thinking about phrasing

    - Not practicing phrasing

    - Playing with tension and other technique challenges

    - Chasing the notes

- Benefit your repertoire learning and feel because it gives you confidence that you know the notes in time

- Prepare you for the use of the click in studios, musical theater and other productions

- As for the *Pattern Practice* — Skippy will keep you honest and stave off denial or imprecise self-assessment. Like the good friend who tactfully lets you know that you have some parsley stuck between your teeth, Skippy will prevent you from thinking you know something when in reality (meaning: in time!) you do not!

Psst, Skippy, you, um, got some parsley, um...

Skippy will keep you on track and make your practice vastly more effective. (I am not exaggerating — he is a superstar!)

For the *Pattern Practice* you *will* need a metronome. This is absolutely non-negotiable, no ifs, no buts, no excuses! Here's why:

- Following the unwavering stoicism of the metronome will greatly help you develop your skills experiencing and practicing music in your mind.
- Using a metronome correctly transcends finding the right tempo and hitting start. As you progress through this book, I will show you:
  - How you know whether to use a metronome for a specific drill or not
  - How to play and think in time
  - How to track the accuracy of your playing while you are playing, which is essentially the same as playing with other musicians like a drummer
  - What to be mindful of as you use it
  - What determines the best tempo for a particular exercise at any given time
  - A variety of ways to use it creatively in the *Pattern Practice* to drill those important "thinking ahead" skills

Any kind of metronome will work:

- An app (for a fancy version check out the *Time Guru* app)
- A complimentary metronome inside your browser (*https://www.google.com/search?q=metronome*)
- A free-standing battery-powered one (see *ArisBassBlog.com/Resources* for my favorite model)
- Or a good old-fashioned wind up one such as Skippy himself!

Just make sure it has an easy to reach on and off button and that you like the tone. Personally, I prefer woodblock tones to bleeps and beeps as they sound more pleasant and — often are shorter and have a more defined attack, which helps with accuracy.

Nice-to-have features but not essential for our purposes:

- A "downbeat" option, meaning the metronome can identify the "one" in the most common time signatures.
- A "subdivision option," meaning the metronome can divide the beat into various subdivisions.

 **TIP:** Smartphones and computers, with their incessant notifications, present hazards to your focus. I highly recommend using a stand-alone model. Put your smartphone into a different room and focus on *Pattern Practice* in a distraction-free zone.

Many creative ways for metronome use exist, such as going at incredibly slow tempos, eliminating random metronome beats or placing the beat at unexpected spots in the subdivision (the latter two can be done using an app or Digital Audio Workstation). These great drills will help your internal sense of timing, your pocket, and your technique and speed. For the *Pattern Practice* we use the metronome first and foremost to expedite your fretboard knowledge by helping you to think ahead, so Skippy will perform in quite the traditional way. In this book, Skippy is the star and a true genie in a lamp.

Genie Skippy — Call on him and he helps you make the magic happen!

FURTHER RESOURCES AND SUPPLEMENTAL MATERIALS

The book you are holding in your hands is a complete, stand-alone resource. If, however, you wish for additional support or assets, we offer several, such as:

- A wallchart with all patterns, area maps, and all the practice tools you need
- Practice groups
- A course and a course with support ("Cohort")
- Additional Pattern Paper for download (in various versions)
- Resources for teachers and other supplemental materials

Please visit *ArisBassBlog.com/PatternSystem* for details.

I highly recommend you use all of these tools within the context of this method. To get the full benefit, study the system as we are presenting it here.

THE OPEN AREA

What Do I Call the Open Area?

On the bass, I call the area between fret zero (i.e., the open string) to fret four the *Open Area*.

One-finger-per-fret will set you up so that you can play a chromatic scale without shifting. Each finger has its assigned home.

Play the following notes and say all note names:

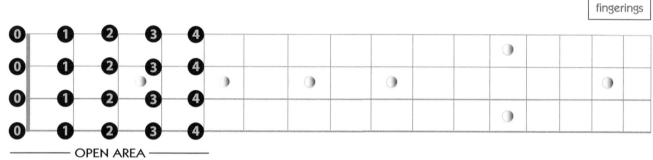

OPEN AREA ───────
frets 0 through 4

We typically number the left-hand fingers on the bass as follows:

    1 = index finder

    2 = middle finger

    3 = ring finger

    4 = pinky

    0 = no finger, the open string

NOTE: For the *Open Area*, the fret numbers coincide with the fingering numbers, so finger #1 plays the first fret, finger #2 the second fret and so forth.

Now I pick out and name only the notes in the key of G major, like this:

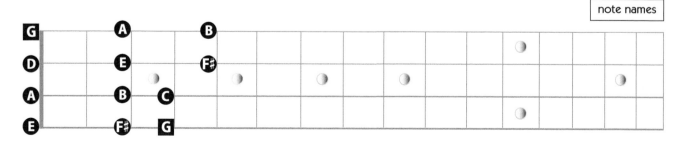

Now translate this to fingering:

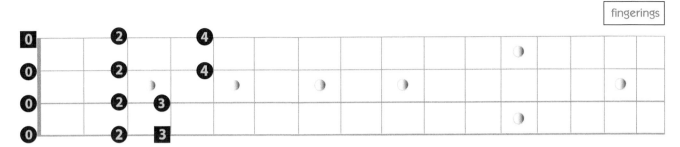

fingerings

Notice that in *The Pattern System* we always go from the lowest possible note to the highest possible note in that area. Our defined area here, the *Open Area*, comprises frets zero to four.

The pattern above — correctly named "The *Open Pattern* or *Pattern Zero* of G major" — contains all notes of the G major scale but does not start on the tonic. The low E and F♯ — while part of the scale — do not mark the beginning of the scale. Because of the way it sounds, your ears may tempt you to rename it the "E minor scale." After all, it will sound like all notes relate to the first note you played, E, hence making it E minor. In this case, try to hear it as G major, starting on the sixth scale degree below the tonic. The good news is that if you view the patterns this way, every pattern contains every mode of the major scale. We will talk more about this later. For now, pay attention to the shapes and the location of the tonic of the major scale within that shape — it serves as a sonic and music theory reference.

Writing Out All Keys – Open Area "Area Map"

Your turn to write out all fifteen keys!

Wait a minute, I get to do all the work?

Yes, Skippy — and for good reason: you will retain the information much better by writing it out yourself.

Writing

I mentioned in the introduction that we integrate writing your own patterns as a valuable learning tool. Rather than me writing out pages and pages of patterns and scales for you, I want you to write them out yourself — and by hand.

The Romans knew: *Scribendo Discimus* — we learn through writing! For that reason: do the assignments with a good old pencil and use the paper in this book! If you do the assignments on a computer, you will start to copy and paste a lot — which is a good exercise for symmetry but robs you of the learning you will experience by writing it by hand.

The process of handwriting your own patterns accomplishes several important things:

- Handwriting deeply engages your mind. Think of it as one way of learning how to materialize your thoughts.

- You create your own unique visual of these patterns, and this unique image will become the basis for your visual recall (just like your unique hands form the basis for your kinesthetic recall).

- Putting in the work yourself ensures that you will value the information more, which in turn makes it easier to recall.

▌▌▌ **NOTE:** You can find many of the solutions to the exercises you will work on throughout this book in the appendix — or for a complete listing of all patterns, go to *ArisBassBlog.com/ PatternSystem*. You can also access the included videos and find all patterns there.

▌▌▌ **TIP:** Use a pencil and an eraser. Or try erasable Frixion™ gel pens or markers — they "pop" even more than pencil. Because we will be using these diagrams in visualization exercises, their look proves very important. You could make empty circles and just add the number/note names in. But in your mind's eye, you see big dark dots easier than thin pencil outlines. That is why I recommend erasable Frixion™ pens and markers. The markers have some thickness to them, which accelerates the filling of the dots and squares. If you use a saturated color for the dots and squares, you can add fingerings or note names with the gel pen on top. If you make an error, just erase and redo!

VIDEO 3 ▶

The Open Area Diagrams

In the space below, write out all 15 keys. You will do these at least two times. Hopefully more!

These are the options I suggest you write out:

The circles with note names, Key of C, *Open Area*

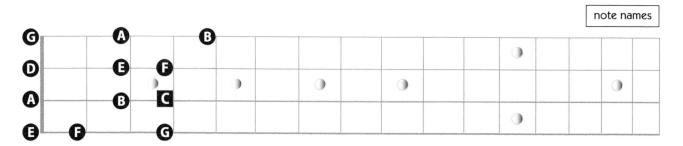

note names

The circles with scale degrees, Key of C, *Open Area*

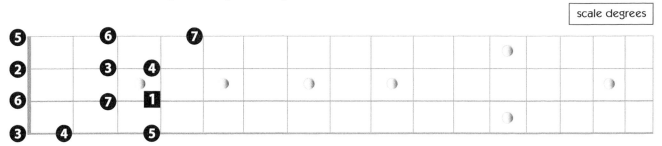

The circles with fingerings Key of C, *Open Area*

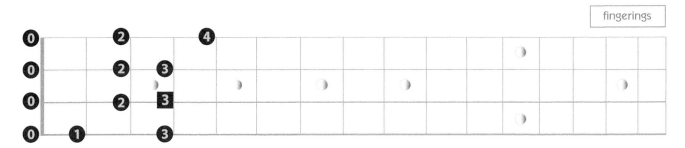

Just the circles (optional, but recommended for visualization purposes) **Key of C,** *Open Area*

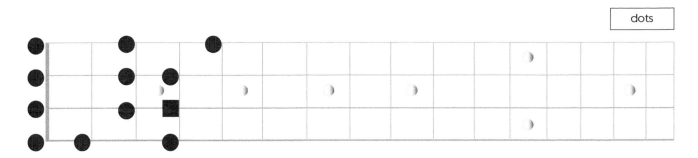

In the beginning, I recommend you write out several, if not all, of these options. This is excellent practice that will help you ingrain these scales in your memory. It also serves you to become familiar with the process of writing out your own patterns — a crucial part of this system.

TIP: Make your diagrams look neat. Even if you would describe your handwriting as "horrible," take your time and give it your best shot. Pattern paper for 4-, 5-, and 6-string basses is available at *ArisBassBlog.com/PatternSystem.*

REMEMBER: In *The Pattern System,* you will not go from root to root (for now!). **Instead, I want you focused writing out all the notes that belong to a certain key in that specific area.**

Make sure to stay in the *Open Area* between frets 0 to 4.

A good place to start is to find the root of the scale (i.e., the tonic) and fill in the notes above and below the root according to your knowledge of the key signature or scale.*

Here is another example in the key of D:

note names

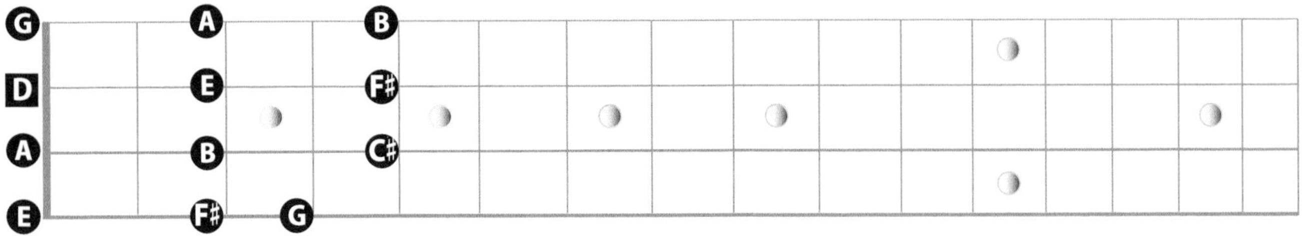

scale degrees

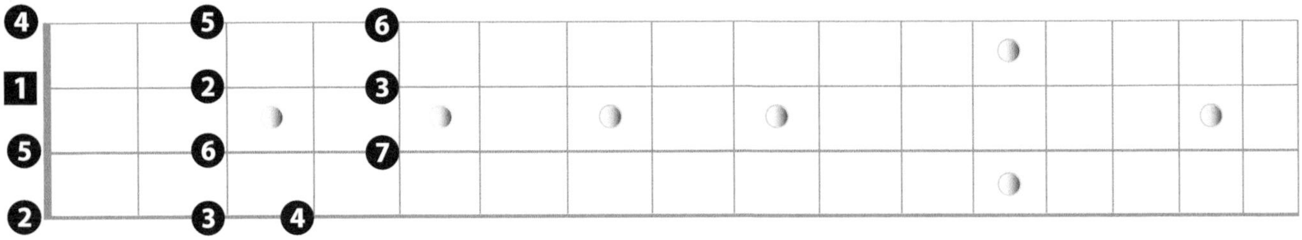

fingerings

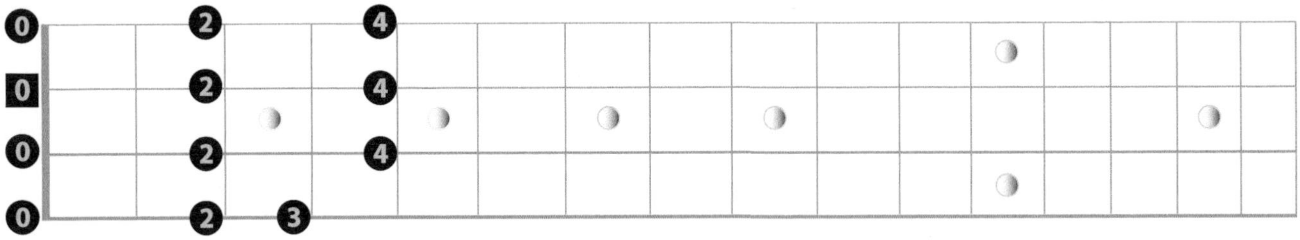

dots

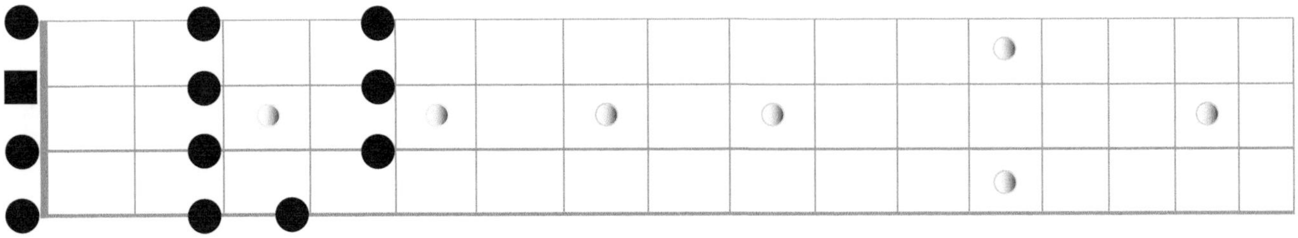

* If you do not know how to create and name scales correctly, please refer to *Music Theory for the Bass Player*.

LIKE THIS

Now play this pattern a few times, like this:

- Ascending and descending. Start from the lowest note and play to the highest, then reverse direction.

- Start from the highest, play down and back up.

- In order to calibrate your ears to the key, also do this:

  - Start on the tonic, go all the way up to the end of the shape.

  - Turn around, go all the way to the bottom end of the shape.

  - Turn around again and land on the tonic you started on.

This brings your ears up to speed, helping inform you if you got it right or not.

Your turn to write out the diagrams!

Staying in the *Open Area*, write out all the scales in order of the Cycle of Fifths using circles/squares starting with note names, then scale degrees.

Write the **flat keys** out in the order of the cycle to the left, i.e., descending fifths (C, F, B♭, etc.).

Write the **sharp keys** in the order of ascending fifths or the cycle to the right (C, G, D, etc.). This will help you get used to writing the patterns and finding all the keys.

Check each scale by starting it from the tonic, playing the entire shape in either direction and ending on the tonic. That way you can check them with your ears.

I have written out the order for you on the pages that follow. Just fill in accordingly!

Open Area – The Flat Keys – Note Names

C

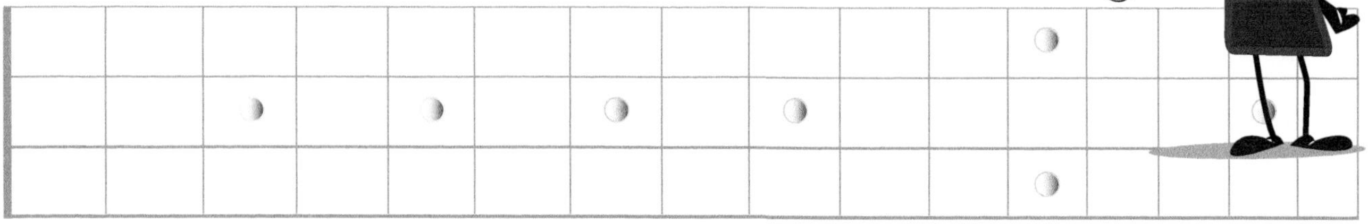

F

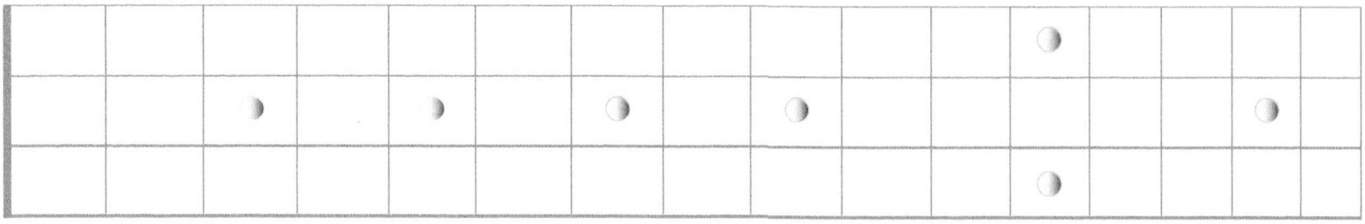

B♭

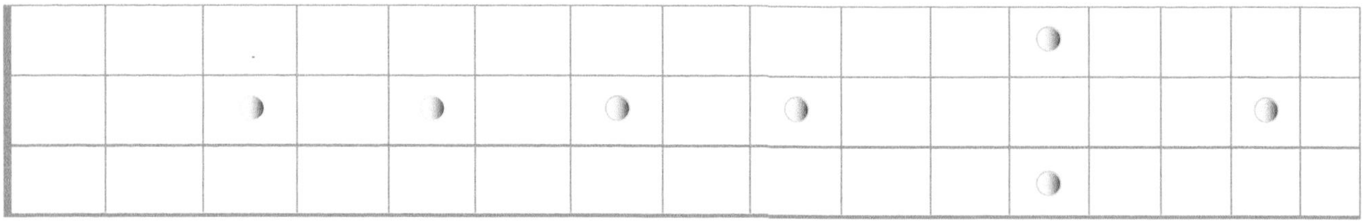

E♭

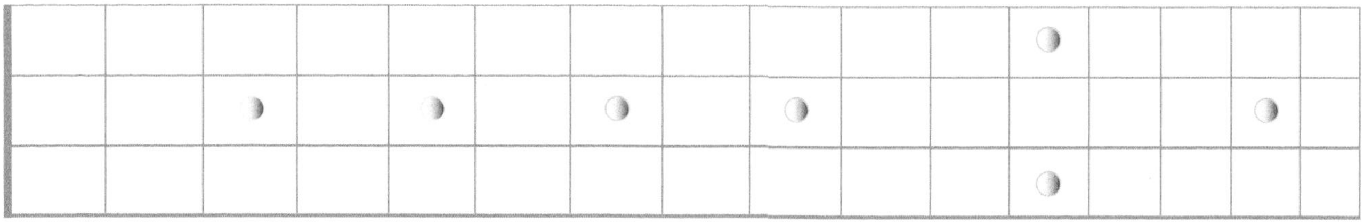

A♭

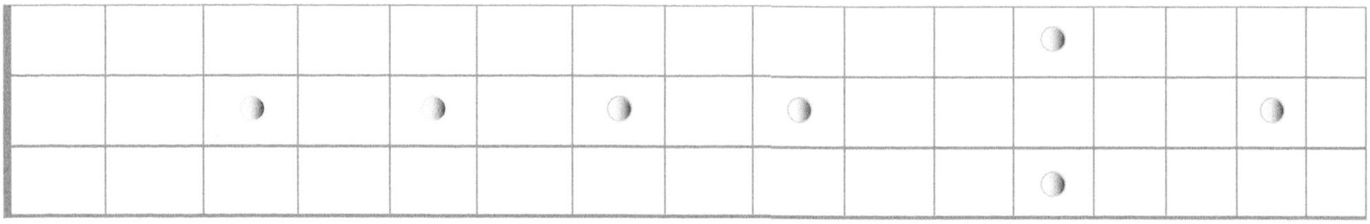

Db

Gb

Cb

Open Area – The Sharp Keys – Note Names

G

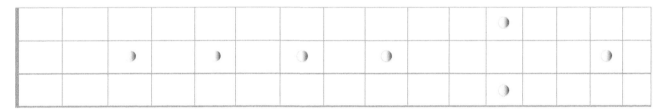

D

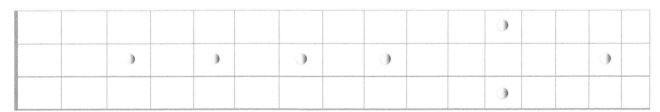

A

E

B

F#

C#

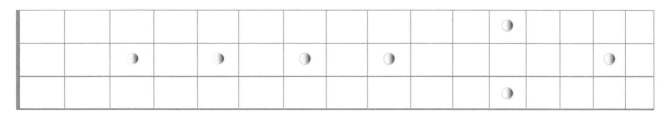

Open Area – The Flat Keys – Scale Degrees

C

F

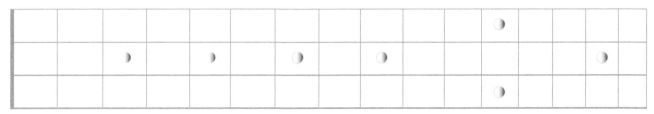

B♭

E♭

A♭

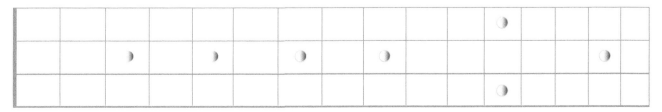

Db

Gb

Cb

Open Area – The Sharp Keys – Scale Degrees

G

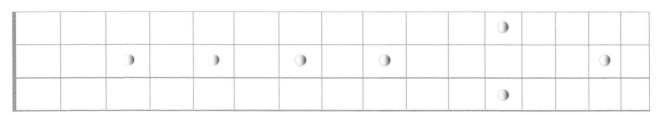

D

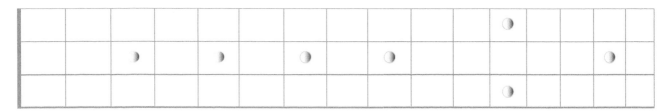

A

E

B

F#

C#

Now that you have written out all the keys in the *Open Area*, let's practice them.

Practice each scale in the following manner:

- Ascending and descending saying note names, scale degrees, and fingerings
- Descending and ascending saying note names, scale degrees, and fingerings
- Ascending only saying note names, scale degrees, and fingerings
- Descending only saying note names, scale degrees, and fingerings
- Starting on the root, all the way up, all the way down, and then back up to the root

TIP: You don't have to work on all of these in every practice session. Start with just a couple of keys, say the fingerings one day, nothing the next, note names the next. Start the shapes ascending on even calendar days and descending on odd ones. Keep it varied — switch things up! No need to execute any of this perfectly before trying something new! On the contrary, keep things moving, fresh and interesting.

Saying elements out loud

If you hear yourself say it, you will remember it better. I will often ask you to underscore your practice by saying out loud what you are playing.

Doing so makes it more memorable and helps you double-check to ensure what you think you are playing matches what you are in fact playing.

Saying note, chord or key names adds the conceptual layer of knowledge (more on that later). It will strengthen the connection between the names of things and where they are on the bass. Your sight-reading will also benefit immensely.

This is what you will say out loud:

- **Fingerings** — these cement the knowledge of the pattern and add a layer of awareness as to which fingers you are using. This is a great place to start the habit of "saying while playing."
- **Scale degrees** — how will the next note sound? These remind you of the relationship of each note to the tonic and each other! If you know the traditional practice of Solfeggio using "moveable Do," as in "Do, Re, Mi…", then you know how powerful this way of thinking is. I prefer going straight to numbers rather than adding an extra layer using syllables. Numbers are reflected in many chords (Cmaj7, F6, Dmin7♭5), and they represent a "sound." As an extra challenge, try keeping the tonic in your inner ear (or sing it) while playing the pattern. This also strengthens your awareness of each note to the tonic and turns *Pattern Practice* into a powerful ear-training tool!
- **Note names** — great for theory, communicating what you play, sight-reading drills as well as for notating music.

- **Keys and chord names** — (which are covered later) for when you practice chord progressions and changing keys.

- **Nothing** — There will be times when saying words out loud while you practice will slow you down (at least initially). That's okay since speaking out loud engages your analytical/conceptual mind. Of all the different "minds," the conceptual one is the slowest. The benefits of engaging it by speaking are still well worth the effort, but as an alternative, just say nothing. Simply play and focus on all your non-verbal experiences. Before long, you will be able to "switch modes": play by patterns alone (visual, kinesthetic), play by conceptual understanding (the names and theory of the materials), or a combination of both. The aural component is always present — always listen to what you're playing. Much more on these channels of perception in *Chapter 7*.

If the prospect of multitasking like this seems daunting — don't worry. This often presents quite the challenge in the beginning. Start with saying the fingerings, which are the easiest to do; then say scale degrees (and relate the numbers to the sound of the scale degree!); then say note names.

Remember that **doing just a little bit at a time will go a very long way here. Start with a slow tempo.** The way I structured this system, you will easily find your way. Just like all my students, if you hang in there, you will get there, step by step!

Because of the various notes we have available as open strings, the *Open Area* presents the only area on the bass where each scale has a completely unique shape. On a four-string bass, only four of the major scales do not contain any of the open strings, namely F♯ and C♯ and their enharmonic equivalents G♭ and D♭. On the six-string, all keys involve open strings and have a unique shape.

Technique Tip: Use the one-finger-per-fret setup!

- Great news! In the *Open Area* you never have to shift — every finger has its assigned fret. Even if not actively pressing that fret, it's best to have the finger hover close to that fret.

- This makes sight-reading easier as each finger has its place — no need to look at the fretboard to figure out where a finger needs to go.

- It enables consistent fingering of common shapes all across the fretboard.

If you have trouble with one-finger-per-fret in the lowest area of the bass, make small micro-shifts until your fingers have become limber enough to stay close to the frets without shifts.

VIDEO 7

- *The Pattern System* works well with the one-finger-per-fret approach, where the visual and kinesthetic representations reinforce each other. You will particularly come to appreciate this fact when we leave the *Open Area* as there are only five other patterns in total.

- This setup allows for a more consistent tone because shifts are minimized.

- Keep your hand relaxed. If you find yourself over-gripping, let the fretting hand drop, take a breath, relax, and pick it up again. Most issues with the one-finger-per-fret setup in the lower register have to do with too much tension and working against yourself. I have very small hands myself and have no problem navigating a full-scale bass in the lower register. We have several tips to help you with this in upcoming sections, but *Music Theory for the Bass Player* contains an extensive section on technique (in *Chapter 12*).

NOTE: If you play a five- or six-string bass, I invite you to learn the *Open Area* for your number of strings. For this purpose, download and print five- or six- string paper at *ArisBassBlog.com/PatternSystem*.

Now that you have written out all these shapes, you have created an overview of the *Open Area*. Your fingers are getting used to these keys and shapes, to one-finger-per-fret, and to starting and ending on the highest or lowest note rather than only going from the root to the octave. A great start, and so much more yet to come!

Practice Tip: How Do You Know if You Really Know a Shape?

The short answer is — when you can recall it instantly and play it from any starting point in any direction. Aim for knowing the shape as a visual image or shape in your mind.

If you are unable to find the shape without saying the note names they describe, it means that there is a lack of familiarity with the shape. Similarly, if you can only play the shape by starting and ending with the tonic, it means your knowledge is coming from your ears rather than the shape itself. **It is very important that you know the shape from all directions and as a combination of visual, kinesthetic, aural and conceptual representations**.

If necessary, bring back the diagrams, look at them until you have them memorized. Saying fingerings (while playing or while just looking and imagining the fingers move) can help greatly in getting the shapes down.

Saying note names affirms the notes and will also greatly facilitate your sight-reading and music theory. That said, it shouldn't become a crutch, as mentioned above.

Once you have left the *Open Area*, only five shapes remain to be memorized. So in many ways, *Areas 1-5* will be easier to learn.

 What about the keys that occur twice?

There are three keys that occur twice in the cycle:

F♯ or G♭, C♯ or D♭, C♭ or B.

Of course, these enharmonic shapes will look the same in terms of black dots, fingerings, and scale degrees. However, they will differ in their note names. You will think differently when you conceptualize a scale as D♭ as opposed to C♯, for example. **Do both versions!** These keys do occur, and you want to be comfortable with them. To test how different the sharp versus flat versions feel, say the note names of G♭ versus F♯, or B vs. C♭ back to back.

So yes, you will be repeating a few shapes where just the title is different and all else is the same. Still, do it! **You learn through writing. It constitutes mental practice. It firmly embeds these patterns in your mind when you create them yourself from scratch in numerous variations.**

 Are you always playing one-finger-per-fret? What about situations of recurring octaves or fifths, such as songs like Taste of Honey's "Boogie Oogie Oogie" or Donna Summer's "I Feel Love"?

Within the system, we use one-finger-per-fret fairly strictly because it is good to have a system to follow as you learn. In practical applications, you can approach your fingering with more freedom and use what works. But you will find that being able to use one-finger-per-fret adds a level of flexibility that you otherwise don't have. It will contribute to much smoother shifts in many playing situations and give you many more options. Adhere to it strictly in this book.

Scalar Studies
Two-Note Groupings

Scalar studies cement your knowledge of the patterns, present a terrific technique workout and give you materials for grooves, fills and solos.

Note grouping drills (and soon interval studies) help you to:

- Further ingrain the patterns by changing up the order of notes
- Cement your knowledge of scale degrees
- Introduce effective variations of the tonal material that you can use in fills, solos and runs instead of just scalar sequences
- Increase your comfort of the one-finger-per-fret fingering and give you great finger fitness
- Create a library of cool licks — these interval studies are great material for solos and provide a good alternative to purely scalar lines

NOTE: Rather than write out note-for-note what to play, making this purely a reading exercise, I want you to find the sequence yourself. I am starting you off with a few measures to give you the idea of the exercise. Then you take over! I will also write out the descending version as there can sometimes be more than one way to reverse the exercise. Your task will be to correctly transpose the exercise into the various patterns and keys yourself!

While I could write it all out for you in all the keys, I remind you that you will realize a much bigger benefit by figuring out these exercises for yourself. That way you commit them to long-term memory!

Don't be surprised when some of these runs start showing up in your fills and solos! You might like the way it sounds.

Practice saying out loud:

- Note names
- Scale degrees

Saying scale degrees can be especially challenging in the beginning, so feel free to go slow and without a metronome at first.

In the examples below, I show you how to connect two-note groupings in a simple way. You will encounter many more variations on note groupings throughout the book. I am demonstrating this in the key of D, in the *Open Area*:

VIDEO 8

Here is another example, in the key of A♭:

Your First Exercise

Improvisation exercises present the perfect opportunity to make these patterns "stick." They will help you ingrain the shapes further and give you a taste of the creative freedom we are going for here because you are practicing the frequent and instant recall of this information in a musical context.

Pick one of the *Open Area* keys. Practice it. Then try the following *groove and fill* exercises:

In the notation examples below, beat one is defined in rhythm and pitch — it is the "groove kernel," the part that stays the same.

Beats 2, 3, and 4 are notated only as a rhythm using slash notation. Improvise with **notes of the scale using only the *Open Area* patterns (frets 0 to 4)**. Repeat the exercise in one key for several repetitions, then move on to the next key.

Improvisation Blueprint:

Aim to use all the notes of the shape over the course of the exercise. Scalar runs always sound driving. To create contrast, also experiment with repeating notes, such as in bar 4 above. Overall, aim for scalar runs at this stage. Vary the starting point of your fills and make it groove by playing with steady timing and consistent tone qualities (e.g., tone lengths, dynamics)!

Creative Exploration: Listen Closely!

Ask yourself:

- What effect does a scalar run have compared to a more static one, such as bar four?
- What is the effect of an ascending run versus a descending run?
- Pay close attention to the note on beat three of each measure, a heavy beat. Make it a chord tone and observe the effect. Then make it a non-chord tone. What do you notice? For what situations might you choose one over the other?

Finding words to describe music and how it makes you feel helps you understand many aspects of it. Besides deepening your appreciation, this will also facilitate the analysis of styles and shape the creation of your own lines. If you feel a bit lost answering the above questions — try contrasts.

For example:

- Driving versus static
- Moving the groove forward versus laying back
- Playing "inside" (chord tones on heavy beats sound very inside and stable) versus dissonant or suspending (non-chord tones on heavy beats tend to have that effect)
- Playing an ascending line can create a lift, whereas a descending line can create the sense of a pull towards gravity

Mind you, with all the above examples, one option is not inherently "better" than the other — it depends on context and what you are looking to express!

 Groove and Fill Exercises are fun and all, but if I play like that in a band situation won't it sound too busy?

Yes, it might indeed! We designed this exercise to give you flexibility and a thorough knowledge of the notes being used, not necessarily to play like that in every single measure of a tune! In a band situation, use your artistic judgment as to whether something fits the song or not. A few fills in carefully selected places are way more effective than overplaying.

How do you know when and where a fill "fits"?

It typically does not work so well if your line interferes with or steps on the melody or someone else's lick, riff, fill or break. Ask yourself if the fill enhances the story or energy of the song or if it's just meant to impress everyone with awesome virtuosity. Too many fills, consequently making every bar sound different, will prevent you from establishing a steady groove.

So why are you recommending this exercise then?

Besides helping you ingrain the various patterns, it provides you with an opportunity to focus on practicing the fundamentals of the *"Art of the Fill."* Imagine the value of having an endless repertoire at your fingertips and the freedom to use it when it makes sense.

Realize the power of trying a variety of options and asking yourself questions like the ones I asked above.

What you are striving for is for the instrument to "disappear" in your hands so the music can flow through you without inhibition. Aim for not having to guess or fish for notes. These exercises help you know what notes and note combinations will sound like before you actually play them. Imagine the freedom that comes with that!

TIP: Want to try a bass solo of a different kind? Try a groove solo! Use essentially the "groove and fill" exercise as a starting point! A groove solo will keep the dancers dancing and still gives you the option to improvise. The fills can be longer, go into every range of the bass and be more elaborate. Have fun!

TEST YOUR UNDERSTANDING #1

1. Does a pattern always start on the root? ☐ Yes ☐ No
2. How about always ending on the root? ☐ Yes ☐ No
3. Which frets does the *Open Area* encompass? _____
4. Why could you run into a bit of trouble practicing *The Pattern System* on a short-scale bass and then playing a long-scale fretless at the gig? _____
   _____
5. Imagine the following patterns in the *Open Area* on the fretboard (use your bass if needed). What note is the highest note that is part of the pattern and what finger plays it?
   a. F major __
   b. B♭ major __
   c. E♭ major __
   d. A♭ major __
   e. D major __

  **BLUEPRINTS FOR PRACTICE**

At the end of each chapter, I offer a suggestion for a concise practice plan that you can follow. You will pick up a lot of material as you work through this book. Practicing everything in all keys and all areas may seem overwhelming. Rest assured that **you do not need to practice everything everywhere at the same time**. If you follow the system, you will cover all the bases.

I have distilled down several non-negotiable exercises and spread them out into a manageable practice plan. There is utility in skimming many exercises and practicing others really well! Mainly: There are only so many hours in the day and often we must be selective on what we can focus on.*

- If you are a hobby player, go at your own pace! **Keep moving along**, come back to some drills later, and remember that **even a little goes a very long way! Recognize the exercises are merely a goal. Work towards it at your own speed.**

- If you are an aspiring pro player or on an academic track, **put in the time and reap exponential rewards.**

As you move through the chapters, the material in this section will continue to grow. Teachers may find the additional teaching resources helpful. Check *ArisBassBlog.com/PatternSystem* for resources.

A few more Tips:

- I encourage you to make your own practice planners and lists, and check off the exercises off as you go.

- Do not get stuck on a particular exercise or vow to only move on once it's "perfect." You will revisit similar exercises over and over. Keep going!

- Remember that going slowly but steadily helps you get there faster.

- I will tell you in later chapters how to be your own coach. If something is too hard, throttle back. Tips for this will follow. You are in control. Keep going!

- Quality over quantity — focus and pay attention to the details (note names, click, etc.). This is demanding mental work. Allow yourself a short break when you need to refresh your ability to focus.

- Aim your attention at regular practice rather than practicing a lot one day and not at all on others. Five times a week for fifteen minutes is better than two hours on one day.

- If you are in an academic environment or are working through this with a qualified teacher, count yourself lucky. Having tests and a witness is extremely powerful in this process!

If you would like additional resources and support, including practice groups, and courses, please find them at *ArisBassBlog.com/PatternSystem*.

---

* If you are looking for a guided structure and many more new exercises, check out our additional resources. Info is at *ArisBassBlog.com/PatternSystem*.

Abbreviations used in Blueprints for Practice:

PP: *Pattern Practice.* Unless otherwise specified, this refers to major scales. In later chapters you will do various triads and pentatonic scales in **Triad PP** (Triad *Pattern Practice*) and **Pentatonic PP** (Pentatonic *Pattern Practice*).

SS: *Scalar Studies.* This refers to interval studies, note groupings and other drills designed to help you ingrain the patterns technically.

IE: *Improvised Explorations.* These exercises help you use the patterns in creative contexts and to inspire to find your own creative language using the patterns of music.

BLUEPRINT FOR PRACTICE #1

Written Homework: Write out all *Open Area* diagrams into the book (note names and scale degrees).
   pp. 22–27

Practice:

1.   PP: Practice the chromatic scale in the *Open Area* as described ascending (fingering = 0,1,2,3,4) and descending (fingering = 4,3,2,1,0)
   Say note names: sharps ascending and flats descending.
   Bonus: Say note names: flats ascending and sharps descending. **p. 16 • Video 1**

2.   PP: Practice C and the flat keys in the *Open Area* as described:
   • Ascending/descending
   • Descending/ascending
   • Starting on the tonic(s)
   • All ascending only
   • All descending only
   Say fingerings, scale degrees, note names. **p. 21 • Video 5 and p. 28 • Video 6**

3.   SS: Practice two-note scalar groupings in the *Open Area* in the keys of C and in all of the flat keys.
   Say fingerings, scale degrees, note names. **pp. 31–32 • Video 8**

4.   IE: Practice *Groove and Fill* improvisation exercises in the keys of C, F, B♭, E♭, A♭ in the *Open Area* with a metronome or jam track. Treat each key as a separate exercise. **pp. 33–34 • Video 9**

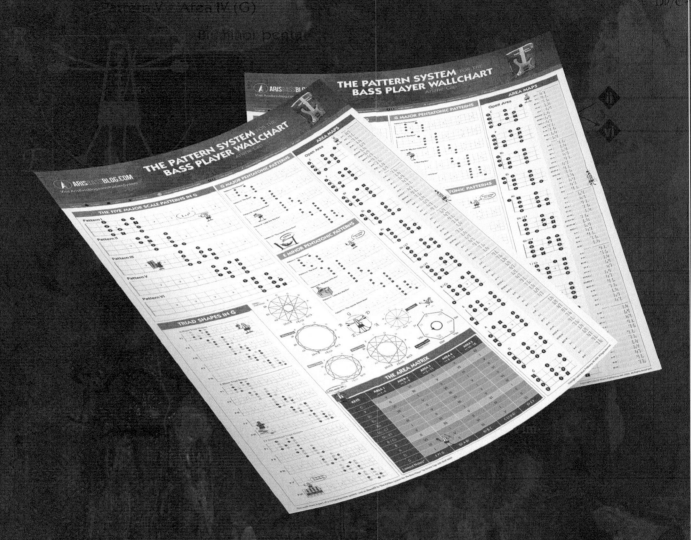

The Five Shapes

FIVE SCALE PATTERNS TO RULE THEM ALL

No need to travel to Mordor! Once you have worked on the *Open Area* with its unique pattern for each key, you will rejoice in the fact that in the following areas, things get a bit easier. Without open strings in the mix, this system uses only five scale patterns for all keys. They repeat over and over — truly five patterns to rule them all! And some may even look familiar from the four-string *Open Area*.

▌▌▌ **NOTE:** The power of the "five scale patterns to rule them all" truly becomes apparent when we explore the *Shapes within the Scale Shapes*. The first and quintessential step — getting these scale shapes or patterns ingrained in your mind — will pay off exponentially as you will quite literally know them "inside and out!"

Mastering the Five Scale Patterns

The First Three

First, you will learn the five patterns all in one key, up and down the neck. You will be doing that in the key of G, which has just one accidental and is the relative major key of Em. Therefore, G lends itself well as a starting key. In addition, G starts with *Pattern I* in *Area 1*, which — as you will see — makes it a great key to stake out the map of all five patterns.

I am starting you off with the *Root Pattern* (aka *Pattern I*), then *Pattern V*, followed by *Pattern III*.

Patterns derive their names from their lowest note (in relation to the tonic of the major scale). This is true for all shapes except for *Pattern I,* which should be called *Pattern VII,* or *VII/I.* However, this obviously is a bit cumbersome. Also, technically, the term *"Tonic Pattern"* would be more precise since the central note of a key is called the tonic*, but *"Root Pattern"* stuck over time and seemed to ring a bell with my students. It starts with the seventh note of the scale, but the root (and in this case tonic) follows as a quick second note in the sequence. Therefore, we just call it the *"Root Pattern"* or *Pattern I* (abbreviated as *PI*).

▌▌▌ **TIP:** As in the *Open Area*, remember that starting on one of the tonics, then ascending to the highest note, then descending all the way down to the lowest note and finally going back up to the tonic helps you hear the pattern in the context of its key. Make sure that you don't become dependent on starting with the tonic. You want to have the shape under your fingers without relying on the auditory cues. In upcoming exercises, you will switch keys on the fly (just as music does!). I want you to know these patterns so well that you can start *anywhere*, including at the top of the shape, at the bottom of the shape, or anywhere in between.

More tips on this learning process will follow. At this point, your goal is to get the shapes totally under your fingers.

---

* The distinction of "tonic" versus "root" will come in very handy once we work our way through the diatonic triads.

This is what I mean by *knowing the pattern*:

- The shape — get it into your muscle memory.

- Take a mental snapshot of the diagram so you can see the shape in your mind's eye.

- Know the **name of the pattern.**

- Be familiar with the **location of the tonic(s)** within the pattern.

- Say the **fingering** out loud when you practice.

- Also, the **scale degrees.**

- And the **note names** (again, speak them out loud at times).

- Have the pattern in your muscle memory from all directions (including starting on top, the bottom, or anywhere else).

- Be able to play these shapes quite **fast**. Faster than you could think scale degrees or note names. You don't want to reinvent the wheel each time; rather, you want to have instant recall. (Remember, there are only five!)

Skippy reinventing the wheel

Pattern I or "Root Pattern"

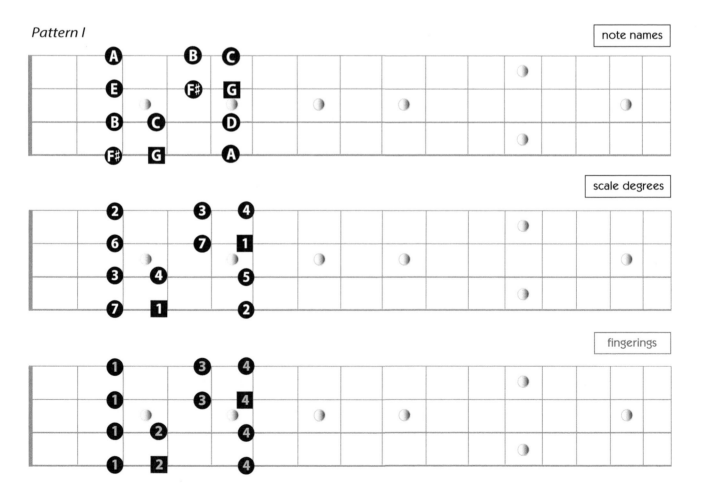

LIKE THIS

- Play it starting from one of the roots — all the way down, all the way up, back to the root.
- Play it starting from the lowest note, then ascend and descend.
- Play it starting from the highest note, then descend and ascend.
- Play it starting from random spots within the pattern.
- Do the above saying fingerings out loud.
- Then saying note names out loud.
- And also saying scale degrees out loud.

In the *Root Pattern*, the roots of the major scale occur twice, namely on the E- and D-strings.

Observe that only these two fingers ever play the root in any of the five major scale shapes: **the second finger or the pinky.**

This is true for all five patterns. *Remember this vital fact – it will help you find the patterns all over the fretboard in future exercises!*

NOTE: *Pattern I* already revealed itself in the *Open Area* as Gb/F# major!

Pattern V

No exceptions here: *Pattern V* — true to its name — starts on the fifth note of the major scale. In G major, this is D. As always, play from the lowest note in the pattern to the highest. Find the D on your E-string on the tenth fret.

VIDEO
11

Pattern V

note names

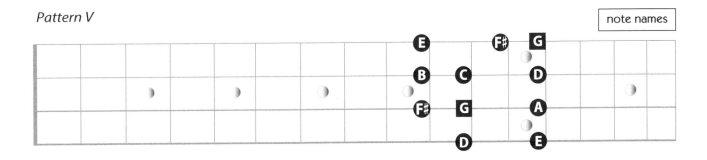

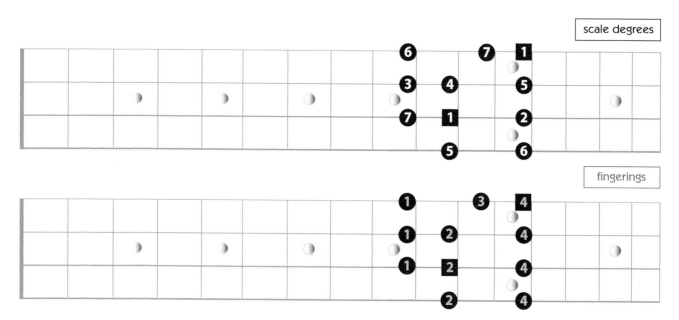

Practice *Pattern V* in the same way you practiced *Pattern I*, by saying fingerings, note names and scale degrees. Practice using all your senses, zoom in on what you are doing by focusing your awareness just like you would in meditation. In addition, mechanically train your muscle memory by playing the shape over and over "by rote." Stay aware of the locations of the roots and focus on smooth movements in your hands. As always, aim for familiarity from any starting point and in any direction.

> Just like *Pattern I*, the major roots occur twice in *Pattern V*, namely on the A- and G-strings.
> And again, pinky or second fingers play the roots!

NOTE: The specific "challenge" of this pattern is that it starts with the second finger.

TIP: Notice how Pattern V contains a big part of *Pattern I*. In essence it is *Pattern I* — plus two notes below:

Pattern V

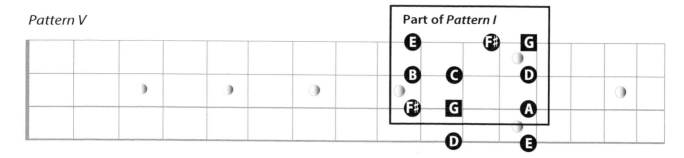

If you had an extra string on top, such as a five-string bass tuned E A D G C (AKA tenor tuning) or a six-string bass, you could even include *Pattern I* in its entirety above *Pattern V*. (As mentioned, I recommend practicing the shapes four-string style first. However, everything repeats, so once you have the hang of four-string style, you can fairly easily extend the shapes to the low B- and high C-strings that exist on five- and six-string basses.)

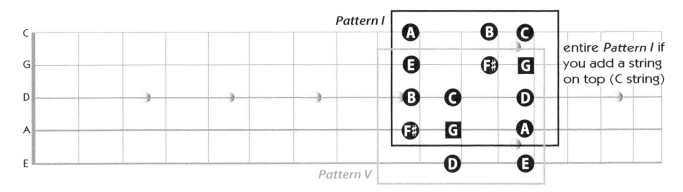

entire *Pattern I* if
you add a string
on top (C string)

Pattern V

▌▌▌ **NOTE:** *Pattern V* has already shown up in the *Open Position* as B major, with the addition of
the open E!

Pattern III

The third note of G major is B, so *Pattern III* starts on the note B on the E-string. We viewed *Pattern V*
as the same as *Pattern I* with two notes below the shape (the D and E).

You could view *Pattern III* as the upper part of *Pattern I* with two notes on top (interestingly, again,
D and E, the two extra notes that you found on the lowest string in *Pattern V* you now find on
the highest string in *Pattern III*.

VIDEO
12

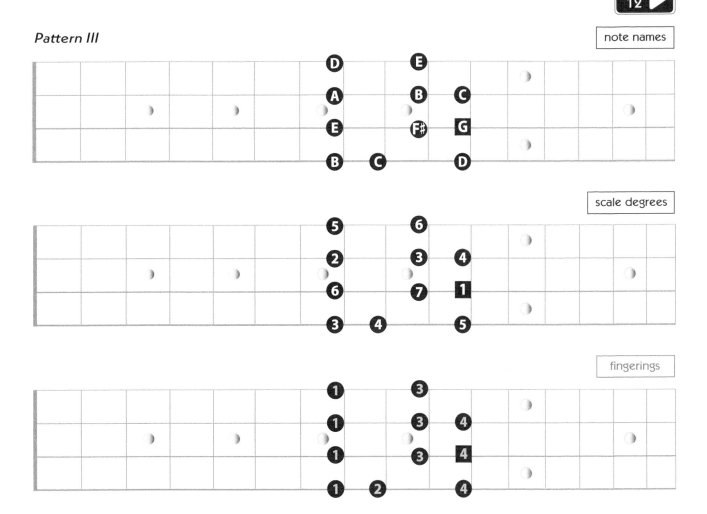

Pattern III features the root only once— namely on the A-string — fingered by the pinky. Pattern III starts with the first finger but ends with the third finger — so be mindful of the correct fingering when playing it descending.

Practice as discussed earlier.

▌▌ **NOTE:** *Pattern III* already showed up in the *Open Area*: D♭/C♯ major reveals itself as *Pattern III!*

The "Crab" Fingering

- So far you learned *Patterns I, III,* and *V*. I have two more for you: *Pattern II* and *Pattern VI*. Both feature a one fret shift of the left-hand position that I call "the crab." A crab on the beach walks sideways. Here, our hand shifts by one fret and similarly "walks sideways" — hence the name. Here is what this "crab shift" looks like, performed in succession for demonstration purposes (numbers are fingerings). I start out and end in the one-finger-per-fret position and achieve shifts of whole steps by alternating the "small hand" and stretching to one-finger-per-fret during the shift. My hand moves sideways…

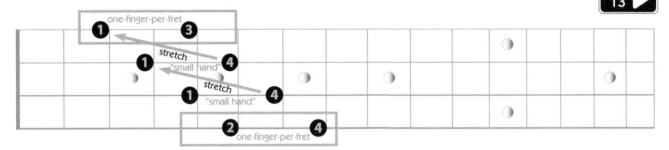

The above notes happen to form the whole tone scale*, a symmetric scale that consists of all whole steps. Check out the fingering: you temporarily leave the one-finger-per-fret position and span only three frets rather than four with your hand ("small hand"), then proceed to stretch the hand to encompass four frets again, to get back in the familiar one-finger-per-fret set up. Make sure to watch the video. This is a smooth and elegant way to shift position by one fret without losing your place. Make sure to practice this movement as demonstrated, until you are comfortable doing it without looking at the fretboard.

The whole tone scale has several good fingerings, this is just one of them in order to demonstrate "the crab."

Skippy says, make sure to get the fingering right…

---

* See *Music Theory for the Bass Player*

Pattern II

Pattern II features "the crab" in action between the A- and D-strings.

Then, take note of the fingering on the upper two strings:

Recognize this sequence with the root under the second finger! Essentially the upper part of *Pattern II* looks just like the two lower strings of *Pattern I*, just an octave up!

VIDEO
14

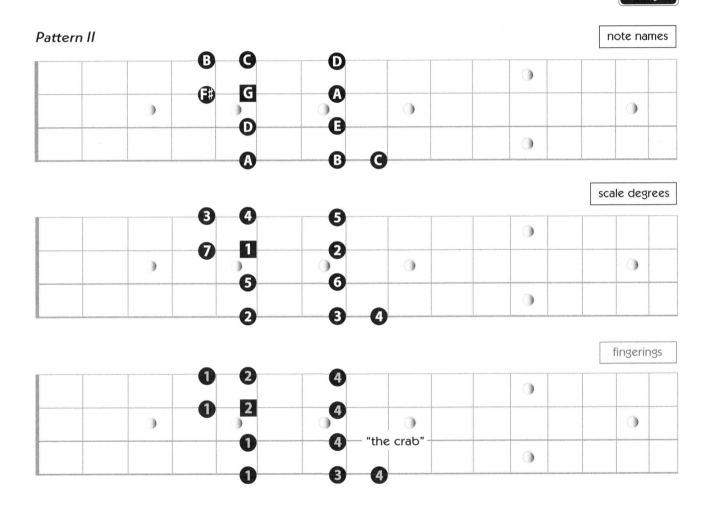

Pattern II

note names

scale degrees

fingerings

"the crab"

Pattern II features the root once, on the D-string.
"The crab" shift occurs on the A-string.

▌▌▌ **NOTE:** There is a second reason why *Pattern II* looks quite familiar. You can find it in the *Open Area*: E♭ major in the *Open Area* looks almost like *Pattern II!* No need to finger "the crab," however, because the open strings (open D and G in this case) eliminate the need for a shift!

Pattern VI

Pattern VI also features "the crab," and the ➊ ➋ ▮4▮ sequence on the G-string.

Since *Pattern VI* starts on the sixth scale degree, you can hear the sound of the relative minor from the lowest note: ➏ ➐ ▮1▮

This realization will help you memorize it, but as discussed elsewhere do not think of the patterns as "modes." Each pattern contains all of the modes. At this time, we are focusing on the major scale and learning the shapes associated with it.

> Like *Patterns I* and *V, Pattern VI* features the tonic twice — always once with the pinky and once with the second finger. Notice the location of the tonics on the E- and G-strings. "The crab" shift occurs on the D-string.

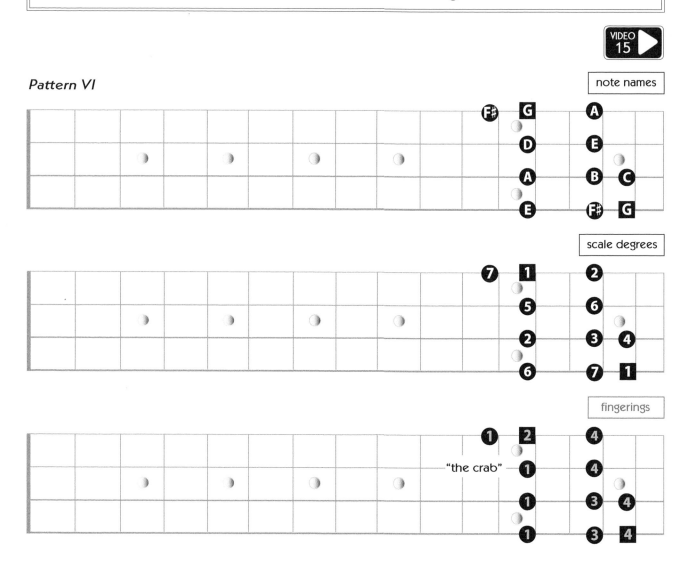

VIDEO 15

Pattern VI

note names

scale degrees

fingerings

"the crab"

▐▐▐ **NOTE:** Just like with all the other patterns, we can find this shape in the *Open Area*, in this case as A♭! Again, no need for "the crab" shift here because you have the open G-string to play the seventh scale degree.

Overview of the Five Major Scale Patterns in the Key of G Major

The diagram below shows the five "Scale Patterns" next to each other on the fretboard. Notice the overlap between the patterns — how neatly each consecutive pattern picks up exactly half of the shape of its neighbors — they fit like puzzle pieces. Each pattern occupies its specific *"Area"* of the bass and the areas overlap by two frets.

VIDEO
16

Pattern I

Pattern II

Pattern III

Pattern V

Pattern VI

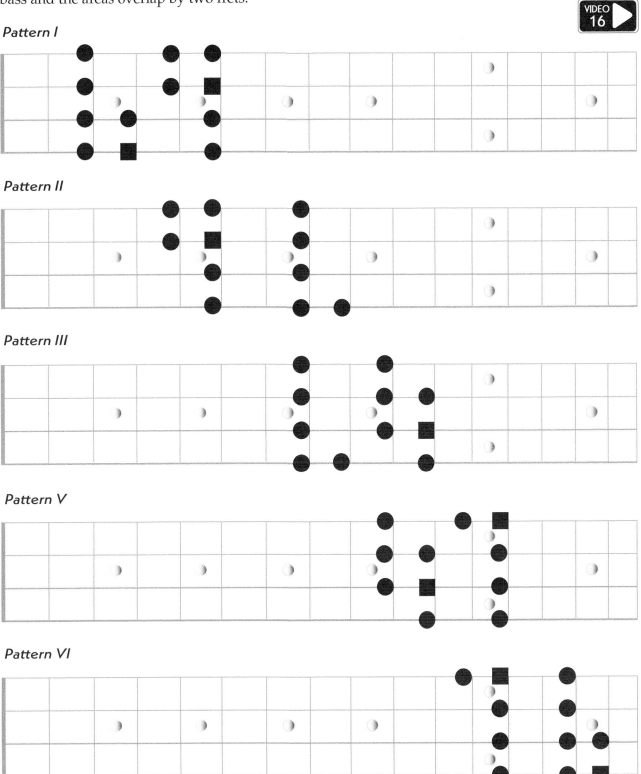

And here once more, all next to each other on one fretboard:

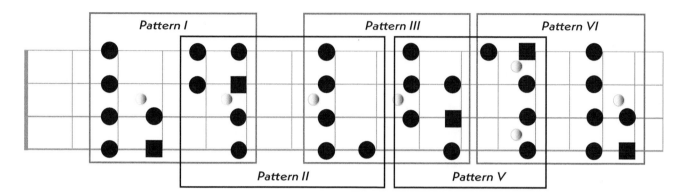

Symmetry and Micro-Shapes

You have already encountered a lot of repetition in *The Pattern System*. Knowing *Pattern I* gives you half of *Pattern II*, for example.

We have the bass fretboard's repetitive layout to thank for that:

Tuned in fourths, this layout proves very practical for fingering all the shapes that show up in diatonic music as well as non-diatonic music — at a finger-friendly distance. *The Pattern System* beautifully takes advantage of this symmetry and places it under your fingertips as economical shapes.

I encourage you to study the above overview diagrams and look for repetitions and overlaps. If you feel inspired, make copies of the overview diagram, and draw repeating patterns with a marker. In particular, I want you to see the following:

Three Micro-Shapes

If you zoom in on all the shapes and on each individual string you can identify just three "micro shapes" — patterns on a single string — that make up the major scale and all its modes:

The Three Micro-Patterns of the Major Scale and Its Modes:

#1 **1** **2** **4** or **1** **2** **4** (2 could be the root or not)

#2 **1** **3** **4** or **1** **3** **4** (4 could be the root or not)

#3 The whole step on its own on a single string. It never features a root.
The whole step can occur fingered:

2 **4** (as in *Pattern V*) or

1 **3** (as in *Pattern III*) or

1 **4** (as part of "the crab" in *Patterns VI* or *II*)

Repetition

Shapes repeat! Find the ones with the major root involved.

Notice that whenever a three-note micro-shape contains the root, that same micro-shape repeats right after without the root:

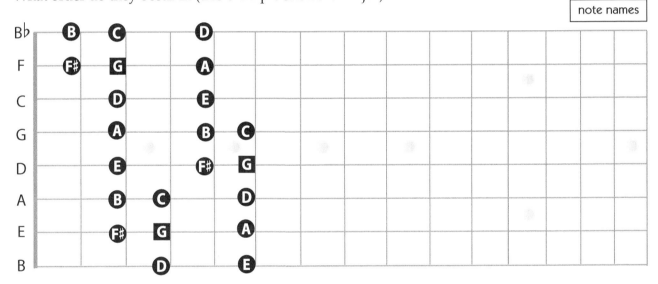

There are many more *Shapes within Shapes* you can find, including other important shapes such as triads and pentatonic scales. Some of these we will explore in more detail later.

What Extended Range Basses Teach Us

Above I showed you what the five shapes look like spread out across the fretboard horizontally. But what if we could keep going with these shapes when we reach the last string?

If you had an eight-string bass you could line them all up, one after the other. I encourage you to check out the diagram below. Mark out all the patterns from the low B-string to the high B♭-string. What order do they occur in (this example shows G major)?

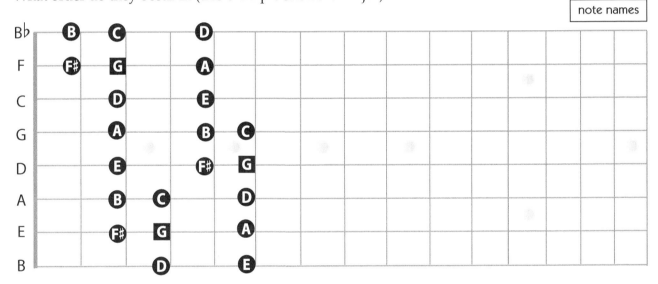

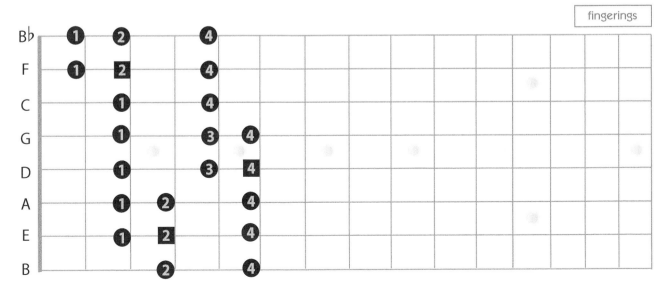

If you did the exercise on the previous page correctly, you would arrive here:

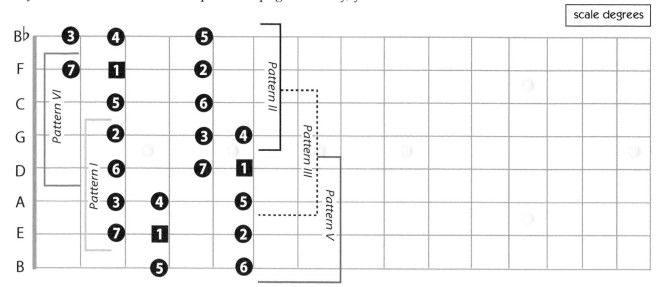

scale degrees

The order of patterns from lowest string to highest happens to come out as: *V, I, III, VI, II*. If we added yet another string after the high B♭-string (and E♭-string!) we would start over, with *Pattern V* again!

Another helpful graph:

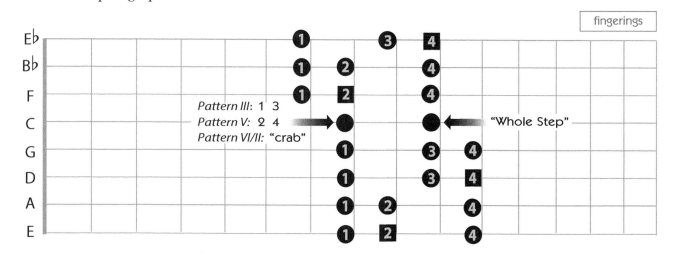

fingerings

Pattern III: 1 3
Pattern V: 2 4
Pattern VI/II: "crab"

"Whole Step"

All these observations help you understand how the bass works. But to gain practical use from these realizations and these shapes, we need to practice them in action (the "meat" of this book).

NOTE: Five- and six-string players interested in writing out the patterns for five or six-string basses: once you have all five shapes in G under your fingers four-string style and have a handle on the "crab fingering," you can write the patterns out for the extra strings. You'd be going against my general recommendation to study *The Pattern System* **four-string-style first** because of its better visualization properties, but I understand that some advanced players will want to use all their available strings right away. Download five- or six-string pattern paper from my blog at *ArisBassBlog. com/PatternSystem*, and adapt all the patterns as needed. Keep in mind that this means that you not only have to adapt the shapes themselves but also the naming. The lowest note names the pattern, so the G major pattern in *Area 1* turns out to be *Pattern V* on the five-string and six-string. Many items in this book, the *Area Matrix* and *Shapes within Shapes* will then have different names.

Just rename as needed. And whenever a shift occurs, you must finger it as "the crab." Recognize that *Pattern III* will now be a "crabby" pattern, as will *Pattern I* on the six-string bass.

Some of my students opted for the version they perceived as "more ambitious" and "more complete" and went the five/six-string route, but many returned to four-string style after a few practice rounds. The visualization and symmetry of the four-string system makes it easier to learn. Once mastered, it transfers easily to the extended strings. I leave it up to you. Mind you, I am not saying you need to use an actual four-string bass, I am just advising to ignore the low B- and high C-strings respectively when doing this method four-string style.

Example: G major

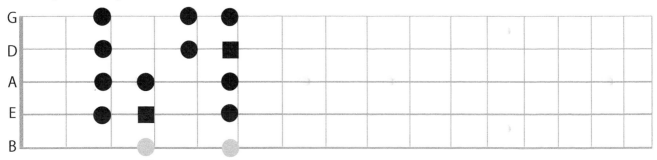

The addition of the notes on the B string turns
Pattern I into *Pattern V* in *Area 1*

Recap: Which Finger Plays the Tonic in Each Pattern

On the E-string:	On the A-string:	On the D-string:	On the G-string:
Pattern I **2**	Pattern V **2**	Pattern II **2**	Pattern VI **2**
Pattern VI **4**	Pattern III **4**	Pattern I **4**	Pattern V **4**

Seen yet another way:

Pattern I has the root **twice**, once on the E-string, once on the D-string

Pattern II has the root **once**, on the D-string

Pattern III has the root **once**, on the A-string

Pattern V has the root **twice**, on A- and G-strings

Pattern VI has the root **twice**, on E- and G-strings

▌▌▌ NOTICE:

- **The major tonic only occurs with fingers 2 or 4.**
- *Patterns II* and *III* are the only two with one tonic.
  All other patterns feature the tonic twice.
- **Remember that the lowest note (scale degree) of the pattern gives it its name.**

Rote Learning

I am usually not a big fan of "rote learning" — which means learning through (often mindlessly) repeating a movement over and over — I much prefer focused and awareness-rich practice, as well as mental practice. However, getting the shapes into your muscle memory by playing them "by rote" does help in this phase.

Practice each pattern repeatedly — all of them — still just in the key of G major.

Make sure to know the shape itself, the name of it, and where the root (or roots!) reside(s) within the shape.

- Practice each pattern ascending and then descending (Play *Pattern I* up and down, then shift to *Pattern II*, play that up and down, etc.)

- Descending and then ascending (Play *Pattern I* down and up, then shift to *Pattern II*, play that down and up, etc.)

- Practice all of them ascending only (*Pattern I* up, shift, *Pattern II* up, etc.)

- Then all of them descending only (*Pattern I* down, shift, *Pattern II* down, etc.)

- Practice *Pattern I* up, then shift into the position of *Pattern II* and descend that, then ascend *III*, descend *V*, ascend *VI*. Reverse as you make your way back down the fretboard.

- Also do the above sequence starting with *Pattern I* descending, like this: descend *Pattern I*, ascend *Pattern II*, descend *Pattern III*, etc. and reverse back down the fretboard

▌▌▌ TIP: Try rote practice while watching a movie. No need to plug in your bass, just pick a pattern and run it over and over. In commercial breaks, reaffirm what pattern you are studying and find the tonic(s).

For the more focused practice (not watching a movie!), say the following out loud:

- Fingerings
- Note names
- Scale degrees
- Say "tonic" whenever it occurs

- The name of the pattern as you start
- Say nothing, just focus on playing the notes — make them sound as beautiful as possible (strive for even note length and dynamics, smooth connections, expressivity — as if you are playing the most beautiful melody).

Test: How Well do You Know The Patterns?

This test will reveal how well you know the patterns.

Come to the bass cold, without playing any patterns beforehand. Then play (still only in G):

- *Pattern III* descending
- *Pattern V* starting on the A on the 12th fret
- *Pattern II* descending
- *Pattern III* ascending starting on its tonic
- *Pattern VI* descending
- Play only the tonics of all the patterns

NOTE: I frequently remind you in my courses to "keep moving," even if you haven't mastered a specific exercise yet. We designed our materials so that you revisit important touch points over and over, using slight variations. So, by moving on at about 80% proficiency, you practice with greater efficiency. I make an exception with these shapes, however since they are so foundational. Just five in total — know them well — then (and only then) move on.

STARTING TO USE THE METRONOME (PART II)

Set your metronome and practice each shape as well as the five *Major Scalar Patterns* slowly and with a click. This feels vastly different than playing without a click because you now have to focus not only on what to play (which note) and how to play it (which finger, how loud, etc.), but also when to play it.

When you first learn a shape, leave the click off. Once you start to get more familiar with the pattern, start using the metronome to make your practice much more effective.

There are beneficial ways as well as detrimental ways to use a metronome. I will provide more guidance in upcoming chapters as well.

For now, you will find yourself switching the click on and off as needed. I only want you to use it once you have the shape(s) confidently under your fingers.

Rules for Metronome Use

If you have the click running, make sure to listen to it and adhere to it.

Are you working on an exercise that you cannot quite execute yet with the click, even at a slow tempo? In that case, I suggest you eliminate the click and practice what still needs work. Once you have obtained a bit of fluidity, switch the click back on at a slow tempo and play to it. **I cannot overstate the importance of this.** If you have the click running but you ignore it, you are effectively practicing to not listen — you are disconnecting your own internal timing from the one (the click) you hear in the room. You can easily see how this can become a problem on the bandstand. Refrain from this bad habit! Be adamant!

**When Skippy speaks,
he demands everyone listen to him!**

The Most Challenging Spot Determines the Tempo

When you play a pattern — or in later chapters a combination of patterns — you will encounter different keys, shapes, and transitions; some of them will be easy, some will be tough. The goal is to play the whole exercise at a consistent tempo. *Therefore, you must set the tempo no faster than the most difficult part allows.* This may mean that you will feel a bit unchallenged during the easy parts. This, however is great because you can use this opportunity to:

- Think ahead during those easier spots.
- Observe yourself — while still thinking ahead — correct your posture (not just your fingers and hands), breathe consciously, scan for tensions, etc.
- Listen to your tone.
- Place the notes exactly on top of the click as if you tried to make the click and your note one single sound.

Always write down your tempos. This provides a great measure of the pace of your learning. Keeping track of your progress helps move you along!

Experiment with subdivisions. If you need a very slow tempo to get through an exercise, try setting the click to eighth notes, triplets or even sixteenth notes. This will give you a more direct sense of the beat, rather than diverting your attention by trying to sync up with a very slow beat. (A metronome setting lower than 55 or so makes it harder to feel the flow.)

Also explore playing eighth notes, triplets or even sixteenth notes as the click taps out quarter notes. It will help you vary the experience of the patterns.

VIDEO 21 ▶

▍▍▍ **HINT:** Imagine you are practicing at a slow but even tempo throughout compared to "winging it" and speeding up over the easy parts and slowing down when the going gets tough, when faced with:

- A key with more accidentals
- A technically challenging jump
- A new area of the bass
- A harder sequence (see later Chapters)

Doing so will set you up for practicing (and hence reinforcing) sloppiness and *overestimating the degree to which you know the exercise.* As I mentioned when introducing Skippy, he will be a trusted friend who holds up a mirror to you. Make him proud!

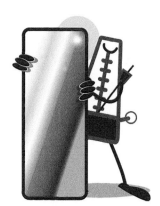

**Skippy mirrors the accuracy of your
playing right back at you**

▍▍▍ **HINT:** If your metronome has a downbeat feature (meaning every fourth beat for example is distinguished by a different pitch or sound) turn it off and make all clicks sound the same. For the connection exercises in later chapters the downbeat feature will come in very handy. For now, leave it out. Make him proud!

TIP: Play these exercises as if they were beautiful music. Practicing the patterns is a great opportunity to listen for even tone, steady tempo, and clean buzz-free notes. If you strive for a beautiful tone when playing these exercises, you teach yourself to develop a great "default" tone. I call the "default tone" the tone we resort to under stress or when we are unsure of what we are doing! For example, if you cannot hear yourself or a band mate on stage or if someone goes into the wrong section, good tone and solid feel usually suffer first. Take advantage of these exercises and make your "default tone" — your automatic tone — a good one! Pay attention to this! It makes a huge difference to the way you sound.

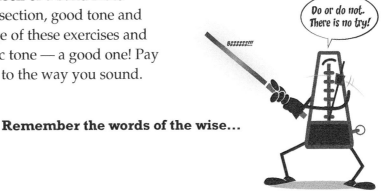

Remember the words of the wise...

I am used to playing scales in a different manner. For example, I prefer playing up the neck in some keys rather than staying in one position. I am quite comfortable with my way of doing it. Why should I change it and why do you not talk about these types of fingerings?

It's great that you have worked out approaches that work for you.

The goal of this method is to expand your possibilities. But not just that — focused, structured and disciplined practice will train your musical mind in a unique way. Keep doing what works for you in addition to giving this system a thorough workout. You may find that you have expanded your horizons dramatically and you now have more choices available to you.

We sometimes gravitate to playing certain keys in certain ways that stick with us which makes for incomplete knowledge, often locking us into a limited number of familiar shapes. Does breaking out of that sound appealing to you?

The Pattern System aims for fluidity in all keys, all over the fretboard, and in all directions. Going up and down the neck has many advantages. We call this playing diagonally. When we are playing diagonally, we are connecting patterns across different areas of the bass. Once you have the five shapes in all areas down, this will become quite natural. We will tackle different keys and areas soon. In a later chapter, I will also show you how to connect the patterns (which will likely include your current way of playing the scale).

Will this system help with reading music?

Reading on the bass is challenging, just like on the guitar. On the piano, every pitch occurs only once. Every octave follows the same pattern and visual appearance. On the bass — the same note (which means the same pitch) occurs two to four times on the fretboard — except for the four highest and the four lowest notes. This makes sight reading on the bass a bit harder because we must decide which of the possible positions for each pitch we will choose and come up with a reliable fingering at the same time. *The Pattern System* makes this very easy by putting each note into a helpful context such as a key or scale and associates it with a corresponding pattern. The search time for the notes on the fretboard is minimized and you'll have practiced default fingerings that work.

Learning to read music on a staff forms the perfect adjunct to *The Pattern System*. We are creating a companion book on reading to go hand in hand with this method. Tackle it at the same time or after you have worked through *The Pattern System*.

 So isn't this just the CAGED system?

The CAGED system (famously named after chord shapes on the guitar) shares one thing with *The Pattern System* — that is the five shapes themselves. This is where it ends. How we practice the patterns, how they are presented here, how they are combined with improvisation, how we shed them in the connection exercises, and how we pay attention to shapes within shapes (highly applicable musically) is unique. Also, by "patterns" this system does not just refer to shapes on the fretboard, even though that is an important aspect, but to the many kinds of patterns found in music. In this book you will mostly work on scales, triads, intervals, and chord progressions. Many, many more patterns exist and warrant systematic study. You have barely scratched the surface, yet you are learning a solid foundation that will benefit you with everything else you study. Keep going.

Like Skippy demonstrates, just knowing the shapes still keeps you caged. You unlock the cage and the magic happens when you know the patterns so well that you can break completely free.

Scalar Studies

Three-Note Groupings

Continuing from Chapter 1's two-note groupings, you now move to three-note groupings! Enjoy what this will do for your technique and get ready to have it influence your runs and fills!

Three-Note Groupings

In the examples below, I show you all the patterns in the key of G. I have added a few fingerings for orientation at times.

Reminder: In *The Pattern System* we always go from the lowest possible note to the highest possible note in any given pattern. The example I wrote out for you is in the key of G major, and it starts on the seventh note of the scale.

Practice saying out loud:

- Note names
- Scale degrees

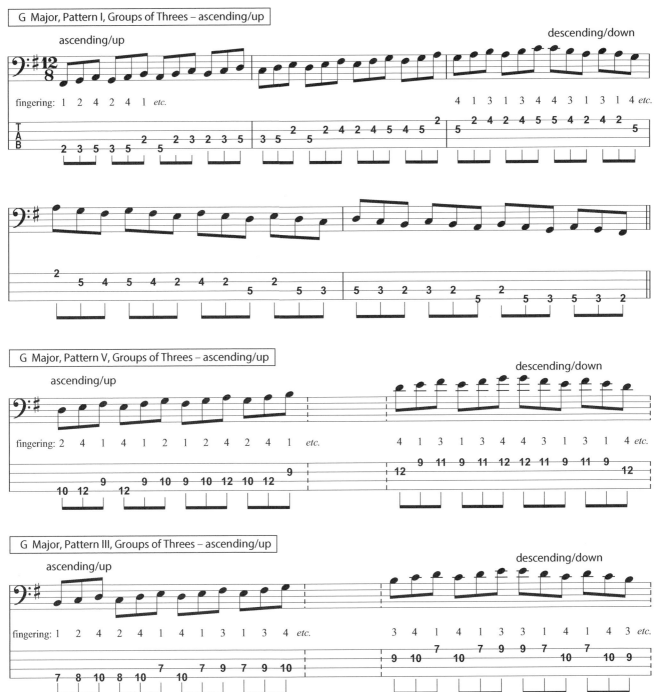

Groove Within a Pattern

Now that you have practiced the five shapes a bit, let's put them to work in an improvisation exercise. Using the shapes creatively will help you get them under your fingers even more.

For the first exercise, pick a pattern. Start by visualizing the entire shape. But now, instead of playing the shape in its entirety and in order, bring in your creativity. You don't need to be comprehensive anymore — but rather inventive! — as long as you stay within the shape.

Instructions

Start by picking one of the five shapes in G. In my example below, I am using *Pattern III*. **Stay inside your chosen pattern for the entire exercise**. No shifts, other than the "crabs" from *PII* or *PVI*.

Choose a slow tempo to start; we are playing in 4/4.

Now follow this blueprint:

1 bar of groove – 1 bar of fill.

Groove on the *odd bar numbers*. Play a repetitive figure, always starting with the root on beat one. For the groove, consistently play the same figure, no variations.

In the *even bars*, fill using any one of these strategies:

- Play a part of the pattern in either an ascending or descending direction — in order
- Repeat one or more notes or phrases
- Make it a meandering sequence (up a bit, down a bit, up a bit more, etc.)
- Experiment with jumps and scale fragments
- Try an angular or disjointed string of notes

As always, observe the effects of each concept and describe it in words. Combine the various concepts and come up with your own. Resist the urge to just jam! Instead, stay in the learning zone and work with one of the suggested assignments from above.

TIP: Rather than trying to play a bunch of fast and complicated notes, take it easy until you get the hang of it. If you are new to improvising, have an eye on the downbeat. Make sure you don't lose the 4/4 count and feel (set the metronome to a downbeat every 4 beats) because turning the beat around does count as a grave violation and would incur a fine.

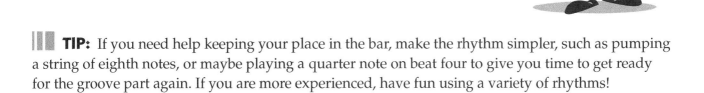

**Skippy will write you a ticket
if you turn the beat around...**

TIP: If you need help keeping your place in the bar, make the rhythm simpler, such as pumping a string of eighth notes, or maybe playing a quarter note on beat four to give you time to get ready for the groove part again. If you are more experienced, have fun using a variety of rhythms!

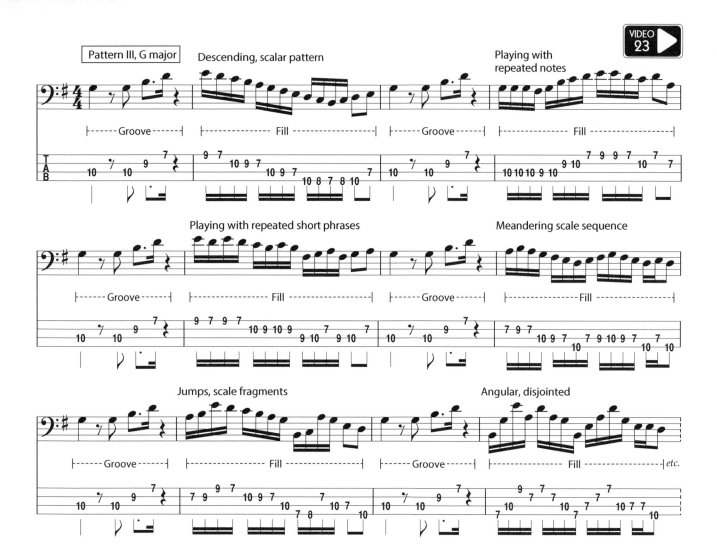

PURPOSE: This exercise will give you a sense of freedom within the constraints of the pattern (and the beat). This is suitable for a variety of levels — again, start with all eighth notes at first, if needed. Explore the musical effect these various approaches have. Pick a topic — such as "angular/ disjointed" or "descending scalar patterns" and riff on it. Describe the effect it has. Where and how would you use this?

All Five Shapes Across the Fretboard

Instructions

Once you have practiced improvising in all five patterns of G in the above manner, tackle combining all five in one exercise:

- Groove on the low G
  - Fill *Pattern I*
- Groove on the low G
  - Fill *Pattern II*
- Groove on the low G
  - Fill *Pattern III*
- And so forth

You will switch areas a lot which will cement your knowledge of the locations of these shapes.

TEST YOUR UNDERSTANDING #2

1. Without playing *Pattern V* ascending first, play *Pattern V* in the key of G descending.
    What is your highest note and which finger plays it? _____
    What is your lowest note and which finger plays it? _____

2. Still in the key of G, play *Pattern III* descending.
    What is your highest note? _____
    What is your lowest? _____

3. Still in the key of G, play *Pattern VI* ascending.
    What is your lowest/highest note _____ / _____
    and which fingers play them? _____ / _____

4. Still in the key of G, play *Pattern II* descending.
    What is your highest/lowest note _____ / _____
    and which fingers play them? _____ / _____

5. What is more important, knowing the shape or knowing where the tonic is?
    ❑ The shape   ❑ where the tonic is   ❑ both are equally important

6. True or false: each pattern contains the tonic twice.   ❑ True   ❑ False

7. What gives a pattern its name? _____

8. True or false: all patterns stay in a four-fret span.   ❑ True   ❑ False

9. Why is there a picture of a crab in this book on bass patterns? _____
    _____

10. True or false: Patterns always go from root to root.   ❑ True   ❑ False

11. How many patterns are there? _____

12. How many micro-shapes (on one string) do the patterns consist of? _____

13. True or false: There are six areas and five patterns in this system (or, including the *Open Area* patterns: 15 total).   ❑ True   ❑ False

14. True or false: Within this method any finger could effectively fret the major scale tonic.
    ❑ True   ❑ False

15. True or false: *Pattern I* should really be called *Pattern VII* because it starts with the seventh note of the scale.   ❑ True   ❑ False

BLUEPRINT FOR PRACTICE #2

Practice:

1. **PP:** The *5 Scale Patterns* in G, root → up/down → root; root → down/up → root; ascending and descending; descending, and ascending; ascending only; descending only; *say fingerings, scale degrees, note names*
    p. 41–46 • **Video 10, p. 52** • **Video 18**

---

2. **SS:** The *5 Scale Patterns* in G in two-note groupings ascending/up and descending/down *(Chapter 1)*;
    p. 31-32 • **Video 8**
    Say fingerings, scale degrees, note names

---

3. **SS:** The *5 Scale Patterns* in G in three note groupings ascending/up and descending/down *(Chapter 2)*;
    p. 57 • **Video 22**

---

4. **PP:** *Open Area* sharp keys all descending only; **p. 28** • **Video 6**
    Say fingerings, scale degrees, note names

---

5. **IE:** *Open Area*, sharp keys: *Chapter 2* Groove and Fill Improv (one bar)
    Just two keys to start: A and E
    With a jam track or metronome; stay in one key throughout the exercise; **pp. 58-61** • **Video 23, Video 24**

---

6. **Bonus SS:** *Open Area*, sharp keys: Scalar Groupings in two *(Chapter 1)*; **pp. 31–32** • **Video 8**
    Just two keys to start: B, F♯, C♯

3 Coming Full Circle

A New Order: Coming Full Circle

In the *Open Area*, you practiced the **flat keys** in the order of falling fifths (counterclockwise direction): C F Bb.

And the **sharp keys** in the order of ascending fifths (clockwise direction): C G D.

As a starting point, this made sense. In the *Open Area*, it is easier to go from keys with fewer accidentals to keys with more accidentals (which is harder).

Now, as we continue up the bass neck area by area, I will organize the keys by going all around the cycle*.

For the *Pattern Practice*, using the cycle in both directions enables you to practice 12 keys in a sequence such that only one note changes with each key change.

C F Bb Eb Ab Db Gb/F# B E A D G C

At first, you start with no accidentals; then you add flats until you reach six flats, quickly convert them to six sharps in your mind, and continue subtracting a sharp with each key until you reach zero again.

We could achieve the same by going to the right, in ascending fifths (C, G, D…). I like to list the keys in the direction that proves musically the most relevant, namely in the direction of the cycle to the left, counterclockwise or the "Cycle of Falling Fifths."

What About the Enharmonic Keys?

Of course, practicing this way means you skip a few enharmonic keys. While enharmonic keys sound the same, their different note names prove relevant in *Pattern Practice* because of the way we conceptualize the key by saying note names as part of our practice.

The enharmonic keys are, of course:

- F# (six sharps) and Gb (six flats)
- C# (seven sharps) and Db (five flats)
- Cb (seven flats) and B (five sharps)

F# and Gb prove a tossup in terms of difficulty as they sit at the six o'clock mark of the cycle with either six flats or six sharps. Cb and C# seem harder, however, because they have more accidentals than their enharmonic counterparts B and Db, respectively. These keys — laden with seven accidentals — may come your way in your musical life, so do include them in your practice, especially when doing note name drills.

---

* We will include more ways of organizing and practicing the keys in a later chapter as well.

Also, while seven accidentals may strike us as harder at first, keep in mind that C♯ forms a C major scale with every single note sharpened, making it quite accessible (The same is true for C♭ with every note flatted).

As for the six o'clock mark on the cycle, you must decide whether to go with flats or sharps. I recommend you switch it up — on even calendar days, practice the key with six accidentals as F♯, on the odd ones as G♭.

**Talking about enharmonics,
Professor Skippy Einstein has a theory...**

 Why do you call the circle to the left the "Circle of Descending Fifths" and not the "Circle of Fourths"?

I favor this naming because:

- It gives an appropriate nod to the interval of the fifth, which sits at the base of our tonal and tuning system.
- Traditionally we call it the circle of fifths, not fourths.
- Who is to say an interval is always automatically ascending? Don't forget the descending direction!
- Inversions of each other, fourths and fifths relate to each other, but the fifth most certainly started it all (being an early overtone and fundamental sound).

More importantly, it illuminates the importance of the V ⟶ I resolution, or, in other words, hightlights a movement that occurs in music all the time. More on this below.

The V–I Resolution

If you navigate through the cycle to the left, you are encountering falling fifths because each time you move to the next key, you are essentially playing a V ⟶ I.

Play through the cycle to the left (tonics only) and hear the"falling" effect. No matter what octave you are in — you might play C up to the higher F or down to the lower one, and then F to the higher or lower B♭, etc.; try to find the sound of tension (for example, C) releasing (in this example, F). C stands for the dominant chord (V chord) of F. F for the dominant of B♭, and so forth.

When you play through the cycle in this direction — no matter in which octaves — it feels like you are somersaulting downhill and cannot stop:

**Skippy demonstrates
the gravitational pull of
the V ⟶ I resolution**

You can enhance this effect by making the V chord a dominant seventh chord:

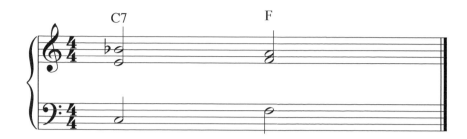

In the above example, C7 resolving to F major pulls even stronger because of the resolution of the dominant seventh's tritone to the tonic and third. (This is a very stable sound.)

To hear the effect of the V pulling down to the I, play through the cycle:

C to C7 ⟶ F to F7 ⟶ B♭ to B♭7 ⟶ E♭ to E♭7 ⟶ A♭ etc. Tension ⟶ release. High energy ⟶ release of energy.

To contrast this, listen to the cycle of ascending fifths (cycle to the right):

C G D etc.: this sequence has an upward, lifting effect. (The song "Hotel California" follows an ascending fifths progression.)

Versus, again, the falling fifths:

C F B♭ E♭ has a falling, descending effect. (Any song featuring a IImin–V–I progression, for example, gives prominence to the movement of falling fifths with the roots of these chords, for example, in B♭: Cm7–F7–B♭. C, F, B♭… the cycle to the left.)

All of this to say: organizing the keys in the order of the cycle of falling fifths has many benefits; hence we start there. The pleasing sound that comes from this direction hails from its frequent use in music where the V falls into the I, like water falls down a waterfall. Therefore, I prefer calling it "descending fifths."

If you need a refresher on the properties of the tritone, the relevance of the fifth, the difference between the diatonic cycle and the chromatic cycle, please refer to *Music Theory for the Bass Player,* which Skippy can often be seen studying ferociously…

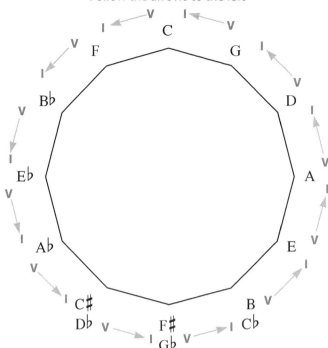

Descending Fifths
Follow the arrows to the left

Skippy demonstrates going 'round the circle to the left...

Staying in One Area

With the five shapes under your belt in the key of G, you now enter the next stage of this journey: music played on the bass in one area. When playing tunes, you often find yourself in one area of the instrument and need to react to various chord changes — you want to do that with minimal jumps and optimal confidence.

You might assume that we will now learn each key horizontally (up the neck), but that would be incomplete because it would mean we'd always have to start from the beginning and then match up the shapes to find them up the neck. In order to do what music does (i.e., move from one chord change to the next as you find yourself in whatever area of the bass), you want to be able to switch to the next key in that same area you happen to just find yourself in — immediately without thinking. In order to achieve this, you will now leave the horizontal plane and turn to the vertical plane, similar to how you approached the *Open Area* — and learn the patterns "area by area."

What do we call an *Area*?

An area is the smallest range on the fretboard that all keys represented by one of the five patterns can fit in. An area on the bass comprises the span of either six or seven frets.

This system divides the bass into six areas — one for each pattern plus the *Open Area*:

- The *Open Area* stretches from fret 0 (open) to the fourth fret. In this area, each key has its own distinct pattern.

- The "regular" areas allow for five distinct shapes for each key — the "five patterns" in our system (see "Overview of all Five Major Scale Patterns" in *Chapter 2*). There could also be seven or more. For the bass, being tuned in fourths, the five patterns approach has proven the most effective way to learn this system. If you learn the five main shapes, you will be ready for most playing situations and can easily add and substitute extended shapes as needed.

- I will guide you through creating your own *Area Maps* for each area. Drawing out the patterns in all keys for each area will deepen your learning and help you grasp them in less time. Once you have reached the octave on the bass neck, you'll create the *Area Matrix*, a spreadsheet that lists each key's pattern area by area. This will prove to be a great resource for quick reference.

Area 1

We define *Area 1* as the area between frets 1 through 6. No open strings, nothing beyond fret 6.

Below, write out the patterns of all 15 keys in *Area 1*.

You can use any of these strategies to find the correct pattern to fit into *Area 1*:

1. Find the tonic(s) of the key in this area and extrapolate the pattern by knowing where tonic(s) are in any given pattern shape.

2. Alternatively, find the lowest note of the key on the E-string in such a fashion that you can create the pattern without any open strings. If you encounter open strings or would have to resort to stretch fingerings (that won't fit a pattern!), just start with the next higher note. **Remember: the lowest note will be the name of the pattern and will help you identify the pattern easily by scale degree.**

3. A third strategy involves knowing the notes of the scale in that area and seeing the pattern pop out, then delete any extra notes beyond the pattern shape.

I recommend you try either of the first two methods and use the last one to check yourself.

Try All Three Strategies in the Key of D

Strategy 1: Finding the Tonic

Tonic on the A string could mean either *Pattern III* or *Pattern V. V* would not fit within *Area 1* (grey box) so it follows that it must be *Pattern III.*

Strategy 2: Finding the lowest note of the scale

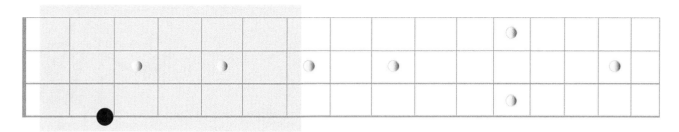

The lowest note that you can fit into the grey box that is part of the D major scale is F♯, the third scale degree in D major, so it follows that it must be *Pattern III.*

Strategy 3: If you fit all the notes of D major inside the grey box, *Pattern III* will emerge.

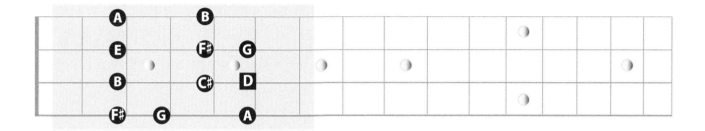

> If you stick to any of these strategies, every key fits neatly into *Area 1* once.
> Only one incident emerges that has two options, namely the shape for D♭ (and its enharmonic equivalent, C♯). Put these into their lower version as *Pattern III* *.

Area 1 Diagrams: The Area 1 Area Map

- Fill out the fret diagrams for all the keys below.
- Write down the pattern name in the space provided.
- Put a square on the tonic.

By now, you know the fingerings of the five patterns, so no need to write those out. Instead, write out note names (strengthening your conceptual knowledge of the scale) and scale degrees (great awareness for your auditory channel because scale degrees describe sound relationships with the tonic). You can also just make black dots, which provide a great image for visualization. Write neatly; take your time.

Play the patterns on the bass to check your work! You can also check your work by accessing our online resources.

---

* On six-string, you'd have to put D♭ in its higher version, *Pattern V,* because the open C-string would put this key into the *Open Area.*

Area 1 – Area Map – Note Names

C *Pattern* _____

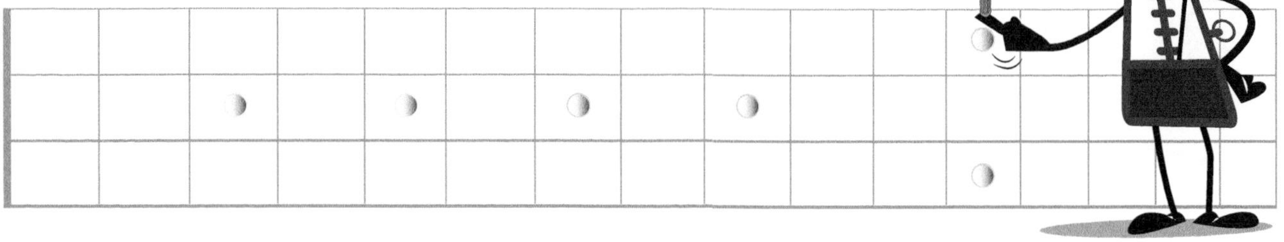

F *Pattern* _____

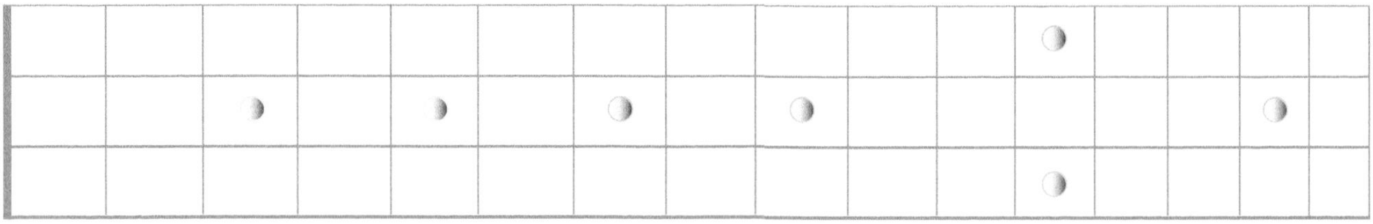

B♭ *Pattern* _____

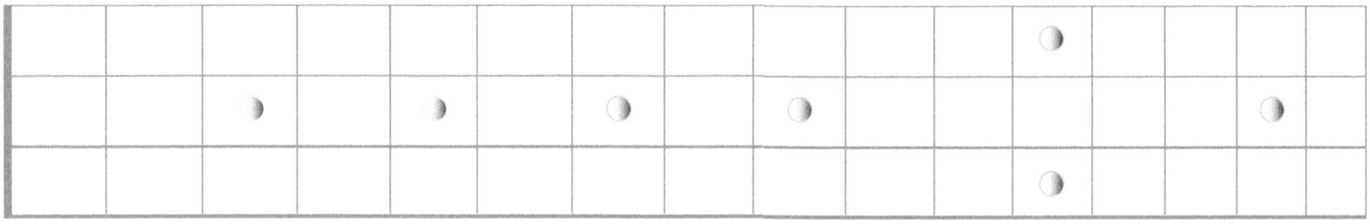

E♭ *Pattern* _____

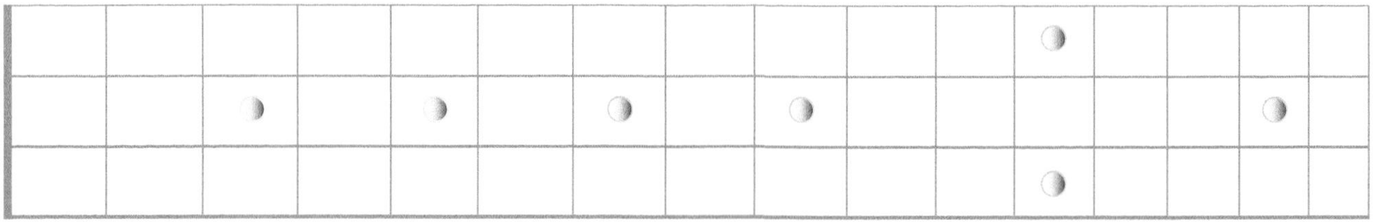

A♭ *Pattern* _____

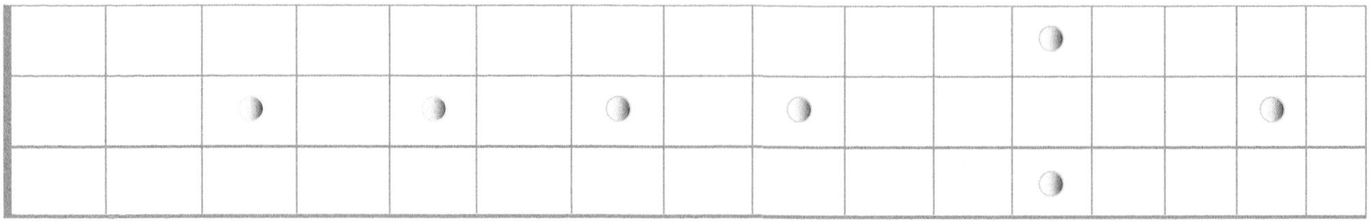

D♭ *Pattern* _____

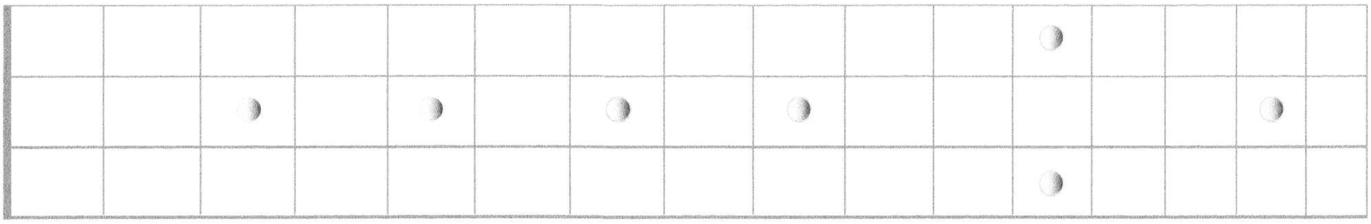

G♭ *Pattern* _____

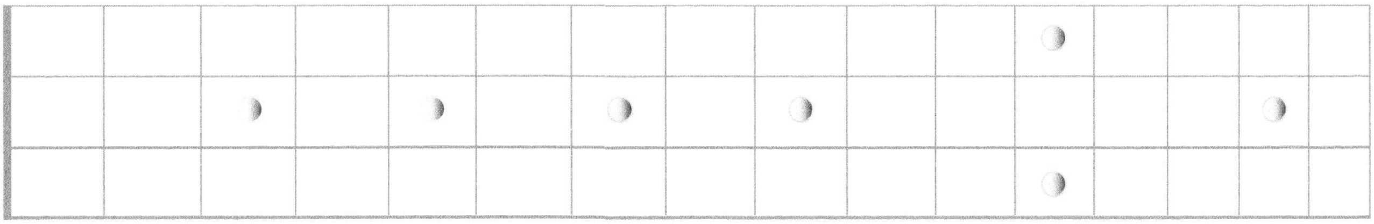

B *Pattern* _____

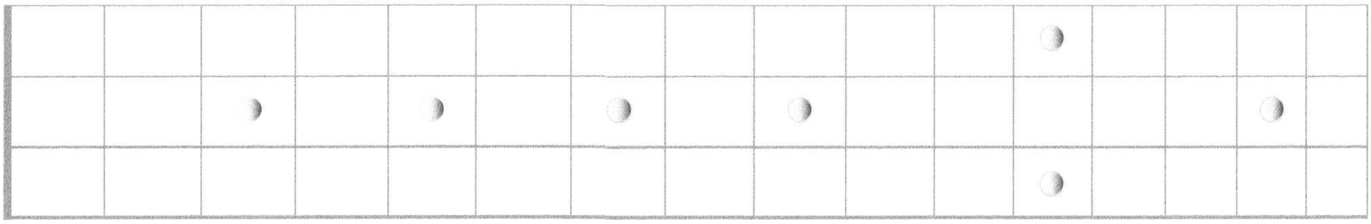

E *Pattern* _____

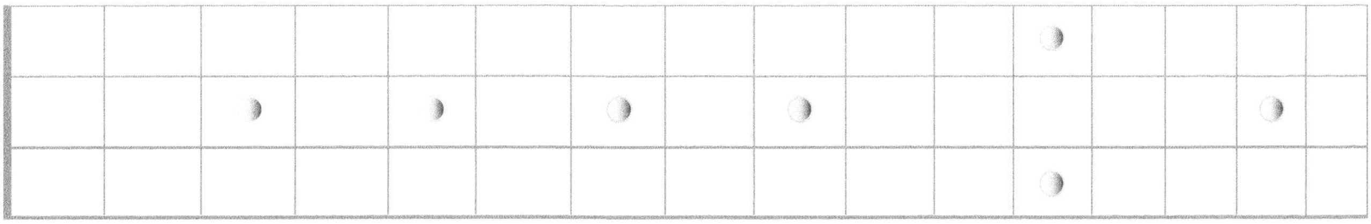

A *Pattern* _____

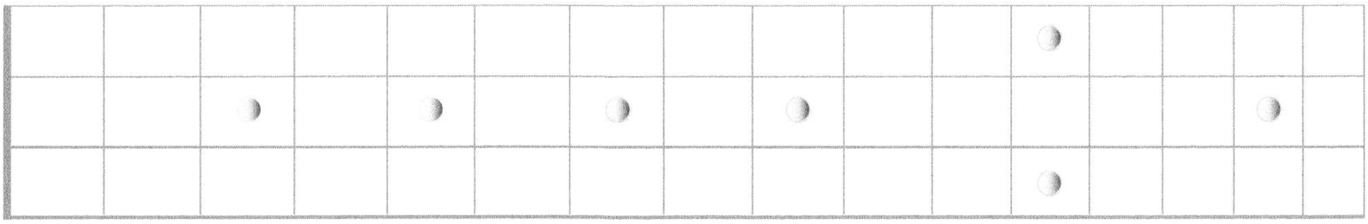

D   *Pattern* _____

G   *Pattern* _____

F♯   *Pattern* _____

C♯   *Pattern* _____

C♭   *Pattern* _____

Area 1 – Area Map – Scale Degrees

C   *Pattern* ____

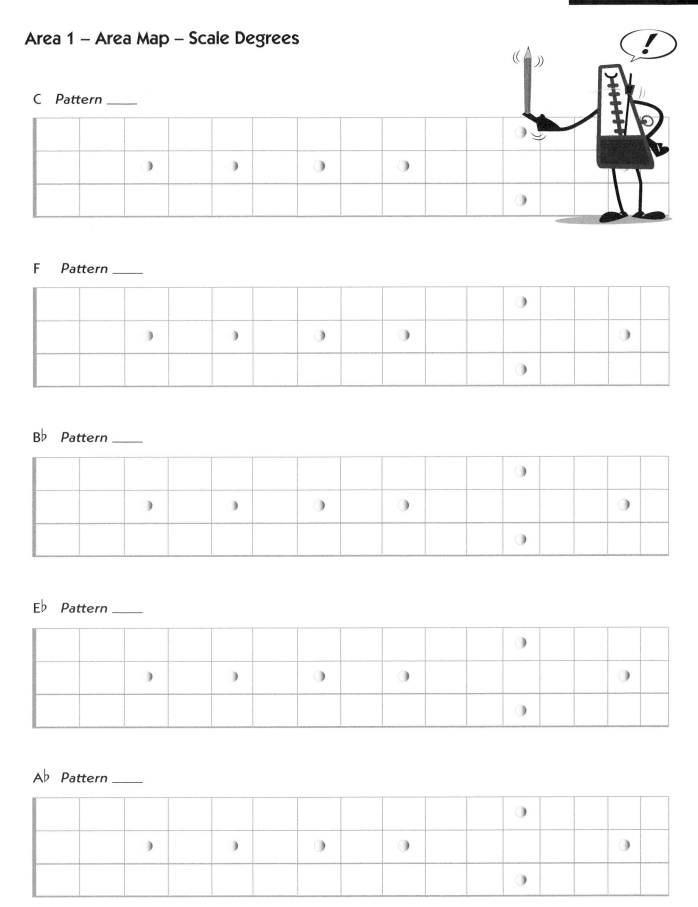

F   *Pattern* ____

B♭   *Pattern* ____

E♭   *Pattern* ____

A♭   *Pattern* ____

Db *Pattern* _____

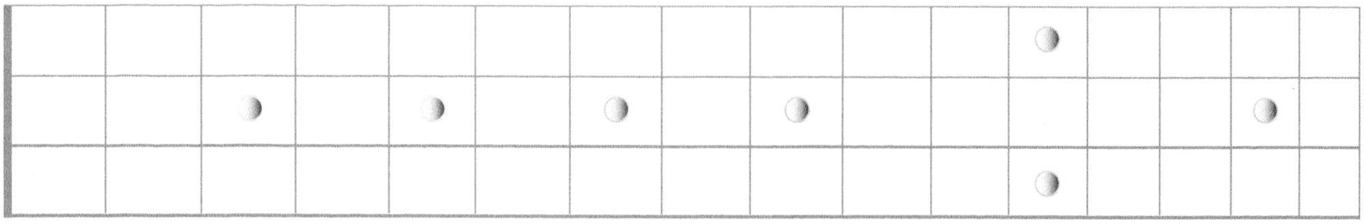

Gb *Pattern* _____

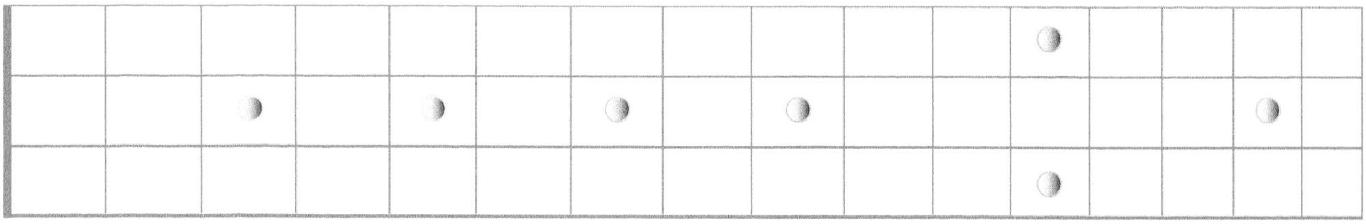

B *Pattern* _____

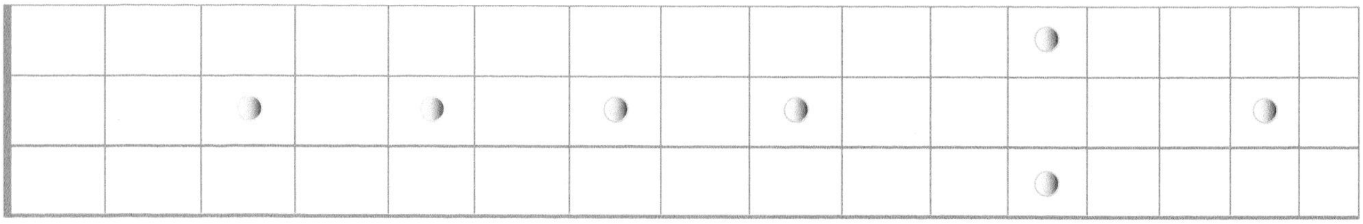

E *Pattern* _____

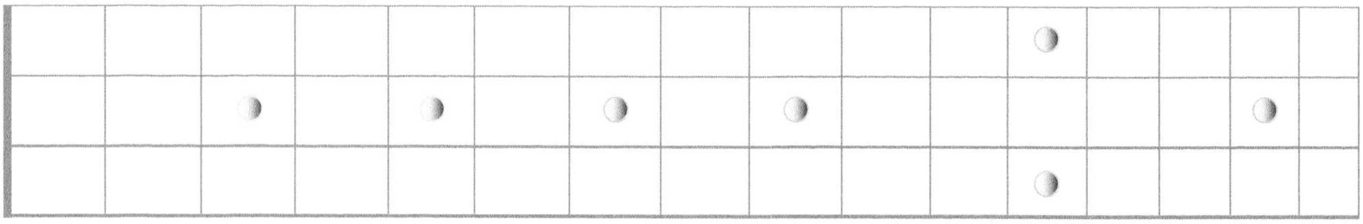

A *Pattern* _____

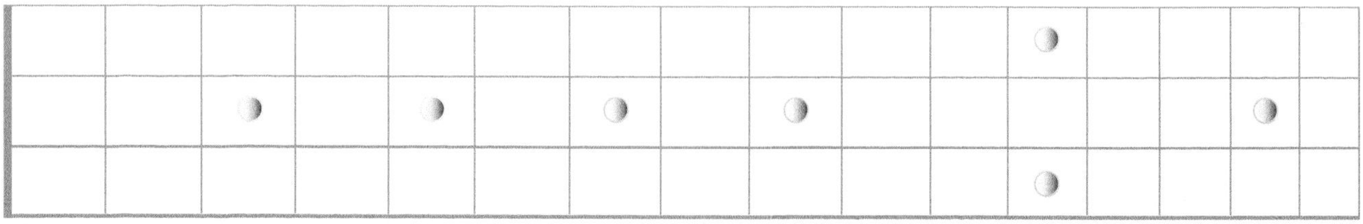

D *Pattern* _____

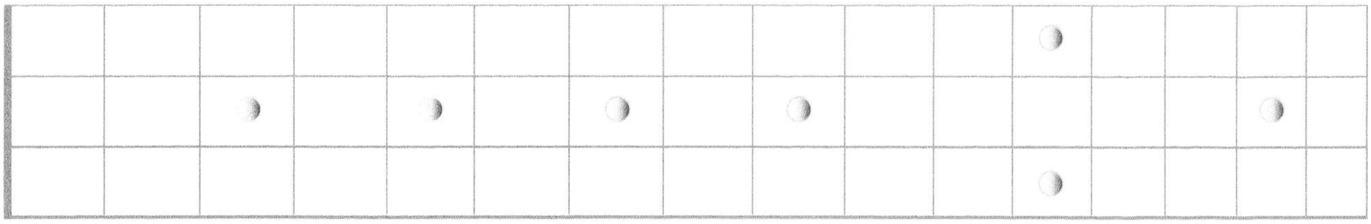

G *Pattern* _____

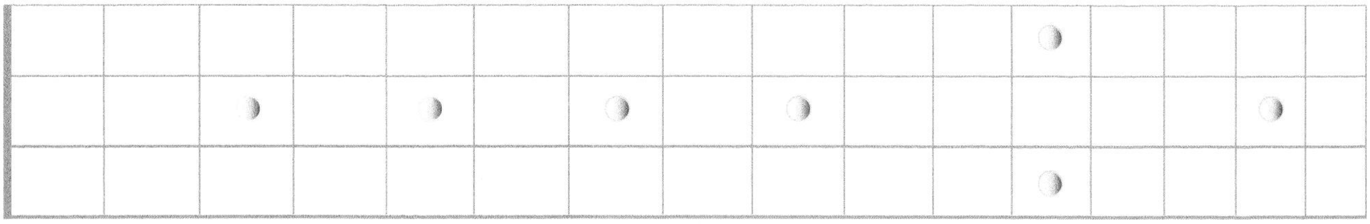

F♯ *Pattern* _____

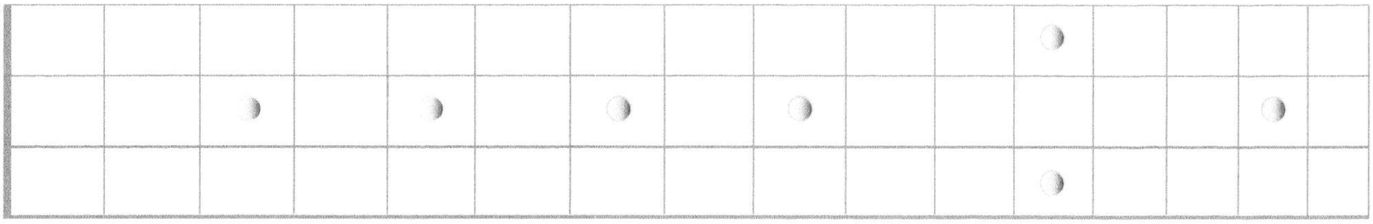

C♯ *Pattern* _____

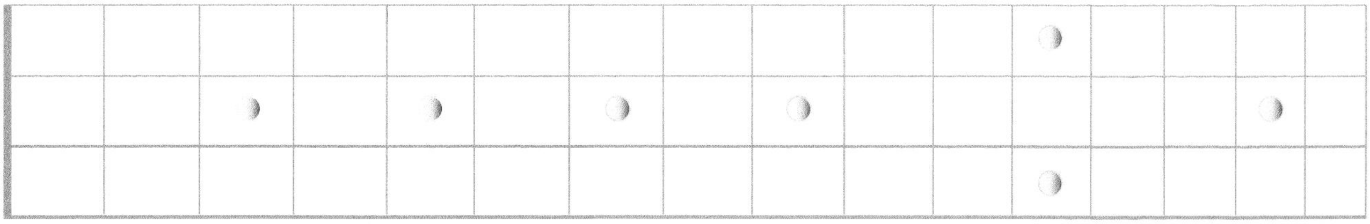

C♭ *Pattern* _____

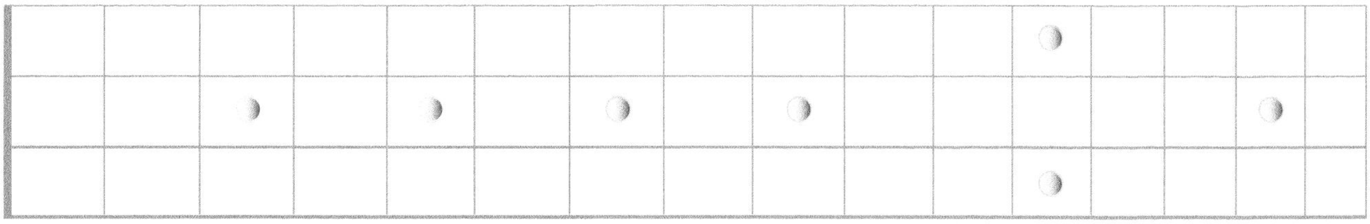

First, look at the sheet and create a mental image of the pattern. Eventually, recall it from memory only. Practice all keys in the order of the cycle counter-clockwise (C F B♭, etc.) until you come around to C again. Include the enharmonic keys whenever you are saying note names.

Phase 1: Practice like this, in the order of the *Area 1 Area Map*:

- Looking at the map, confirm the pattern name, location of the tonic and run the shape:
  - Each pattern individually, ascending, then descending
  - Each pattern individually, descending, then ascending

Phase 2: When you are getting more comfortable with the above, start memorizing the patterns in order and play them like this:

- All ascending only, one after another
- All descending only
- One key ascending, next key descending, next key ascending, etc.
- One key descending, next key ascending, next key descending, etc.

Phase 3: When that begins to get easier, start practicing like this, without looking at the map:

- All keys ascending from the lowest note of the pattern and descending back down without stopping in between keys. Think ahead. What key is coming next? As you play the last few notes of the current pattern/key, think of what the next key will be and which note will start it.
- Then practice all keys descending from the highest note in the pattern and ascending without stopping in between keys. Again, think ahead!

What to say or think while playing the patterns:

- Say note names (great for phases 1 and 2 above).
- Say scale degrees (great for phases 1 and 2).
- Say just the tonic of each key and visualize the pattern in your mind as you play it (phase 3).
- Play the shape and acknowledge the tonic by saying "root" whenever you come across it*.
- Aim to see the shape in your mind before and while you play it.

In Phases 1 and 2, you may need to repeat a key a few times to wrap your mind around it and really ingrain the pattern into your memory. That's totally fine. Acknowledge where the tonic sits in the pattern and use your ears to guide you as a reference point. Once you are comfortable with the individual keys on their own, proceed to play one after another from memory — ideally without pauses when switching keys.

Here is an important aspect to remember: aim to play these exercises at an even tempo. Surprisingly challenging, but very important! Luckily we count on Skippy to come to the rescue!

---

* I prefer saying "root" rather than "tonic" because the word "root" has only one syllable. I will tackle later why we distinguish between "tonic" and "root."

METRONOME REMEDIES: CHEATER BEATS (PART III)

Skippy's main function serves in training you to think ahead in time. While you are playing one shape, be planning for the next one — what key, what shape, where does it start?

Without the metronome, here's what typically happens:

- You breeze through the first key (at a fast tempo)
- You pause to think what comes next (without any tempo)
- You breeze through the next key (at a different fast tempo), etc.

This gives you the illusion of knowing the shapes when you really don't. At least you can't recall them while the music is playing, which is one of the crucial skills you are developing here.

Remember: the only knowing in music that counts proves to be knowing in time!

Skippy helps you think ahead. He holds a mirror up to you and keeps you honest.

Set the metronome to a slow tempo. The exact tempo varies from player to player. A fast tempo does not mean better. On the contrary, err on the side of being slower at first! See my tip on finding the best tempo below.

The Concept of "Cheater Beats":

Initially, you may need an additional step here before being able to switch keys in time with the metronome running. I have developed a concept that will help you — I call it "cheater beats":

- Play the first shape, then let a predetermined number of beats go by before starting the next key. Make it 4 beats at first and then take it down to 2, for example. See what works for you but choose a number **and then stick to it.**

I need to stress this: stay consistent in the number of cheater beats! The whole point of them resides in learning to think ahead in time.

If you lose yourself in the cheater beats and find yourself varying their number, do this:

- Say the next key and pattern in the rhythm of the cheater beats.
  A few examples below, from easier to harder:

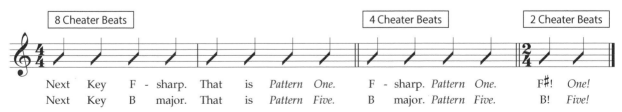

If saying the key and the shape seems too hard, say just one of the two. Vary which one you are using!

▐▐▐ **TIP:** Some students find it hard to speak out loud while playing. The cheater beats are a great way to ease yourself into accomplishing this feat. Start at a very slow tempo. Do it, even if just once. You will be richly rewarded if you do because it helps you get into the *Zone of Learning* (more on that later, but for now, consider this: The magic happens in that zone!).

With a bit of practice, you can take the cheater beats down to 2 beats. Then 1. Then skip them entirely. Experiment with just saying the key on the downbeat.

HOW TO PICK THE TEMPO: The toughest spots and hardest key transitions tell you the tempo to use. If you can barely make it in the tough transitions (typically around the six o'clock mark of the cycle), choose that tempo! And yes, this may mean that a few of the easier keys and transitions come easy, almost too easy!

This is a good thing because it provides you with opportunities to:

Use the time to think ahead! And if you still have mental capacity left, use one of these powerful ideas during the easier keys:

- Check your technique*
  - Are your left-hand fingers close to the fretboard?
  - Do you place the fingers close to the fret?
  - Check that your right-hand index and middle fingers are consistently alternating.
  - Scan for tension in your shoulders, arms, hands, or face.
  - Are you breathing evenly or holding your breath?

- Check your tone
  - Are you getting a fret buzz?
  - Is each note speaking clearly, or are there skips and choked notes, etc...?

- Check your phrasing
  - Pick a phrasing — legato (all notes smoothly connected. It's the hardest one!), staccato (short), or anything in between.
  - Advanced: try a swing phrasing as if you are walking a bassline.
  - Are you playing each note with similar note length, especially when shifting during a "crab?"
  - How about volume? Do you detect a difference between the sound of the index and middle fingers plucking?

- Check your timing
  - How precisely can you place your note on top of the click? Can you "erase" the click with your note? (For the *Pattern Practice*, I do not recommend practicing playing ahead of the beat or behind the beat. Do these types of exercises when learning repertoire or practicing specific groove exercises.)

---

* For more information on technique, consult my book: *Music Theory for the Bass Player*.

- Say out loud
  - Note names
  - Scale degrees
  - "Index-middle-index-middle" (referencing the right-hand alternating)

So much to pay attention to in the *Zone*. If you feel "bored" at a slower tempo while doing certain keys, use the remedies above. They work rather quickly against boredom!

 If you practice like this, even just a little bit — with this kind of focus, patience, and discipline — I can assure you that this method will work wonders for you. 10 minutes of practicing, using the exact processes described above, blows decades of mindless repetition out of the water. I have seen the effects of this kind of deep work with hundreds of students.

I also know that this approach can be demanding to do on your own. Having a teacher trained in this kind of instruction and a physical classroom or online community to do this with can make all the difference. If you are looking for further help, please refer to our resources at *Arisbassblog.com/PatternSystem*.

If you practice on your own and hit a roadblock, remember to:

- Set the tempo according to the toughest spot.
- Think ahead and focus on a detail from the list if you have space for it.
- Keep a log of the work that you have done. When doubts arise, this will help you to verify what you have already accomplished.
- And the most important tip of all: stick with short frequent bursts.

Do short, frequent bursts rather than hours of mindless practice!

Set a timer! If you do this right, you may be a bit exhausted after two or three minutes in the beginning. Slowly increase your focused practice time to ten minutes.

And, after each practice session: celebrate. Be happy about the work you have done! (More on that later!)

TIP: For *Pattern Practice*, avoid tempos slower than 55 bpm. It's quite difficult to get into a steady rhythmic flow at such a slow tempo. If you need a tempo slower than that (totally okay if you do — some do, some don't!), let two clicks of a faster tempo go by or feel the rhythm in subdivisions such as two or more beats per click.

▌▌ **NOTE:** You do not need to do all the variations of the above exercises in every single practice session. Just keep switching things up, keep it interesting. This will also keep all your neurons interested and alert. As soon as you are becoming better in one way of practicing, approach the same routine from a different angle as described above (descending only, saying note names, metronome, etc.…). The learning curve can be very steep in the beginning, but you will appreciate the satisfaction that comes from getting better quickly and practicing at a higher efficiency.

Definitions

What is a scale?

A scale is a set of notes that follows a formula of intervals. In this book, we only concern ourselves with the major/minor diatonic system — in other words, the major scale and its seven modes; as well as with several shapes within this scale, including triads/arpeggios and pentatonic shapes. A scale, its diatonic triads and modes are **music theory constructs** that are essential to master because music utilizes them in so many beautiful and recurring ways.

What do you call a *Pattern?*

In this book, we define a *Pattern* as the shape formed on the fretboard by the notes of a specific musical concept such as scales and chords. There are many more patterns in music, such as chord progressions, melodic patterns, rhythmic patterns and so on. This book predominantly uses the fretboard shapes formed by the major scales and some of the shapes contained within, such as diatonic triads and pentatonics. **The major scale forms five distinctive shapes within a given area on the bass.** Patterns are formed because of the nature of the scale and its realization on an instrument (the bass) that is tuned in fourths.

Imagine a pattern as a "pool of notes"; also as a reservoir for shapes within those patterns — modes, pentatonic scales, triads, chords, interval series. Each of the five patterns contains blueprints for many shapes — patterns within patterns — that we will study systematically. With practice, we will turn these into a powerful basis for true freedom on the fretboard.

Many think that by teaching patterns, one can circumvent the need to learn to read notation or shortcut the recommendation to understand music theory. While these approaches exist, this book does not count as one of them. What I teach here and how I teach it goes way beyond "just moving some patterns up or down." To just know the shapes will only be superficially useful. *The Pattern System* constitutes a learning system that includes not only the systematic, comprehensive, and creative study of the patterns but also mental training, self-coaching, focusing and improvisation. Improved technique is a great side effect of all of this, too.

What do you mean by *Area?*

An *area* on the bass is the region of either five frets in the *Open Area*, or six or seven frets (in *Areas 1* through *5*) in which the patterns of all keys occur.

Why are there five *patterns*? Why no *Pattern IV*?

The major scale consists of seven notes, yet we prescribe five patterns. Theoretically, we could create a pattern starting from each scale degree. While certainly possible, we prefer to work with five patterns. Here is why: take a look at the two "missing" ones below.

G major *"True" Pattern I* (extended fingering – three notes per string)

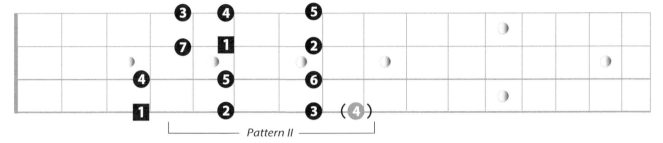

G major *Pattern IV* (extended fingering – three notes per string)

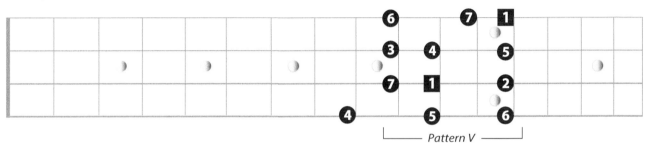

"True" *Pattern I* ("our" *Pattern I* starts on the seventh note of the scale) as well as *Pattern IV* use "extended fingering" (stretching over five frets on one string) and cover three notes per string consistently. They have their uses for special applications such as speed licks or tapping, but in *The Pattern System*, we do not spend much time on them because:

- As you see, the existing patterns are easily covering their notes — IV essentially equals "V plus one note," and *Pattern I* turns into a cumbersome *Pattern II*.

- Because they use extended fingerings, they are — at least initially — much more challenging. "The crab" shift circumvents this.

- Once you are comfortable in the system presented here, adding extended scalar patterns for creative applications proves very easy.

- As soon as you have mastered the basics of the system, you can easily combine patterns so that you will gain all the benefits of these extended fingering shapes as well.

 Why do you place D♭ as *Pattern III* in *Area 1* rather than as *Pattern V*? It would be so nice not to have to make that jump!

D♭ could fit into *Area 1* as *Pattern III* or *Pattern V*. Either works. I tried both versions and settled on the lower one: D♭, being a harder key, comes easier in the lower register at first. Since we will soon move up the neck, it won't make a difference in the end, but it seems a bit easier in the beginning.

The reason you are noticing it as a "jump" lies in the direction we have been practicing the patterns so far. With A♭ preceding D♭ — when practicing the cycle to the left — it feels like a jump down to stay in the area. Had we moved D♭ up to *Pattern V*, you'd just feel G♭ as a jump down. In order to stay in one area, you have to jump somewhere; else, you will continually weave your way up the neck.

 Ari, I sat down and created a different *Area Matrix*. It turns out beautifully symmetrical! And I remember it so much easier this way! Why shouldn't I use it instead?

I think getting lost in the symmetry of these shapes and the bass fretboard can be very worthwhile. Any activity engaging you with the fretboard will help you manage it. Many students have sent me their beautifully symmetrical DNA streaks or color-coded patterns. I say go for it creating those! The more you think about these shapes and the symmetry of the fretboard, the better.

That said: Many have tried to make practicing a certain sequence easier, particularly the cycle to the left that we spent a lot of time on in the beginning. They came up with mnemonics (and more) that worked great for that order. But if you do this — you shortcut yourself. **I do not want you to become an expert in playing through these exercises through the cycle in only one certain order.** Your system might work amazingly if you start on a certain note, in a certain area, or go in a certain sequence — but we are not aiming for that. In actual performance, music doesn't always come in a way that fits the specific sequence you worked out.

Rather, I want you to become an expert in:

- Thinking ahead
- Knowing the shapes from all directions
- Acing them on the fly
- Becoming flexible with the shapes within them
- Being fluid with these shapes, so they light up for you as you improvise

Keep in mind that once we plunge into the challenging *Connection Exercises* and are playing through a variety of sequences or exploring *Shapes within Shapes*, that one beautifully symmetrical way you found may not be able to help you.

You will not receive trophies for knowing it one way and one way only. Rather, practicing in as many variations as possible is key!

If my students come into a lesson and tell me they can ace everything I assigned them ascending, you can bet I will ask them to descend. Why? Since I know them and we have found our groove, I trust them! So, if they ace the ascending route (80 to 90% or so suffices, no perfection required!), let's immediately practice the next step!

This brings me to a very important point that I will revisit again and again with Skippy's help. When we talk about the *Zone of Learning*: as soon as you know something a little bit, in *The Pattern System*, change it!

In summary, I welcome you to create your own representations because it shows that you are working with this method at a deep level. As for practicing, I recommend you stick with the system as it is laid out here. I have tested various versions of this system with my students and found the most consistent success with the one presented here.

Scalar Studies
Groups of Three, Descending/Up and Back Down

Remember the note groupings you practiced in *Chapter 2*? In this chapter, I will show you a variation of this drill: we essentially just reverse the order of the group and practice groups of three descending/up and ascending/down. Practice these exercises in *Area 1* as well as the *Open Area*.

Below are examples for this exercise in a few *Area 1* keys.

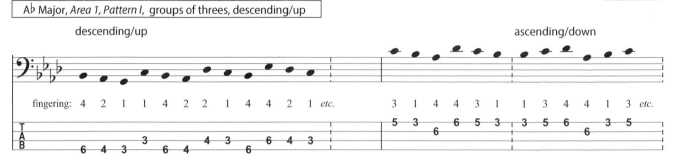

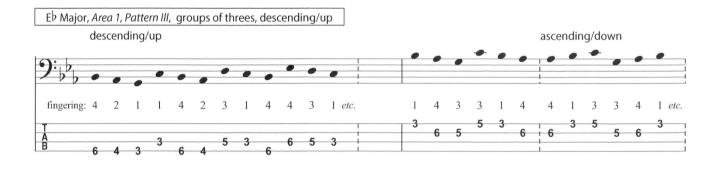

▌▌▌ TIP: I did not give the above samples any meter. Experiment with rhythmic variations. You can view the above as 12/8 and place the beat on dotted quarters, or experiment with a 6/4 feel and place the beat on quarter notes.

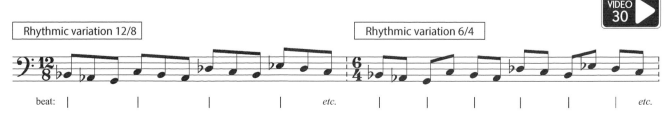

▌▌ **QUICK REMINDER:** Make sure each finger has its assigned fret according to the fingering of the pattern. Take note of the jump of a fourth between each 3-note group. These are typically a little tricky. Stick strictly to the default fingering for each pattern and shift the relevant finger over to the next string, lifting it as little as possible.

Improvised Explorations

Within a Pattern Through the Cycle

In this improvisation exercise, you will improvise "coming full circle": stay in one key for four bars, then switch to the next key without stopping.

Aim to go through the entire cycle doing each key for four measures, then change to the next key without stopping or pausing! If it helps you to have the cycle in front of you at first, do so, but wean yourself off as soon as possible. Use the rhythmic template if you like or come up with your own. As the key change approaches aim to visualize the next pattern in its entirety before the switch. Think ahead!

For now, use the materials from the scale freely, meaning without focusing on specific things like intervals, arpeggios, etc. Use scalar segments and runs, jumps, repeated notes as you please. Work on making musical sense by starting with an idea, such as a rhythm or motive or concept, and develop your improvisation from there.

Many love doing these exercises with a backing track. Please download yours here: *ArisBassBlog.com/PatternSystem*

VIDEO 31 ▶

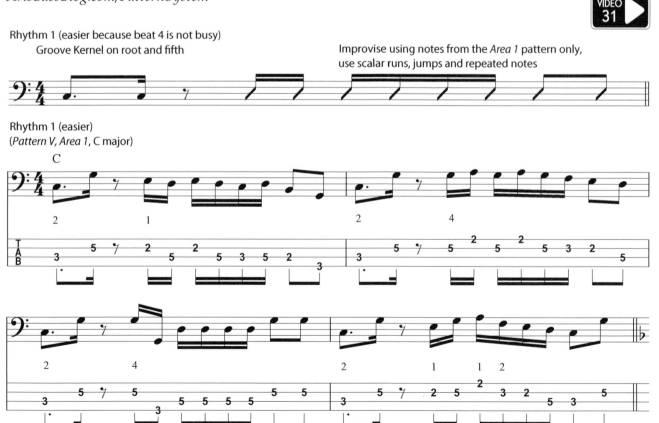

Rhythm 1 (easier because beat 4 is not busy)
Groove Kernel on root and fifth

Improvise using notes from the *Area 1* pattern only, use scalar runs, jumps and repeated notes

Rhythm 1 (easier)
(*Pattern V, Area 1*, C major)

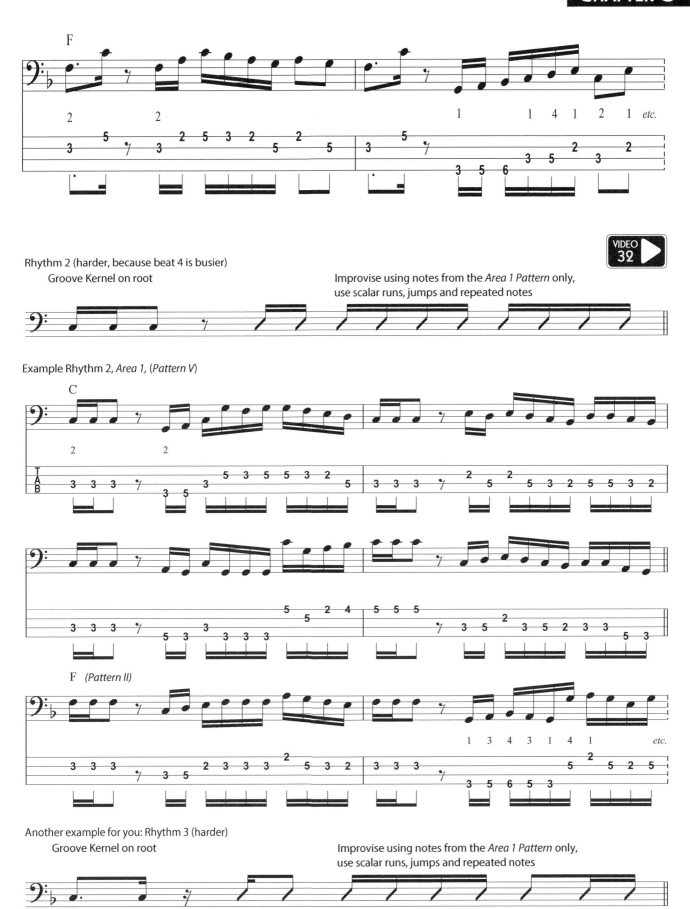

Rhythm 2 (harder, because beat 4 is busier)
Groove Kernel on root

Improvise using notes from the *Area 1 Pattern* only,
use scalar runs, jumps and repeated notes

Example Rhythm 2, *Area 1, (Pattern V)*

F *(Pattern II)*

Another example for you: Rhythm 3 (harder)
Groove Kernel on root

Improvise using notes from the *Area 1 Pattern* only,
use scalar runs, jumps and repeated notes

TEST YOUR UNDERSTANDING #3

1. To find the correct pattern for a key in a respective area, find:

    ❑ a. Any root in the area and extrapolate the shape from there

    ❑ b. The lowest note of the key in the area. That will be the name of the pattern and that will always be correct.

    ❑ c. Either of the above

    ❑ d. None of the above

2. On the four-string bass, there will be a few keys that look the same in the *Open Area* and *Area 1*. Identify those keys: _____/ _____ , _____/ _____

3. True or false: Fourths and fifths remain the only intervals you can repeat over and over and by doing so, hit every single key. ❑ True ❑ False

4. Using the Cycle of Fifths to practice different keys works so well because:

    ❑ a. It contains every key.

    ❑ b. Following the sequence means you only add or subtract one accidental with each change of key.

    ❑ c. Especially counterclockwise, it shows up in many chord progressions, which makes this practice a very applicable effort.

    ❑ d. It has proven to be a great way to organize keys, accidentals and note naming.

    ❑ e. All of the above

5. The Cycle of Fifths to the left can be called the cycle of fourths. Why?

    ❑ a. While technically true (because fourths and fifths are inversions of each other), it proves more practical to refer to it as the "Cycle of Descending Fifths," or the "Cycle to the Left," or the "Counter-clockwise Cycle," because it acknowledges the sound and musical value of the "falling fifth," a strong chord progression.

    ❑ b. Think of the cycle to the left as a never-ending string of V → I releases. You can hear this very strong resolution. Calling it "descending fifths" matches what it sounds like.

    ❑ c. Descending fifths have a stronger gravitational pull than ascending fourths. Naming it fifths provides a nod to that fact.

    ❑ d. All of the above

6. What do we mean by *area*? _____

    _____

7. In this book, what is a *pattern?* _____

    _____

8. Why is there no *Pattern IV?* _____

    _____

 **BLUEPRINT FOR PRACTICE #3**

Written Homework: Write out all *Open Area* diagrams into the book (note names and scale degrees).
pp. 70–75

---

1. PP: *All Area 1* keys as described in the chapter, cycle to the left; **p. 76** • **Video 27**
Record tempo and number of cheater beats, if any: _____ _____

---

2. PP: All *Open Area* keys through the cycle to the left; no more looking at the diagrams; **p. 28** • **Video 6**

---

3. SS: "Groups of 3, descending/up"; pick a few *Open Area* and *Area 1* keys (suggesting F, D, A♭ in both areas)
p. 83 • **Video 29**

---

4. IE: *Chapter 3* improvisation through the cycle to the left in the *Open Area*
p. 84–85 • **Videos 31 and 32**

AREA 2

Welcome to *Area 2*. You are now going up the neck, learning the patterns area by area. The purpose of this is systematic study. *Area 2* is the next area up the neck. It overlaps by three frets with *Area 1*.

Write out all patterns for *Area 2* below.

You do this by taking the *Area 2* patterns and continuing on to the next pattern.

This means:

If *Area 1* Pattern is:	It Becomes This Pattern in *Area 2*
PI	PII
PII	PIII
PIII	PV
PV	PVI
PVI	PI

Area 2 **stretches from fret 3 to fret 9:**

While this seems like a nice-to-know fact, don't worry too much about these fret numbers from here on out. Rather, focus on knowing the pattern for each key in each new area.

Area 2 Diagrams

Write out the *Area 2* patterns and identify the *Pattern Number* in the space provided.

Area 2 – "Area Map" – Note Names

C   *Pattern* _____

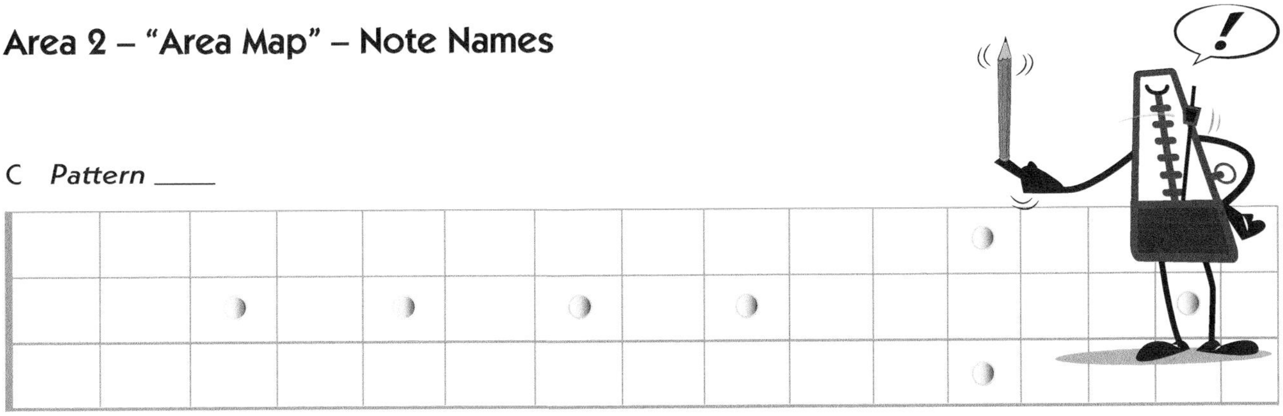

F   *Pattern* _____

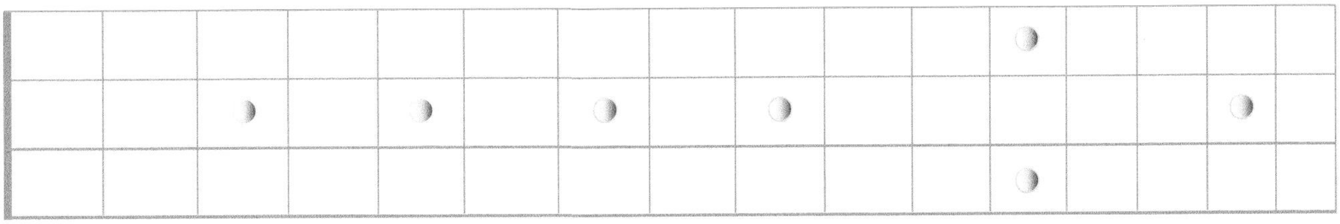

B♭   *Pattern* _____

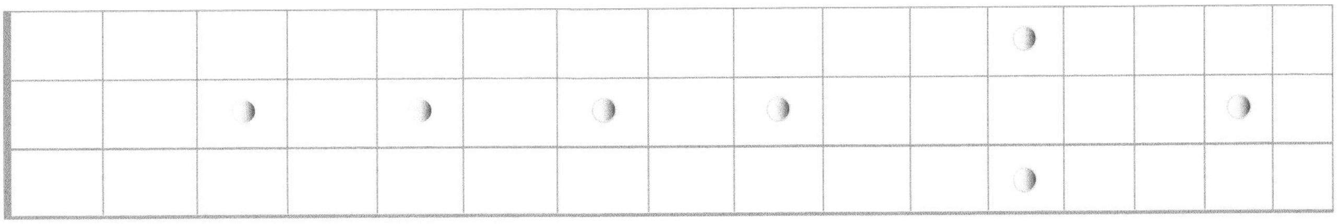

E♭   *Pattern* _____

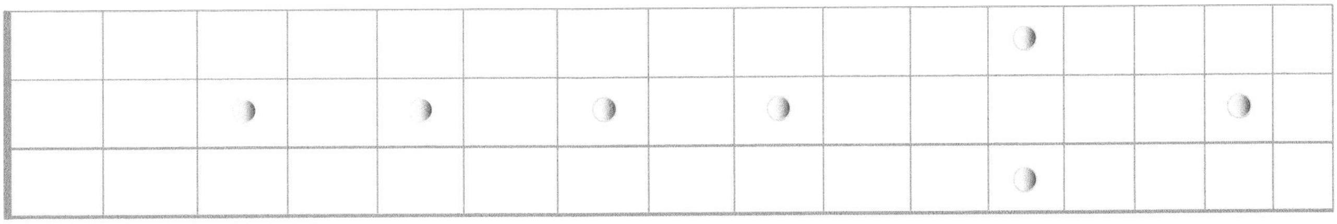

A♭   *Pattern* _____

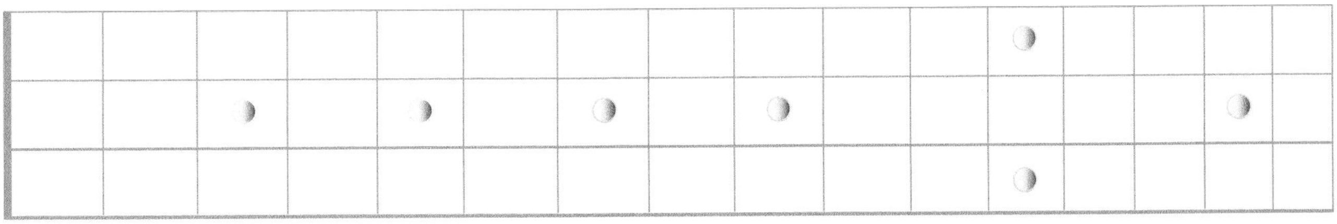

D♭ *Pattern* ____

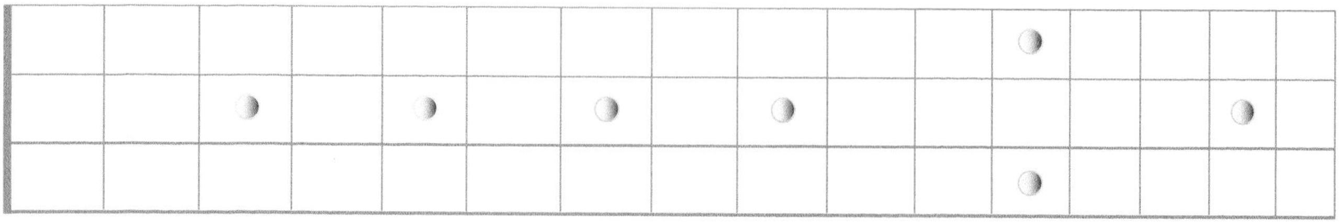

G♭ *Pattern* ____

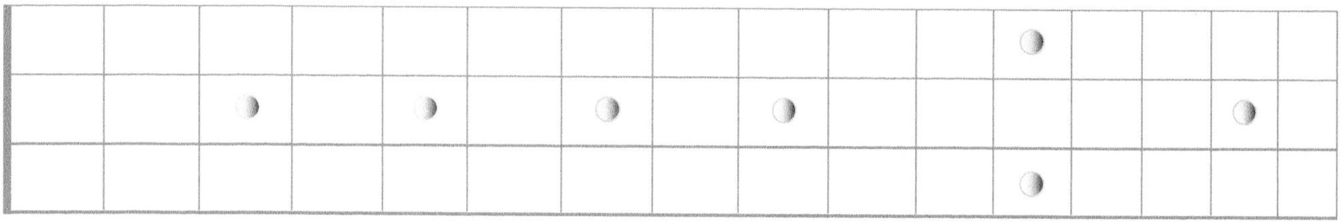

B *Pattern* ____

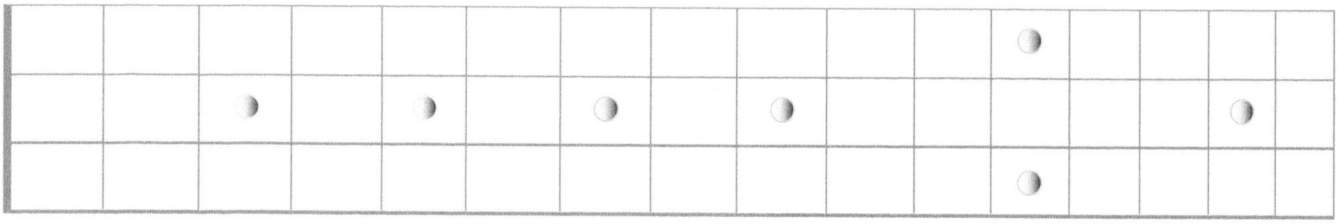

E *Pattern* ____

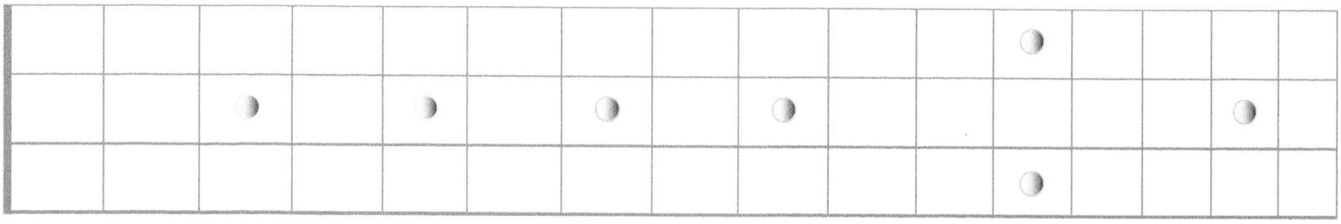

A *Pattern* ____

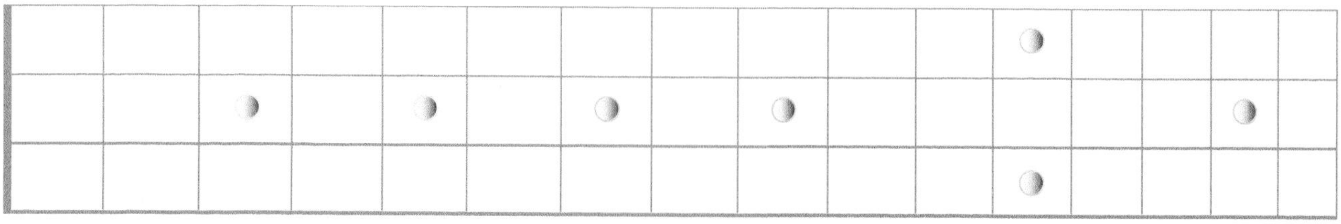

D   *Pattern* _____

G   *Pattern* _____

F♯   *Pattern* _____

C♯   *Pattern* _____

C♭   *Pattern* _____

Area 2 – "Area Map" – Scale Degrees

C   Pattern _____

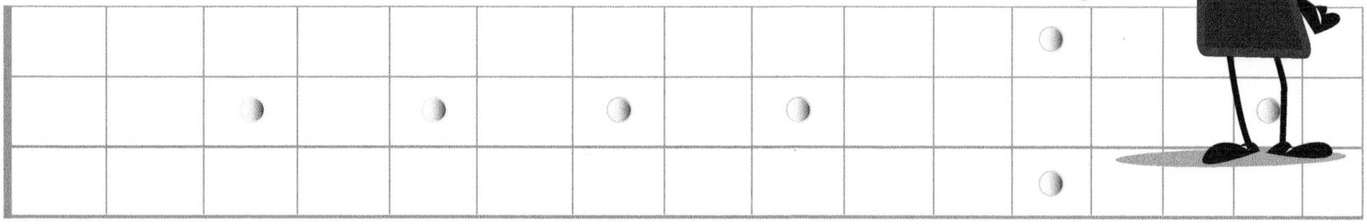

F   Pattern _____

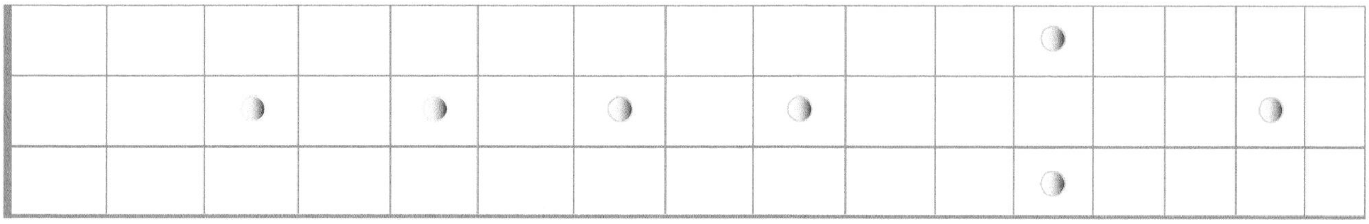

B♭ Pattern _____

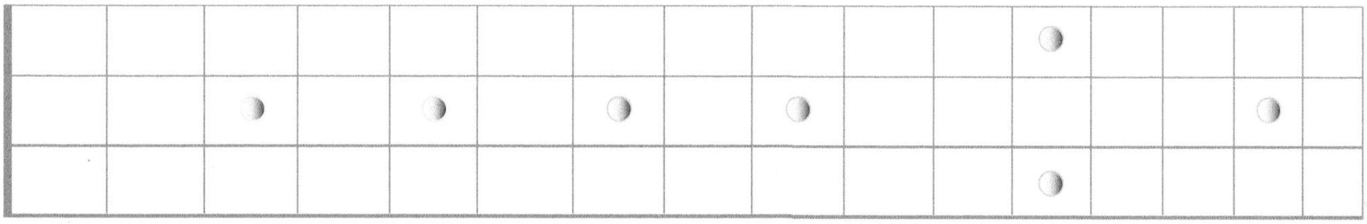

E♭ Pattern _____

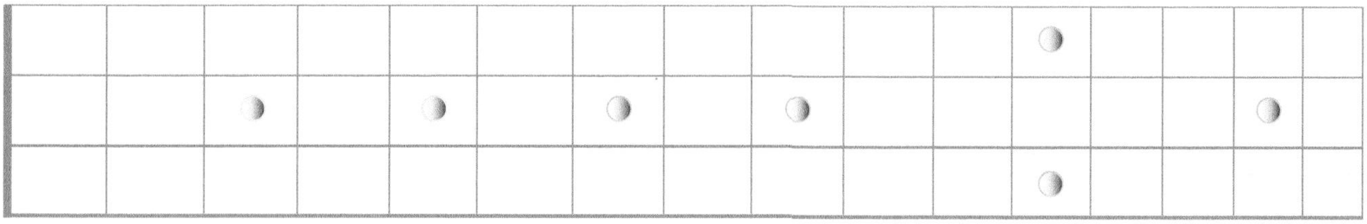

A♭ Pattern _____

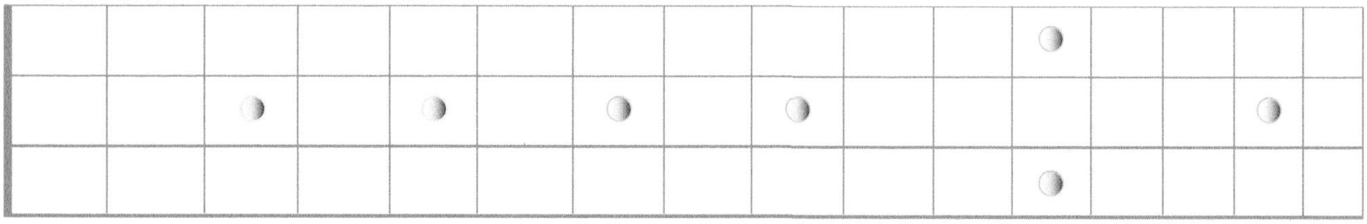

D♭ *Pattern* _____

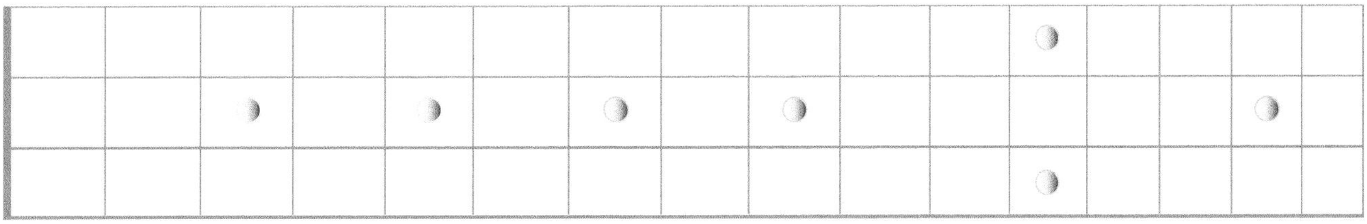

G♭ *Pattern* _____

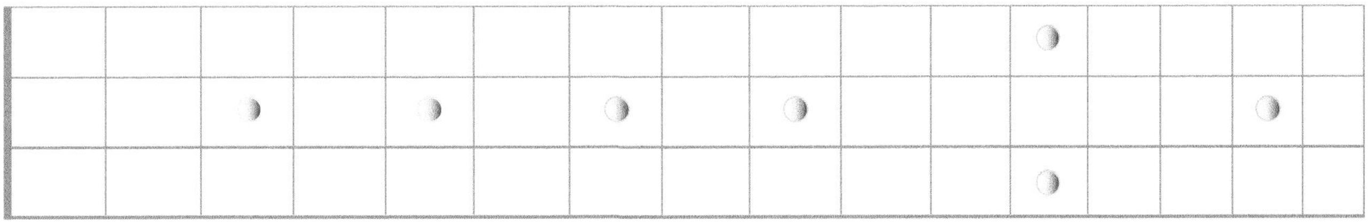

B *Pattern* _____

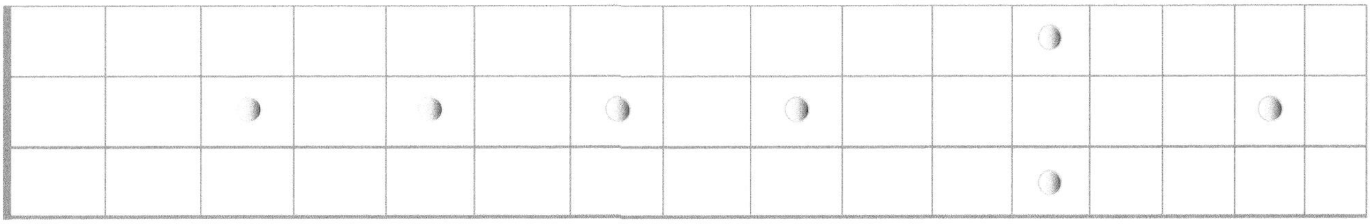

E *Pattern* _____

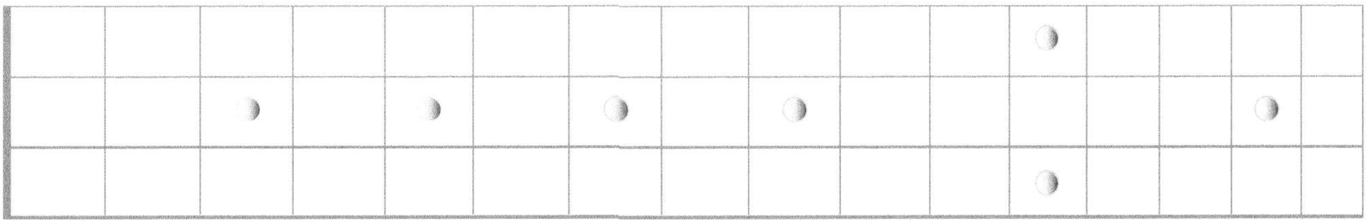

A *Pattern* _____

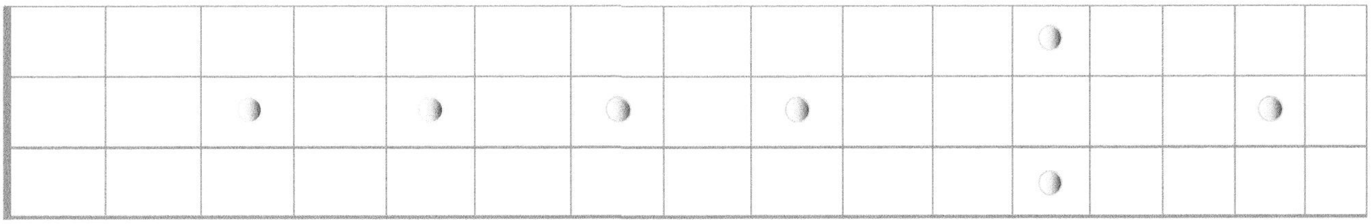

D   *Pattern* _____

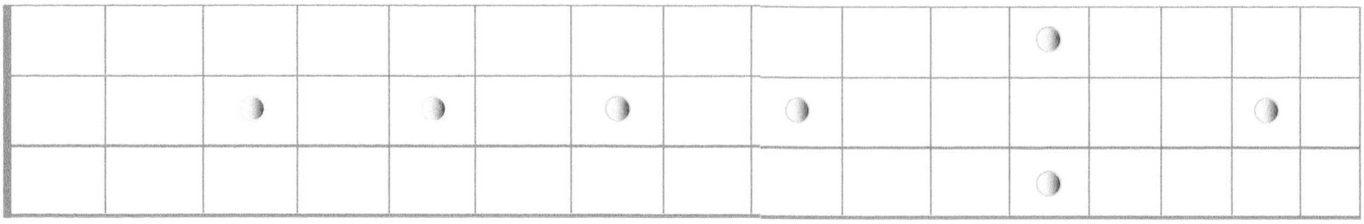

G   *Pattern* _____

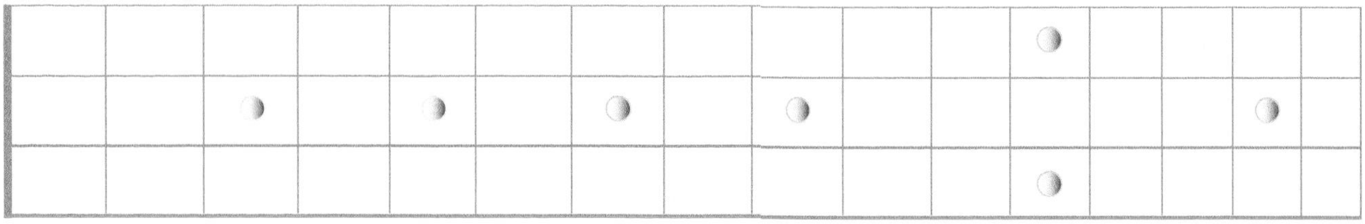

F♯   *Pattern* _____

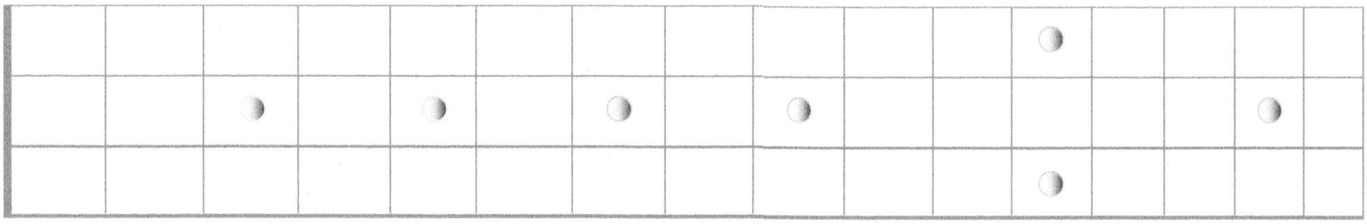

C♯   *Pattern* _____

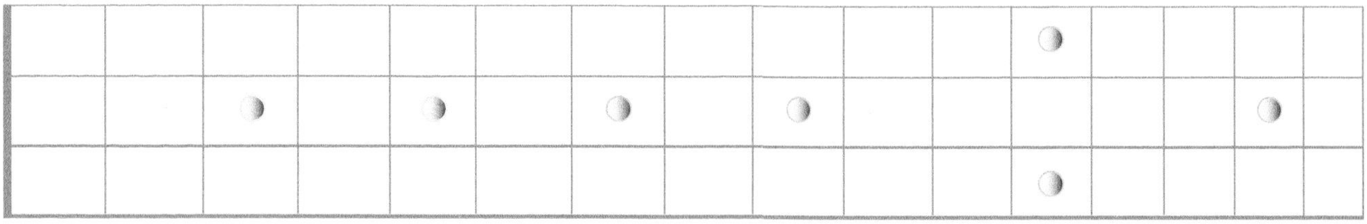

C♭   *Pattern* _____

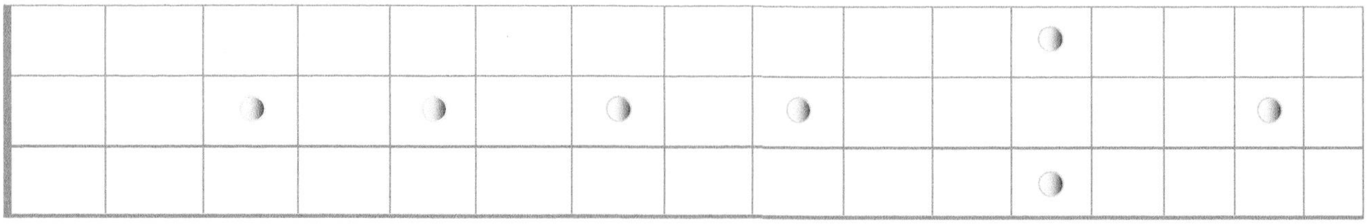

LIKE THIS

Revisit the Practice Like This Section in *Chapter 3* and practice in the same fashion. Use a metronome, include cheater beats if needed.

Now add this new practice regimen to your familiar routine:

- Play one key ascending, the next key descending:
  — Ascend C, descend F, ascend B♭, etc.
- Then, reversed:
  — Descend C, ascend F, descend B♭, etc.
- Also, turn the direction of the cycle around: C G D A, etc.

A Word on How to Turn Around

Sometimes notes occur in the previous pattern as well as the following pattern at the turn around point either on the top or on the bottom. If so, repeat the note.

Here are examples of what turning around could look like. Look for the boxes and fingering guides in the example below. You are in Area 2 — notice how notes could repeat on the bottom or top. Always position your fingers such that you play the fingering for the entire pattern correctly — including the very first note! If you doubled up on that first note, you may need to shift to a different finger.

Practice these exercises without any regard for meter. The downbeats will fall on odd places at times and may be completely unrelated to when the key changes — they are only dictated by the pattern. Just keep going. In the beginning, I recommend just setting the metronome to quarter notes and play one note per click, or even just a note every other click (half notes).

Also, start with C descending, so you practice both directions for all keys.

REMINDER: Strive to recall the whole pattern instantly before you switch to the new pattern or key. Ideally, a snapshot in your mind is all you need to recall it. While your fingers are busy playing the snapshot, you have time to think about the next key. This means you are multitasking on a high level. Getting comfortable in that "zone" proves extremely useful as you play in a musical situation.

Can you do this without stopping in between?

When you can proceed from one key to the next without stopping and stick to a steady metronome beat without cheater beats, you have reached a milestone. It means that you know the patterns and can think ahead while playing them. Since the patterns will flow easier now, you can relax and work on thinking ahead or developing other musical details.

REMEMBER: The metronome forces you to evaluate how well you are doing. At what tempo are you beginning to crumble during the toughest spot? Find that tempo and practice right at that edge. Keep a log of the tempos you practice at so you can track your progress!

"But I Could Do It Perfectly When I Practiced!"

The Flummoxing Phenomenon of Messing up in the Lesson or on Stage

Ever practiced something thoroughly, sounding "perfect" at home just to come into the lesson or on stage to see yourself crumble and fail? It sure has happened to me!

Yeah, I totally know the feeling, Skippy!

This phenomenon can have many causes and many remedies. Most of them have to do with not listening to yourself properly when practicing. **I am presenting two typical examples here:**

1 • Adding "Thinking Pauses" without Noticing

Maybe a run, jump or fill gives you — literally — pause. If you don't pay attention to a steady tempo but instead add random pauses "to think" — you need to fix it! It may be that you are not ready for a steady beat yet — fine, just be aware of it. Switch off the metronome, isolate the toughest spot, and practice it slowly. Then bring in Skippy! Start very slowly. He will help you execute the tough spot in time.

OOOOOOMMMMM!

**Fix it without a metronome,
then bring in Skippy and
relax into it and focus on the beat…**

2 • Practicing Mistakes

If we don't listen to ourselves attentively, another problem tends to emerge — we start to practice mistakes. Maybe we are aware that the note was wrong, but we just redo the note right then and there or skip right past the mistake and move on. This could have very bad consequences. When our mind begins to block out false starts or ignores dropped or extra beats, practice can become a sequence of:

$$\text{Start} \longrightarrow \text{Stumble} \longrightarrow \text{Correct} \longrightarrow \text{Move on.}$$

Sometimes we may repeat this sequence so often that we end up being able to play a spot correctly only after we stumbled over the obstacle first or after that extra thinking pause. We actually perform with that stumble or pause "built-in" to our performance. We might not be aware of this even happening at all! Or if we are, we are quick to tell ourselves that this was "just a false start" — just a "one-time thing." **Meanwhile, we practiced the false start so well we cannot do without it anymore.** And we do not hear it as a mistake anymore either.

It's no wonder that on stage or in the lesson, you stumble again — "just like you practiced it." Yet now — with a witness — the error does stick out and may even surprise you.

Conclusion and Remedies

Habits such as these likely **delude us into miscalculating our capabilities**. I have already mentioned the metronome as a great tool to bring self-deceptions, especially hesitations or pauses, for thinking, to light. Skippy will also point out errors and "false starts" if you set an accented downbeat according to the meter.

An equally powerful method I recommend is to record yourself. In our guided online courses, the posting of student recordings has become a powerful tool for self-assessment and focused practice. When that red recording light goes on, we shift to attention. Practicing this shift proves invaluable!

To summarize — to fix the issue:

- Shift your attention and listen to yourself.
- Identify the issue and isolate it.
- Loop it. No metronome at first, if needed, then with the metronome.
- Go slowly, using the metronome.
- Record yourself.

Whether you are practicing a song or patterns, bringing attention to such details will make all the difference.

**Yes, Skippy will help,
and fewer
slip-ups will happen!**

Am I slow for not getting this quicker?

No, you are not.

Unfortunately, one of the biggest mistakes that many methods, teachers, and students alike tend to make is to disregard the importance of step-by-step and comprehensive practice — most importantly — practice that includes creative application! The assumption is that just by knowing something in theory (such as a scale from root to root!), it will magically be accessible to you when you play a groove, fill or solo.

Not so! And no — it's not you!

Many get stuck on their musical journey somewhere along the way, and they understand intuitively that this plateau has to do with a lack of knowledge about how music is put together.

One way of categorizing how music is put together is to study the patterns of music theory. Once players realize that, they can bravely tackle learning the theory. However, they often do so away from the instrument! Unfortunately, they then realize that all these numbers and letters do not seem to improve their actual playing or result in more confidence when grooving or soloing!

If this is you, let me tell you that this is no fault of yours but a flaw in the approach and methodology you have been using. Follow this system and it will reliably bridge this gap.
The key factors in this approach being that it:

- Is step-by-step and comprehensive
- Uses improvisation
- Applies the click to ensure you are thinking ahead
- Optimizes your practice by employing mental techniques and visualization

The good news is that this is 100% doable with a bit of patience and consistency. Besides my own experience, hundreds of my students have confirmed to me how much this method has helped them.

Stop blaming yourself. Adjust your expectations; don't fight the reality that deep knowledge takes a step-by-step approach.

Over time, the process of recalling all this material becomes quicker as long as you give yourself a chance. You will save yourself a lot of time and heartache by not trying to take the entire flight of stairs at once, but by going step by step.

**Skippy approves of a
step-by-step approach**

Why do you include TAB in this book? I thought only those that are not serious use TAB.

I encourage everyone to learn to read sheet music. If you are just learning to read, utilize our upcoming *Reading Method* that goes along beautifully with *The Pattern System*. As a matter of fact, those two make for a pretty powerful combination since our *Reading Method* uses the patterns you are learning here. More info is available at *ArisBassBlog.com/PatternSystem*.

So, why do I include TAB?

- Because TAB underscores fingerings and shows exactly which position the exercise is intended for.

- It also helps those who may need a bit of help reading or cannot read at all yet.

- Because I want to meet you where you are! If TAB sits in your toolbox and helps you, great! If not, just ignore it!

I agree that it can be a crutch, but I also like to use whatever helps you!

 I want to improve super-fast. What if I practice ten hours a day? How quickly will I get through it?

The most important factor is the depth of your focus. While putting in a lot of hours may help you improve faster, I maintain that focused shorter practice sessions are far more effective than hours of mindlessly moving your fingers. *The Pattern Practice*, with its specific and targeted drills, can get you very fast results. Focus on the depth of focus rather than the number of minutes or hours spent.

I suggest that you divide your practice routine into several 20-30 minute sessions.

You can speed up learning by practicing more each day — but take frequent breaks. If you are doing the exercises correctly, you will feel like you just took a brisk walk or did a workout session. Take short breaks between your focused practice time.

You say to take frequent breaks. Does it matter what I do in those breaks?

In the break, ground yourself, take a stretch, walk around, look out the window, interact with a favorite person, pat your pet, or grab a cup of tea. Resist the urge to jump on a gadget or screen and overload your mind at this moment. Right after your practice session, your mind does valuable processing and integrating. Do not minimize the fruits of your hard labor by immediately jumping onto something fast and flashy. Let what you practiced settle in for a minute and relax. Or move for a minute. It feels nice!

FAQ   Can I ever practice too much?

Be aware that there is a point of diminishing returns that can emerge after a certain number of hours-per-day practiced. I do not recommend working more than three hours daily on this system because it would not enhance learning. It would take time from other important areas of practice and life. I suggest you take one day a week off to give yourself time to process and integrate the material.

This system works on a few areas of study simultaneously. You move through several areas of the bass at once because all the exercises complement each other and further ingrain your learning. You'll integrate it all with improvisation exercises and interval drills. Trust me — it will take hold. Focus on regular practice rather than overdoing it one day and running out of steam the next. Follow a regular pace and reap predictably satisfying results.

Scalar Studies

Interval Study in Thirds (Ascending/Up)

This introduces the practice of playing interval studies within the patterns. Let's start with thirds: play diatonic ascending thirds from every scale step. On top — reverse and descend accordingly.

Think of it as a formula for ascending thirds through the scale — **"two up, one back."** That means: two notes in the scale up (i.e., up a major or minor third) and one back (that could be a major or minor second — essentially, you are playing the note you just left out earlier). Then two up again, one back and so forth. When playing descending thirds going down the scale, the formula reverses: two down (down a third), one (a second) back up, and so forth.

Remember to stay in the pattern only. If you struggle, say out loud: "two up, one back, two up, one back."

Saying scale degrees is very effective with this exercise.

Here are a few examples for this exercise — I am using various keys so that each pattern is demonstrated.

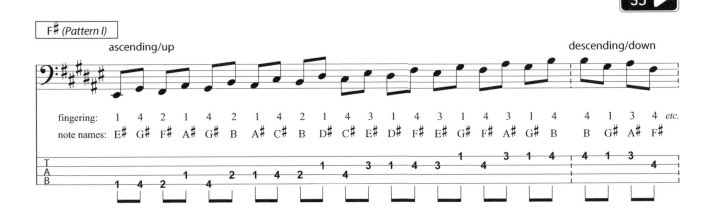

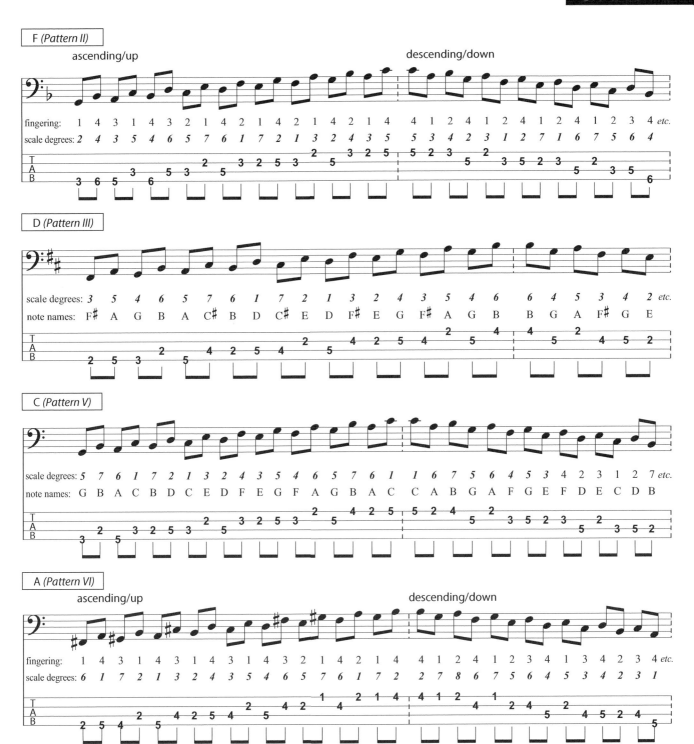

Focus on playing legato, alternating your right-hand fingers, and achieving an even tone and rhythm. Make your left hand/finger movements as small as possible. Press the strings straight down — no bending — to ensure proper intonation.

TIP: Also do these exercises in the *Open Area*!

Proper strategy wins the day (and the groove)!

Pedal Notes Through the Cycle in Area 2

When you pedal, you repeatedly come back to a "pedal tone" — any note can work depending on your harmonic context. Chord tones are typically a good starting point. Pedaling always makes for a certain "wow" factor — perfect for creating peaks in your own (or during someone else's) solo.

NOTE: Pedaling draws a lot of attention, so use it wisely.

Technical aspects:

Pedaling is quite literally "High-Intensity Interval Training," pardon the pun. It creates a terrific workout opportunity for the left and right hand alike. Depending on the notes you play, there can be a lot of string crossing — across the entire bass. Keep your hand calm, minimize movement, and make sure to adhere to one-finger-per-fret for best results!

Pedaling offers opportunities for countless variations:

- Apply a variety of rhythmic groupings (1+1, 1+2, 3+1, 3+3+2, for example, work great). There are examples of this in the following exercises.
- Pedal with the root (sounds stable) or the fifth (sounds dramatic — creates a peak) or any chord tone.
- Pedal with different octaves.
- Open strings work great as pedal notes.

In our course, we go deeply into the musical possibilities that pedaling offers. Try a few of the examples below. Pick a key and practice it for a while. Then move on to the next key. Play to a backing track. Below I am giving you an example for each *Pattern* number in *Area 2*.

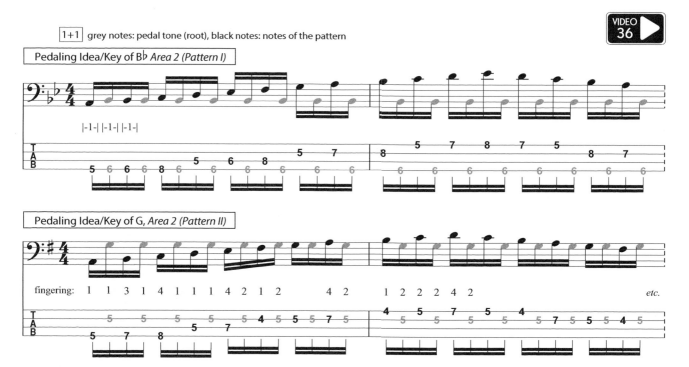

1+2

Pedaling Idea/Key of F, *Area 2 (Pattern III)*

Pedaling Idea/Key of E♭, *Area 2 (Pattern V)*

3+3+2

Pedaling Idea/Key of C, Area 2 (Pattern VI)

If these are challenging, give Skippy a rest at first to figure out the flow of notes, fingerings, and technical challenges. Then bring him in for those winning "Finger Kung Fu" moves!

Skippy is "Karate Click"

TEST YOUR UNDERSTANDING #4

Write the associated pattern for each area and key listed below:

1. *Open Area*– Db major – *Pattern* _____
2. *Area 1* – C major – *Pattern* _____
3. *Area 1* – C♯ major – *Pattern* _____
4. *Area 1* – D major – *Pattern* _____
5. *Area 1* – Eb major – *Pattern* _____
6. *Area 1* – E major – *Pattern* _____
7. *Area 1* – F major – *Pattern* _____
8. *Area 2* – F♯ major – *Pattern* _____
9. *Area 2* – G major – *Pattern* _____
10. *Area 2* – Ab major – *Pattern* _____
11. *Area 2* – A major – *Pattern* _____
12. *Area 2* – Bb major – *Pattern* _____
13. *Area 2* – Cb major – *Pattern* _____

BLUEPRINT FOR PRACTICE #4

Written Homework: Write out all *Area 2* diagrams into the book (note names and scale degrees).
pp. 89–94

1. **PP:** *Area 1,* cycle to the left: one key ascending, next descending, next ascending etc. metronome marking: __ cheater beats if any: ___ **p. 95** • **Videos 33 and 34**
optional: also practice in the cycle to the right

2. **PP:** *Area 2,* cycle to the left: one key ascending, next descending, next ascending etc. metronome marking: ___ cheater beats if any: ___ **p. 95** • **Videos 33 and 34**

3. **SS:** Interval studies in thirds; ascending/up; pick a few keys in various areas (suggesting G E Db in the *Open Area, Area 1* and *Area 2*) **pp. 100–101** • **Video 35**

4. **IE:** Pedaling with the root, cycle to the left, *Area 1* and *Area 2* **pp. 102–104** • **Video 36**

5. **Bonus SS:** *Area 2,* "Groups of 3" descending/up (suggesting keys F♯ Eb C) **p. 83** • **Video 29**

 # Connection Exercises

CONNECTION EXERCISES

In this chapter, I show you the *Connection Exercises* — the *gold standard* of practicing *The Pattern System*. *Connection Exercises* provide a brilliant way to maximize the impact of these abstract drills because they mimic what music does:

You are playing a song, improvising or grooving over the current chord. The next chord change comes your way, and you now want the sound possibilities that go with this new chord change available instantly at your fingertips — in the same area you currently are on the fretboard as well as everywhere else on the bass. Our patterns perfectly organize — "sound possibilities"— and they come beautifully packaged with the best fingerings. They contain the complete knowledge of where notes are everywhere on the fretboard — which, of course, also frees up the possibility to use notes outside of the patterns with knowledge of what that will sound like. From your mind, all these possibilities will flow effortlessly onto the fretboard as you move to the next chord or scale, whether up and down the neck or staying in one area.

This essentially unlocks the magic of *The Pattern System* — to know the notes so well you can forget about them! *Connection Exercises* will get you there.

Connection Exercises are a series of drills where you switch between different patterns of an area according to a certain number of beats — essentially, you are switching "inside" the pattern, not at the lower or upper end of it.

Prerequisites:

Remember that for *Connection Exercises* to "click" for you, you must:

- Know where the tonic(s) is/are in the pattern.
- Be able to visualize the entire pattern!
- Know the five patterns with correct fingering ascending as well as descending! *

Ingredients of Connection Exercises

- An **area** (the *Open Area*, or *Area 1* or *2*)
- A **sequence** of keys (the cycle of descending fifths, for example, which you have been working with a lot so far)
- Determination of what to practice (for now, you are just doing the scalar Patterns, later you will expand to *Patterns within Patterns* like triads, pentatonics, chords, and chord progressions)
- A **starting point** (a key and a starting note within it)
- A **number of beats** (such as 8, but it could be 7, 9 or any other. 8 is a good starting point)

---

* Remember: Knowing a pattern descending means being able to play it descending without ascending it first!

Step-by-Step Instructions

In the example below, you will practice scalar patterns in *Area 1*, going through the cycle of fifths to the left (C, F, B♭, etc.) starting from the lowest note of the (C) major scale using an 8-beat count.

Step 1 • Set a metronome to either a 4-beat downbeat (for two times 4) or an 8-beat downbeat. This means that Skippy will either go…

> **tic** toc toc toc **tic** toc toc toc… (4-downbeat), or

> **tic** toc toc toc toc toc toc toc **tic** toc toc toc toc toc toc toc… (8-downbeat)

Step 2 • Find your starting point (the lowest note of C — *Pattern V* in *Area 1* — is G, so third fret on the E-string, second finger).

Step 3 • Play eight beats — which equals eight quarter notes — of *Pattern V* in C major.

Step 4 • Wherever you land at the end of eight beats switch on the fly to the next pattern in the sequence, i.e., F in *Pattern II*. Keep the same playing direction, play the next note, in this case, A (second fret on the G-string, first finger). Do not pause as you switch scales.

Step 5 • Play F major continuing in the same direction you are currently playing. When you reach the end of the pattern, turn around without repeating the highest (or lowest) note.

Steps 6 and on: repeat this process until you have gone through the entire cycle.

Points to remember:

- Do not interrupt the patterns — no extra notes, no skips, no doubling up on top.
- Seamlessly go into the next note of each new shape. Think ahead! — already know the next scale and its pattern on beat 7 (or even earlier, if possible).
- Don't turn around when you switch keys; instead, keep the direction going until you reach the end of whatever pattern you are in, then turn around and continue through that pattern until the appropriate number of beats have passed.

The entire set of *Connection Exercises* as described above are written out for you in the examples that follow.

The goal is to immediately switch to the new pattern at the top of the beat, with the next pattern's fingering applied correctly from the start. Ideally, you will **see the next entire pattern in your mind's eye** and place your fingers accordingly. I highlighted a few key spots:

- Sometimes you'll have to use the same finger twice (see the transition between A♭ and D♭).
- Other times small jumps and shifts occur (F to B♭ in this next example).

There is only one correct way to do this.

NOTE: First note of new key marked in grey on the next page.

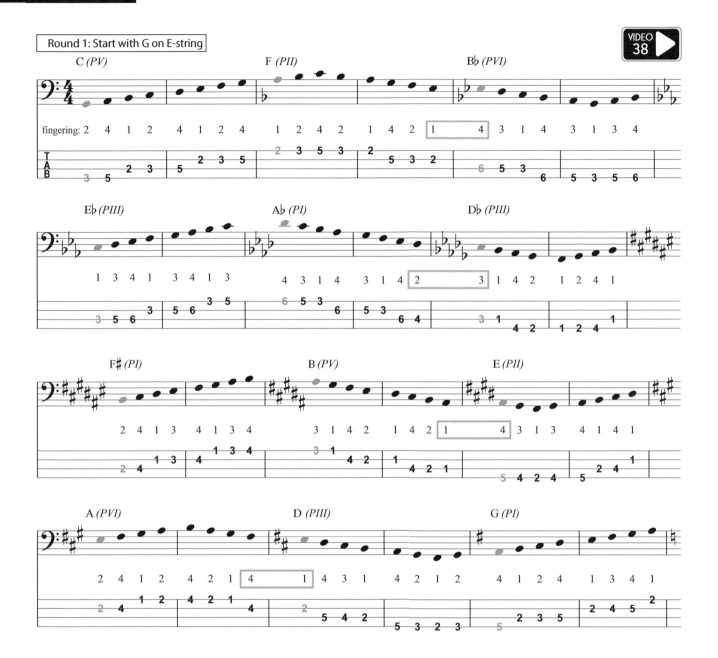

VIDEO 38

As soon as you begin to get the hang of this, vary the starting point within your starting key, so start *Pattern V* of C major — not on the low G, but on the A above it. Or start it from the high C or from a note on the D-string. Wherever you decide to start, just keep going for another round and the chips will fall differently yet again. I have included a few variations using different starting points below.

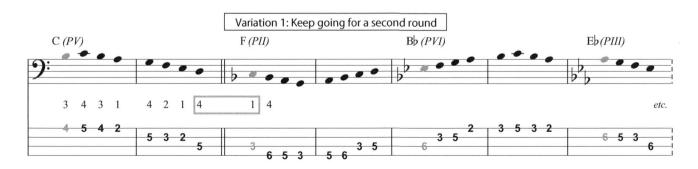

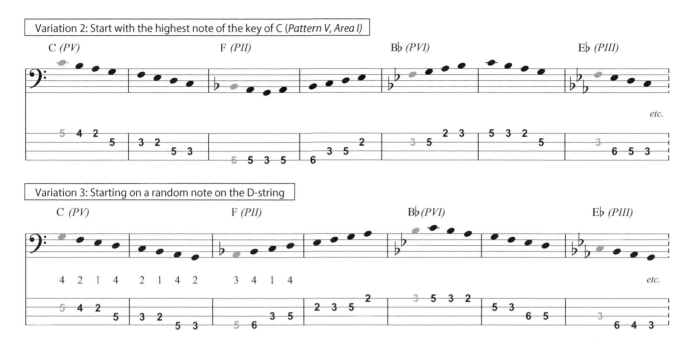

Variation 2: Start with the highest note of the key of C (*Pattern V, Area I*)

C *(PV)*   F *(PII)*   B♭ *(PVI)*   E♭ *(PIII)*

etc.

Variation 3: Starting on a random note on the D-string

C *(PV)*   F *(PII)*   B♭ *(PVI)*   E♭ *(PIII)*

etc.

By varying the entry point, you change the note where the key change occurs. This forces you to draw from your knowledge of the patterns rather than to just learn a sequence by heart.

It's OK to go very slowly at first.

Example Strategies:

- Play half notes at a tempo of 60.
- Use cheater beats (see below for a great trick).
- Or switch the metronome off entirely until it gets easier.

 Hey Ari, I made a cool matrix mapping out the notes when the scales change! So, all I have to learn are the intervals at the point of the new scale! Cool, aye?

Please understand this very important concept: the goal for you is not to become an expert in repeating the above sequence — or any other one for that matter — by learning it by heart. While interesting and impressive, this will not give you the flexible "thinking ahead" ability we are after. Rather, I want you to be able to go fluidly from one key to the next no matter where the change points may fall. You can achieve this by visualizing the next pattern while still playing the current one — then, on the switch, you can seamlessly continue in the new pattern, according to the visualization in your mind. This visualization allows you to join the pattern at any point.

- If it helps you to have the *Area Map* in front of you in the beginning, do it.
- If you can only do it without a metronome at first, no problem! Bring Skippy in as soon as you have a basic handle on the concept, at a very slow tempo.
- And always follow this cardinal rule: as soon as it gets easier, change something to switch things up and continuously challenge yourself.

I am having trouble keeping track of the 8 beats while executing all these mental and finger acrobatics. Any tips for not adding beats or dropping some here and there?

It's not uncommon to lose count of the eight beats with all the multitasking you are doing. This will become easier very quickly. I recommend you experiment with these proven remedies:

- Use your body, sway back and forth to mark out every beat or maybe every other beat. Or tap your right and left feet to mark out uneven and even beats, respectively. Rhythm lives in the body, so use movement to help you feel it there. If you sway every other beat, you will do each side twice to accumulate 8 beats.

- Cheater Beats in Connection Exercises — once again, words to the rescue: Experiment with counting out loud but combine what you say with the pattern names. Many have found this to be helpful (mostly one syllable per beat):

  - C – is – *Pattern* – V – next – is – key – of – F.
  - F – is – *Pattern* – II – next – is – B – flat.

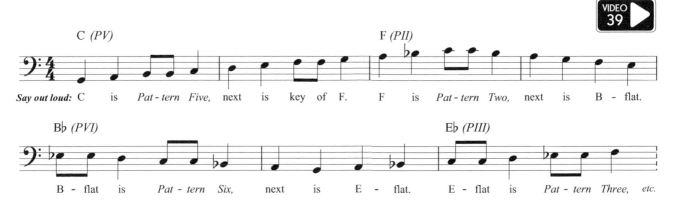

- Remember to set the metronome to an "8" downbeat, so every eighth beat will sound different, which will help you check yourself.

- Or you may find it easier to keep track of two measures of 4/4, which is also much more common than a measure of 8/4, when you are not speaking note names or steps, count 1-2-3-4, 2-2-3-4.

- No need to "sing" these notes. Saying or whispering them works just as well.

 Some students grasp these patterns and the mental processes required to master them quite easily, while others struggle with the underlying logic at first. This doesn't reflect on your musical (or any other!) ability in any way. It typically is just a sign that some fundamentals are not second nature yet. If you have a hard time, these reminders usually help:

- The pattern is named by the lowest scale degree. (Verify this for each pattern by saying scale degrees!) Remember the exception for *Pattern I*, which starts on the seventh scale degree.

- You must know where the tonic is in the pattern. Find the tonic or tonics for each pattern! All other notes in the pattern relate to that note!

- Know the pattern so well that you can recall it instantly — without much thinking so that you can perform it from all directions.

As you learn this, avoid comparing yourself to others. Rather, keep track of your own progress and look forward to your increasingly competent self in the future. Soon enough, you will look back on this chapter of your journey — and smile at how far you've come.

Remember these strategies to keep you moving along:

- Go slowly, potentially without a metronome at first.
- Aim for practicing this just a little bit at a time — but do that every day.
- Do the improvisation exercises with backing tracks to experience the joy of applying these patterns creatively. (For jam tracks, check our resources.)
- Reach out for help. We have communities ("Pattern Cohorts") going through this system together. We also have practice groups, courses, jam tracks, and many other additional resources. (*ArisBassBlog.com/PatternSystem*)
- Progress does not necessarily follow a linear pattern. But, as Skippy wisely points out, as long as you stay in touch with these exercises, you will see great progress over time.

**As Skippy demonstrates,
taking stock of and investing in your practice
pays dividends over time!**

Why are These Connection Exercises so Hard Initially?

1. This is mentally challenging work. You are being asked to think ahead while playing specific notes. This is hard at first. **But know that thinking ahead is one of the most important skills you are learning in this system.**

2. In addition, you must recall all patterns/scales instantly — all while doing something else with your fingers. You must keep track of multiple information streams: the notes you are playing and the ones that come next, the sequence of scales, the fingering, the scale steps and note names, proper execution. **Keeping track of multiple streams of information is a crucial skill for every musician and these exercises are helping you sharpen that skill.**

3. Because your ears may be insufficient by themselves to help you. When you play a scale by ear from the tonic to the tonic, you can easily identify it and do not need to know the fretboard that much at all — you can just hear the sequence of whole steps and half steps. Just knowing a scale like this does not guarantee that you can proficiently use its notes creatively and freely everywhere on the bass and in any order. Connection Exercises with their sometimes difficult switching and starting points pose a welcome challenge here — they force you to know the material on the fretboard rather than allow you to just go by ear. Mind you, I am not suggesting that you don't use your ears. I am encouraging you to **know the fretboard without having to hear the notes first. Visual and kinesthetic knowledge gives you new access points and frees you up tremendously.**

> *Music is a full-minded contact activity, and this is your Dojo!*

With a bit of practice, the fretboard literally lights up with all possible notes of the new key readily at your fingertips.

Ear Training

You can actively integrate your auditory skills and ear training into your practice of the patterns. I don't believe it ever makes sense for a musician to let their ears take a back seat!

Here's how:

1. Say the scale degrees while keeping the sound of the tonic/root in your mind's ear. Scale degrees should not be abstract numbers you are just running through in order, but rather, they should have sonic meaning. Play a root. Then think of it and internally hear the various scale degrees (numbers) in relationship to it.

   - How clearly can you hear it inside your mind's ear? Can you sing the notes?
   - Connect the numbers to sounds. Try to hear the notes inside your mind or sing the tonic as soon as you switch to a new pattern in the Connection Exercises.

2. As you are thinking ahead to the next pattern, see if you can also "pre-hear" the next pattern before you play it.

   - Can you hear the next tonic/root?
   - How about the scale degree with which you start the pattern?
   - Both are great options.

If you are looking to improve your ears, check out our resources section. In *The Pattern System* Course, we show you exercises that will train your ears using *The Pattern System*. We also offer an online course called *Ear Confidence – Six Paths to Fearless Ears*.

TIP: If you are still struggling, then likely one of three things is at play:

- You don't know the five shapes themselves well enough yet.
- Your knowledge of the area needs a bit more practice.
- Counting while playing is hard for you.

Remedies:

- Practice the five shapes in G quite a bit more. Play them descending only for a few days, without relying on having to ascend them first.
- Visualize the key in the area you are in as one single snapshot of the pattern before you play it.
- Go back to playing one key ascending and the next key descending. Think ahead as far as possible — push yourself a little. Play them slowly with a click.

You need to know the patterns so well that you still have capacity to count (or even better, feel!) the eight beats. Strive to get each pattern fully automated, so once you visualize it, your mind is free to focus on the beats and think ahead to the next key.

Open Area: Connection Exercises cycle to the left, 8 beats

Let's practice *Connection Exercises* in the *Open Area*. All other parameters stay the same:

- 8 beats
- Cycle to the left
- Starting with the lowest note of the C major pattern

I am writing out the first few keys below to give you the idea — then you take over. Use your *Open Area* Map if needed, but wean yourself off the written-out patterns as soon as possible. These should not be reading exercises either. You get the best effect by practicing these from memory.

VIDEO 40

METRONOME REMINDERS: CONNECTION EXERCISES WITH A BEAT (PART IV)

In *Pattern Practice*, the metronome assures that you think ahead — one of the most powerful skills in which to train yourself! It will come in handy when you read sheet music, play songs, improvise, or even lead a band.

As bass players, we must be comfortable playing to click tracks in the studio or in coordination with "human metronomes" (drummers), so there are many benefits from playing comfortably in time with a click. To assure maximum success with this system, use a metronome for at least 80% of the time you practice, especially when doing *Connection Exercises*:

- The toughest spot of the exercise determines the maximum tempo.
- One of the many purposes of practicing with a metronome is to sync up your internal timing to an external source, as well as getting used to playing with this reference.
- Unless you are experienced, do not put the click at tempos lower than 55 BPM. If you long to go slower (I encourage you to go as slow as you need to!), pick a faster tempo and let two clicks go by for each note (playing half notes). For example, setting the metronome to tempo 80 means you play half notes at 40 BPM if you play on every other click.

- If the metronome is running, always listen to it and play to it. There are times when you need to wrap your mind around a transition or new sequence, and the metronome may be distracting. If that occurs for you, switch it off, figure out the tough spot slowly, then return to the use of the metronome at a very slow tempo.

- Never practice a mistake — you are practicing a mistake if you make it more than three times in a row. If this occurs, change one thing (for example, set a slower tempo or just turn the metronome off temporarily). Fix the mistake while you are off the timing grid, then bring back the beat and shed.

- Remember to use "cheater beats" if needed. The metronome trains thinking ahead. Train yourself to "think ahead" in tempo (during the cheater beats at first, then without them, while playing).

This is it…

You have definitely found it, the Holy Grail of practicing the fretboard… the Connection Exercises using the metronome.

Hail the Knight of the Round Table!

Scalar Studies

Interval Study in Thirds (Descending/up)

In *Chapter 4*, I showed you how to practice the ascending/up sequence (and descending/down from the top down) using thirds. Let's turn the starting interval around to create the descending/up sequence (and its inverse, ascending/down).

Reminder: The purpose of these interval studies is to:

- Ingrain the patterns
- Learn all the diatonic intervals
- Train your fingers (lots of string crossing here!)
- Jumpstart ideas for licks, fills, soloing, etc.

Descending/up: My examples here are written in *Area 2*, starting you off with a sample key for each pattern:

VIDEO 41

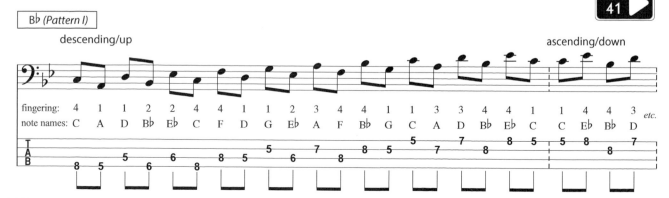

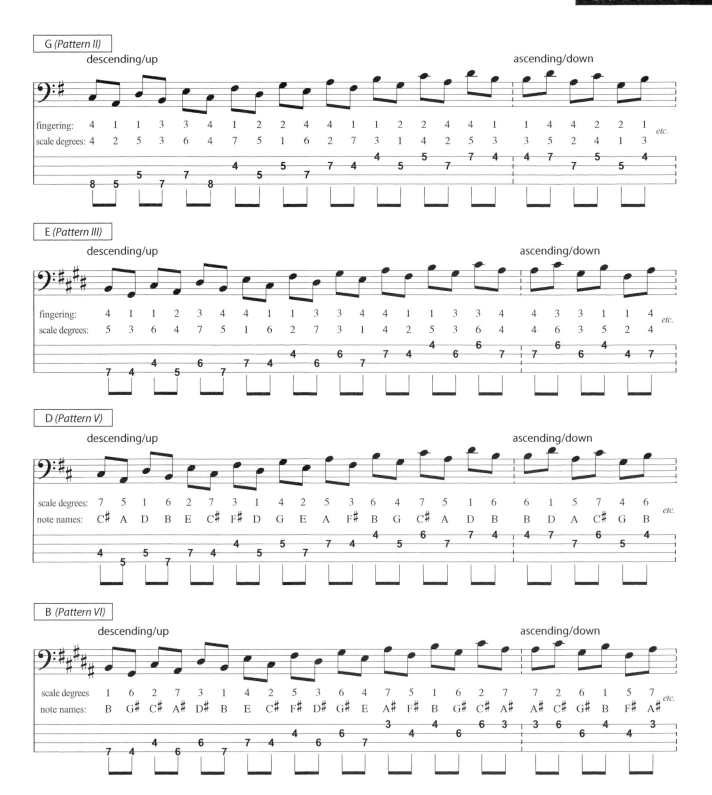

The descending/up sequence (and its inverse, the ascending/down one) poses more of a challenge than the ascending/up (and descending/down, respectively) one because it involves jumps of a fourth (which is a string crossing challenge!).

As a reminder, ascending/up and its reversal, descending/down (exemplified here in G major, just one octave to refresh your memory from the previous chapter):

A trick you can use if you have trouble with this:

Think of two scales "braided together" — watch the color-coding in the note names in the examples below: notice the black and grey note names — the black letters form one complete scale, as do the grey ones. Say every other note name (just the black ones, for example!) — it will help you get the hang of this!

G B A C B D C E D F♯ E G   G E F♯ D E C D B C A B G

B G C A D B E C F♯ D G E   E G D F♯ C E B D A C G B

line (╱) = challenging string crossing

Improvised Explorations

Improvise Connection Exercises

Two-Bar Template

The first exercise that follows features a two-bar rhythmic template. Your assignment is to rhythmicize the *Connection Exercises* exactly as we did them above. Don't change the order of notes; just add the rhythm. How does that feel to you?

Exercise 1: 2 bars, *Connection Exercises, Area 2*

One-Bar Template

Now try a one-bar phrase (harder)

VIDEO
44

Rhythmic template, 1-bar phrase

Improvise, Starting on the Tonic

In this exercise you start each new key on the tonic and freely pick the direction you'll play the scale. Just like before, follow the given rhythmic pattern or invent your own.

Starting from tonics, change direction of playing freely

VIDEO
45

Rhythmic template, 1-bar phrase – start on the tonic, improvise

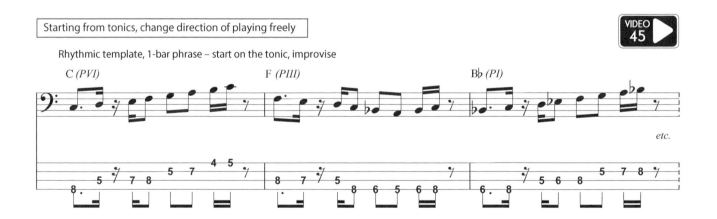

 I can read all these improvisation exercises easily, but I don't play them with your fingering or those "Patterns." I just have my own way of doing it. Why should I change my way just to follow your system?

The purpose of the improvisation exercises is not to simply read them. The written examples are merely starting points and short demonstrations of the given descriptions. Their main function is to ingrain the Patterns (and the diatonic shapes contained within them) through creativity, in order to make them yours and make them stick.

They also provide opportunities to exercise these valuable skills:

- Thinking ahead
- Making quick decisions on the spot
- Keeping track of multiple streams of information simultaneously

In my experience, even some intermediate to advanced players are not fully aware of how they map music across the fretboard — or in their mind. Some develop a set of personalized approaches, devices, and licks that they predominantly rely on. This is, of course, an important part of developing a personal style.

What happens sometimes, though, is that "blind spots" remain.

Things like:

- Not being fully comfortable in certain keys
- Certain areas of the fretboard remaining under-explored (typically the lower strings in the middle register)
- Relying too much on licks, patterns and fingerings that have become comfortable

This system will help fill these gaps and offer many additional possibilities to explore idiosyncrasies and fuel your creativity through the mastery of the fretboard. **Many players also report that this method helped them break through plateaus and come up with fresh ideas for solos.**

In my teaching, I encourage players to keep doing what is already working for them and reserve separate time for *Pattern System* practice. *The Pattern System* is designed to show the student what is possible — both on the fretboard and in the mental processing of music, enabling them to integrate the method into their individual style.

TEST YOUR UNDERSTANDING #5

1. *Connection Exercises* — practice switching keys on the fly to a certain number of beats. This is important because:
   - ❏ a. Music does the same.
   - ❏ b. It is important in music to do everything in a symmetric way.

2. Saying scale degrees out loud is useful because:
   - ❏ a. Each number represents the sound of the note in relation to the tonic.
   - ❏ b. It helps your math skills.

3. *Area 2 – G major – Pattern* _____

4. *Area 2 – G♭ major – Pattern* _____

5. *Area 2 – A♭ major – Pattern* _____

6. Finish this sequence of diatonic thirds descending/up: B♭ G, C A♭, D♭ B♭, etc. _____

7. In *Area 1* there are only three pitches that could potentially be the lowest note of a pattern. Which are they? ___, ____, and ____

8. In *Area 2* there are only three pitches that could potentially be the lowest note of a pattern. Which are they? ___, ____, and ____

9. True or false? If the metronome is on and you are really struggling with a spot, you can ignore the beat. Just figure it out without listening to it then sync up with it again after you've gotten it.
   ❏ True   ❏ False

BLUEPRINT FOR PRACTICE #5

1. **PP:** *Connection Exercises*, *Area 1*, for 8 beats; cycle to the left; say scale degrees/note names/nothing
   pp. 107–109 • Videos 37 and 38
   and p. 113 • Video 40

2. **PP:** *Connection Exercises, Open Area,* for 8 beats; cycle to the left; say scale degrees/note names/nothing
   pp. 106–109 • Videos 37 and 38

3. **SS:** Interval studies in thirds; descending/up; pick a few keys in various areas (suggesting D♭ A F and C♯ in *Area 2*) **pp. 114–116 • Video 41**

4. **IE:** Pick an improvisation exercise in *Chapter 5* and play it in the cycle to the left and then right
   pp. 116–118 • Videos 43 and 45

Sequences and Zones

SEQUENCES

What do I mean by "Order" or "Sequence?"

The word *Order* — AKA *Sequence* — in our system refers to the order you practice the patterns in. So far, you have done the "circle" or "cycle" in both directions. You changed one note from one key to the next.

Now I will expand on this and cover moving between keys by every single interval within the octave. This further reinforces instant recall of the pattern for each key in a given area. More importantly, this is also additional training for keeping track of multiple streams of information — in this case, the key you're in and the sequence of keys you are following. It's also excellent preparation for key changes (modulations).

Contrast key changes (modulations) with chords moving *within a shape* — as in a *diatonic chord progression*! Any diatonic event will clock in as *Shapes within Shapes* in this system (see diatonic triads, chord progressions and pentatonic scales in *Chapters 8* and up!).

Explanation:

- C major – F major – B♭ major • three different keys, hence **three different patterns**
- C min7 – F7 – B♭ major • all from the same key, B♭ major, hence contained in **one and the same pattern**!

The fifth (and its inversion, the fourth), as well as the minor second (and its inversion, the major seventh), are the only two intervals that we can repeat over and over and end up practicing every single key in. Other intervals, however, will need several "rounds" in order to make it through every single key.

▌▌▌ TIP: Always play the starting key in the beginning as well as the end of a sequence. You want the experience of coming from one key and going into the next one. Play the starting key twice!

All Possible Sequences

1 • Moving in Fifths: The Cycle

Only one note changes between keys: Cycle of fifths to the left or right—one—sequence for all keys

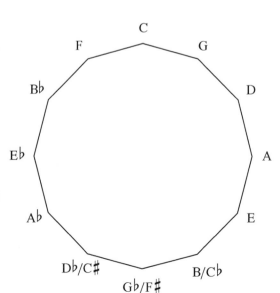

2 • Moving in Whole Steps (Two Sequences)

Now, instead of moving in ascending or descending fifths, you move in whole steps! **Of course, you need to use the actual keys from the cycle because you want the note naming to be correct.**

Don't list your whole step sequence as C D E F♯ G♯ A♯ C.

A key of G♯ major would have one × (double-sharp), like this: G♯ A♯ B♯ C♯ D♯ E♯ F× G♯!

Or, maybe even worse: G♯ B♭ C D♭ — No!

A♯ is equally repellent. Don't go there. Use A♭ instead, with four easy flats!

The cycle has the correct naming of keys already figured out for you. Use it!

So, in order to achieve the correct naming of the keys, you have to break the music theory rules somewhere:

C D E F♯ A♭ B♭ C • between F♯ and A♭ is technically speaking a diminished third (not a major second). For our purposes in this specific context, we call it the whole step or major second (which is the enharmonic interval to a diminished third.)

In the image to the right, I connected all the whole steps to get two hexagons within the dodecahedron (twelve-sided polygon):

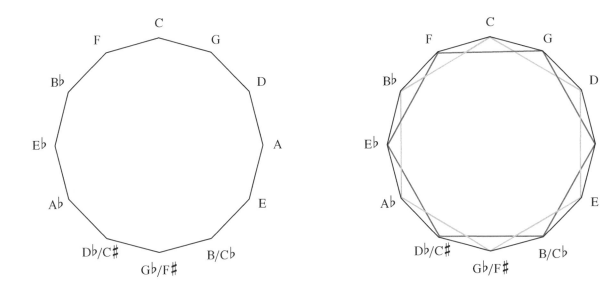

Two rounds of whole steps — two accidentals are added or subtracted from each key to the next!

C has zero accidentals. D (two sharps: F♯ and C♯). E (four sharps: F♯, C♯, G♯, D♯), etc. — all the way to six sharps or flats on the bottom, then subtract two flats at a time until you return back to zero accidentals at the top.

Notice that here too, you can go either to the right (ascending major seconds: C, D, E…) or the left (descending major seconds: C, B♭, A♭…).

3 • Moving in Minor Thirds (Three Sequences)

Mark the minor thirds in the diagram below. If you do it correctly, you will get three squares (3 X 4 = 12). I suggest you use different colors for the different sequences:

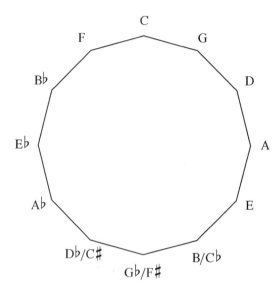

Notice again that sometimes you must use an enharmonic spelling to find the correct name for the next key. Be sure to use the names as they are displayed in the diagram above.

Three rounds of minor thirds – three accidentals are changing from one key to the next!

4 • Moving in Major Thirds (four sequences)

Now you get four triangles (4 x 3 = 12):

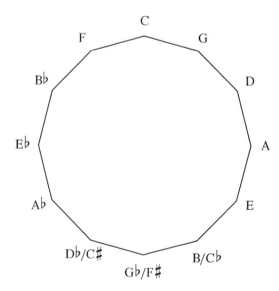

Four rounds of major thirds – four accidentals are changing from one key to the next!

5 • Moving in Minor Seconds (one sequence)

Figure out the complex star shape you get here:

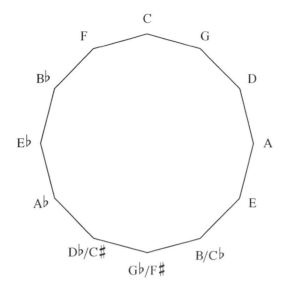

One round of minor seconds – five accidentals are changing from one key to the next!

▌▌▌ **NOTE:** For bassists, when practicing anything in half steps, the temptation is to just move up by one fret each time. True to pattern system fashion, however, you will go area by area, so the maximum of half-step shifts of a shape in any given area you can make is three before having to use a different pattern in order to stay in the area.

6 • Moving in Tritones

The Tritone (augmented fourth or diminished fifth) cuts the octave in half. You get six pairs of keys to practice.

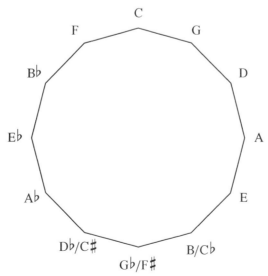

Six rounds of tritones – six accidentals are changing from one key to the next!

That's it. These are all the options!

▌▌▌ **NOTE:** Remember to also practice the enharmonic keys (C♯, C♭, F♯/G♭ respectively) on occasion, especially when saying note names!

▌▌▌ **CREATIVE TIP:** Pay attention to which notes are changing and which stay the same. This will be very useful when you connect keys in musical ways.

It's not F-hashtag, it's F-sharp!

Correct note naming proves important…

 Wait, what about sixths or sevenths? Don't you want to be comprehensive here?

We already tackled them: They are covered by their inversions. For example, sixths are inversions of the thirds. Going up a minor third gets you to the same note as going down a major sixth:

- C going up to E♭: minor third.
- C going down to E♭: major sixth.

It makes sense to think of all the intervals and going in both directions.

For example, the cycle of major seconds to the right:

- You could think of ascending in major seconds (C, D, E, etc.)
- Or of descending in minor sevenths (C, D, E, etc.)

Or, when going in the cycle of major seconds to the left:

- You could think of descending in major seconds (C, B♭, A♭, etc.)
- Or ascending in minor sevenths (C, B♭, A♭, etc.)*

The smaller intervals seem much easier, of course, yet I have also had students who preferred going up at all times. So rather than think of major seconds going down, they preferred minor sevenths going up (which gets you to the same result, of course).

Keep variations that are harder for additional practice. To get started, I recommend sticking to the smaller intervals listed above.

---

* Review inversions in *Music Theory for the Bass Player* if you need a refresher.

Going Beyond the Order of the Cycle

With all the above sequences, you will become very fit at knowing intervals as you will learn them all by heart.

You can also take it a couple of steps further:

Try twelve-tone rows or random sequences! Here are a few for you. Some find this easier as they are now allowed to look at the progression versus having to keep track of the cycle in their head. I still find this an interesting challenge because, yet again, we reshuffled the deck and created additional randomness. Remember, the goal is to be able to instantly recall any scale, not to learn a particular exercise (meaning all the individual notes) by heart.

A♭	F	G	E	C♯	A	D♭	B♭	G♭	C	E♭	F♯	B	D	C♭
E	F	C♭	D	A♭	D♭	B♭	B	E♭	C	F♯	G	A	C♯	G♭

▐▌ **NOTE:** You can create endless rows like these by writing all 15 keys on little pieces of paper and pulling them one by one from a hat. Online 12-tone row generators exist, but you will be renaming a lot of keys (remember, G♯ major is not a valid key!) and you may miss the enharmonic keys!

Enjoy the beautiful symmetry of it all. I also hope you are beginning to look at the Cycle of Fifths as more than just a tool for identifying the key signature!

List Summarizing The Interval Cycles

A great practice tool, use the following list as a reference. We also feature all these sequences on our beautifully designed and useful *Pattern System Wallchart*.

- Top line: the interval
- Second line: Number of notes changing between each key in this sequence
- Third line: How many unique "rounds" or "cycles" you get — even though they might look like squares or triangles!

For the purpose of this graph, I am lumping the enharmonic keys together; keep including them as unique keys in your practice, especially when saying note names!

INTERVAL	NOTES CHANGING	NUMBER OF UNIQUE CYCLES	RESULTING DIAGRAM
Fourths/ Fifths	1	1 cycle of 12 keys	
Major Seconds/ Minor Sevenths	2	2 cycles of 6 keys	
Minor Thirds/ Major Sixths	3	3 cycles of 4 keys	

INTERVAL	NOTES CHANGING	NUMBER OF UNIQUE CYCLES	RESULTING DIAGRAM
Major Thirds/ Minor Sixths	4	4 cycles of 3 keys	
Minor Seconds/ Major Sevenths	5	1 cycle of 12 keys	
Tritones (augmented fourths/ diminished fifths)	6	6 cycles of 2 keys	

If you like mnemonics, remember this:

Key change in:

Whole steps	= 2 frets ⟶	2 accidentals change
Minor thirds	= 3 frets ⟶	3 accidentals change
Major thirds	= 4 frets ⟶	4 accidentals change
♯4/♭5	= 6 frets ⟶	6 accidentals change

However:

Minor seconds	= 1 fret ⟶	5 accidentals change
The cycle	= 5 frets ⟶	1 accidental changes

 A major scale is made up of 7 notes. So, why is there no scenario where all 7 notes change from one key to the next?

There are 12 chromatic notes and 7 notes to a scale, so two notes will always be the same even if they end up being spelled enharmonically.

Between C major and C♯ major, you are seemingly changing every note, but you really are not. If you overlay the fretboard diagrams, you would see the overlap of notes.

C major: C D E F G A B C

C♯ major: C♯ D♯ E♯ F♯ G♯ A♯ B♯ C♯

E♯ (F) and B♯ (C) are the same.

You can see it easier when renaming C♯ to D♭:

D♭ E♭ F G♭ A♭ B♭ C D♭

▌▌ **NOTE:** Thinking about common notes between keys (or patterns) is useful when transitioning between keys: you can use the common notes to create a smooth connection between keys.

 Why do you call it "The Cycle of Fifths"? Shouldn't it be "The Circle of Fifths"?

I already use "circle" for the graphic representation of the notes in diagrams. But there is more to the story…

Iconic bassist Carol Kaye told me during an inspiring one-off lesson I took with her a long time ago that back in the day when you said "Circle," they'd think of you as a classical player — all the Jazzers called it the "Cycle." I have called it "the cycle" ever since. Either is fine, of course.

When using the word in the context of a sequence (e.g., the "cycle of major seconds," the "cycle of minor thirds," etc.), I prefer the word "cycle" because it refers to a repetitive process that eventually returns to its beginning.

THE ZONE OF LEARNING

Above I gave you a tool that creates yet again near endless combinations and opportunities for practice by:

- Choosing a sequence, an area, and a direction
- Varying the starting key
- Switching up the starting note within that key
- Playing *Connection Exercises* with 8 beats, or 6, or 13

And — you are doing scale studies in more and more variations. We will soon add diatonic sequences and *Shapes within Shapes* — which will make all these exercises very relevant to the songs you are playing.

All the above are concrete practicing prescriptions. Follow the *"Practice Like This"* sections as well as the *"Blueprints for Practice"* at the end of each chapter for the most important points, and create your own variations once you are ready.

How you look at everything presented here will make all the difference in your success. Initially, all the seemingly endless combinations of keys and sequences may feel a bit overwhelming. Approach this vastness with a sense of wonder and curiosity as to how deep the goldmine is. This is just the starting point!

Welcome to the path. It just gets more and more interesting and rewarding.

I also hope you are beginning to understand how well the fretboard can be known and how beautifully the patterns of music map onto the fretboard!

Become Your Own Coach

What follows is my heartfelt advice to you on becoming your own coach through this journey. You want to grow into your own coach, not only in the sense of being a cheerleader to yourself but also by identifying and aiming to practice in your "optimal zone of learning."

You can do this on your own or join one of our offerings, especially one where mentor and cohort support can help you along in this endeavor, particularly when you are just beginning to learn this system.

Prerequisites to Reaching Your "Optimal Zone of Learning"

Reaching "the zone" — in my view — consists of two prerequisites:

STEP 1 • Listening to Yourself

By that, I mean not just listening to your playing, but also to everything else that goes on in your mind. This first step is about attitude — Self-assessment starts with a mindset of support towards yourself! Without that, it is hard to listen to yourself and do anything about it other than despair!

We are typically quite good at opening that piece of the zone to someone dear to us. We (hopefully!) display patience and a sense of encouragement to a person we want to support. We believe in their potential for success.

One of the most important things for your success is learning to bring a similar mindset to yourself and carefully adjusting your inner dialogue. If you are quick to put yourself down, I'd like you to shift your focus to diagnosis rather than fighting this likely a bit resistant thought pattern.

Here is what I mean:

Not: *"I crashed and burned!" "I sound terrible!" "Wrong again!"*

Instead, stay calm and look into the detail of what happened:

Example: *"I did well for the first three keys, but then I lost the beat."*

Or: *"When I do Connection Exercises, I seem to get confused when a key with a "crab" movement comes up!"*

Or: *"I tend to lose my place at this particular key change!"*

Identify exactly what went wrong rather than making generalized statements that only talk about failure. **In order for the above to work, you must be able to actually hear what you are playing.** This is a skill that deserves special attention and can be learned. It doesn't always come naturally. Denial and distraction can play tricks on us. Harsh internal voices can drown out anything else we hear.

Help can take on many forms. For example, recording yourself or playing in front of someone who is rooting for you — yet vows to give honest and constructive feedback — can be very helpful here. In our cohort courses, we have had great success with students submitting videos to their online community. Most were a bit hesitant at first, felt awkward about it or dismissive, but all agreed that the benefits were very well worth overcoming their initial trepidation.

When you listen back, you may be surprised at what you are hearing — maybe it does not match what you thought you heard during the recording process. **Listening to yourself while playing is very different than listening to a recording of yourself.** It can be sobering, but the point — again — is to concretely find out what you can do better to get the result you are after and to support yourself through this. Your practice will become much more effective, as well as more enjoyable!

STEP 2 • What precisely to practice

The next step is to take what you are hearing and coach yourself to the next level. To use the examples from above, good remedies could be:

"I did well for the first three keys, but then I lost the beat."

Remedy: "Okay, great, I'll do it again, a little slower, with some cheater beats. I will start at that third key where it gets tougher."

"When I do Connection Exercises, I seem to get confused when a key with a "crab" movement comes up!"

Remedy: "Okay, I close my eyes and try if I can see the entire pattern of "the crab" pattern in my mind's eye before the switch. Or I will look at the Area Map if needed."

"I tend to lose my place at this key change!"

Remedy: "So I will just do those two tough keys back to back a few times."

The *Pattern System* offers great tools to put the above ideas into action. The more you pay attention, the more you will find that direct feedback is built into the system, and this can show you how to effectively self-correct to stay on course. You are operating a cockpit with several levers — set all parameters just right and take off!

You are the captain of your own spaceship...
Set all the levers just right and make your practice take off!

In the Zone... Not in the Zone...

There exists a zone of learning that I encourage you to find for yourself. The aspect of practicing that I will discuss here is finding the right level of difficulty or challenge for yourself. This is, of course, individual. Don't compare yourself to others because it won't tell you much about yourself. It's one thing to try to exactly emulate what your teacher demonstrates or what a player you admire does — typically focusing on specific aspects of playing like phrasing, details of movement, tone, etc. However, it's quite another to only make general comparisons such as: "*He's/she's so awesome, and I sound terrible in comparison.*" This is not helpful at all.

Just focus on finding "your zone."

Like Skippy demonstrates here, the optimal zone of learning is one where you are:

- Hanging on with some effort (but not too much)
- Not crashing and burning
- Not just strolling along easily either

Go Zones

A good warm-up!

Good. You are moving along!

Perfect. In the zone. Working hard and making great progress!

You can aim for maximum effort for short spurts only. Too much of this will set you back.

Victory! Your hard work is richly rewarded!

Avoid Zones

Skippy? Hello? Wake up, Skippy!

A bit too casual — unfocused. You won't make much progress this way.

Too hard! This carries the danger to crash and burn!

You may find yourself in one of the three "avoid" zones at times. If you practice the same thing over and over so, you get bored, or if you push so hard that you feel like you are falling off that cliff, you need to adjust. It will seem like you are slowing down, but you will get to the top much faster and stay engaged rather than throwing in the towel! I show you how in the next section.

Strategies for Success

In *The Pattern System*, if you find yourself in the "crashing and burning" zone rather than the *Zone of Learning* — adjust. The following ideas will lessen the complexity, affording you an opportunity to catch up and take the next step, rather than stumble while trying to take three steps at once.

- Tempo:
    - Leave out the metronome.
    - Add cheater beats.
    - Choose a tempo at which you can execute the toughest spot.
- If you are struggling in a new *Area* or with *Connection Exercises:*
    - Look at your diagrams of the area. Imprint the pattern you have filled out by hand into your mind. Look at the page and a particular pattern — close your eyes and visualize it. See/feel yourself playing it — look again — visualize. Repeat until your mental recall has improved.
    - Start a new area by playing each pattern ascending/descending first through the cycle to the left.
    - Then to the right.
    - Now, try all keys ascending only.
    - Next, descending only — then one ascending, next descending.
    - Finally, *Connection Exercises!*
- Add cheater beats if needed.
- Say the name of the key at the point of switching. Also, say which pattern the key is in.
- If you find some keys are harder:
    - Play that key by rote over and over. Visualize the pattern and the location of the tonic. Then say the note names and/or scale steps. Mindful repetition is the key.
    - Reduce the number of keys you are doing.
        - Do just an excerpt of the cycle. For example, in the cycle of fifths practice, focus on just the keys around the "6 o'clock mark" over and over.
        - Or choose three keys of a major third sequence and loop them over and over.
    - Look at the *Area Map* and take a mental snapshot.
    - Play that key by rote over and over. Visualize the pattern and the location of the tonic.

On the flip side, what do you do if it feels like you are just strolling along and not really exerting much effort? Likely this will happen if you are practicing the patterns in the same order or area over and over. As I said earlier, the goal here is not to make you an expert in a certain drill. Rather, I want you to become more and more comfortable in the "Learning Zone" — where nothing seems quite settled yet. You are multi-tasking at a very high level and really must focus to get through it. That is the sweet spot!

If you need to challenge yourself a little more, change something:

- Change the starting key in your sequence.
- Alter the starting note within the key.
- Turn the direction of the sequence around.
- Use one of the improvisation exercises and apply them.

- Say note names, scale degrees or the pattern number.

- Change the number of beats in the *Connection Exercises* (from 8 to 7, 9, 11, 6?).

- Set a more ambitious tempo.

- Focus on a detail — use the strategies against boredom from *Chapter 3*.

- To step up the challenge even more, you can use "negative cheater beats" — here you say the upcoming key two beats before the actual key change — or even four beats earlier. You'll be playing one scale while planning for the next one. Your mind is training to track more than one stream of information and to think ahead.

I have taught this system to hundreds of students over the years. This is what they have taught me:

- You don't have to do every sequence, every possible combination, everywhere, until it is perfect. But — you do need to keep switching things up!

- Consistency is important for measurable success.

- Keep moving. Don't get stuck in an area or a particular way of doing things.

- Come back to exercises and areas often.

- If you begin to get good doing it one way, change something.

There is definitely a learning curve for thinking in the patterns themselves. You also face the learning curve of learning how to learn and how to coach yourself. **You can use these same principles for song learning, practicing technique, theory drills… even other areas of study in your life.**

 How do I know when to move on to the next sequence or exercise?

At this stage, don't go for perfection. It's a mistake to get stuck on an exercise and push hard until you are frustrated.

Instead, ask yourself:

- Have I understood the concept, practiced regularly, and seen improvement?

- If tested, would I be able to execute the exercise at a slow tempo, with maybe a stutter or two and quick recovery?

If yes, then keep moving on.

If no, throttle it back by a step (tempo, sequence, direction, etc. — as discussed).

If you are in college, be ready for your teacher to test you each week — being held accountable is one of the best ways to improve! Our course offers peer and coach support. We have deadlines, video submissions, practice groups and a schedule! For many, that can make all the difference. Either way you approach it, the goal for you is to learn to be your own coach!

How long should I practice each session?

You can go "Pomodoro-style" — as in the "Pomodoro Method" — and set a timer for twenty minutes. Then take a ten-minute break. Or practice for fifteen. Or ten! Consistency is key. It is better to do ten minutes every day than to cram for five hours straight right before your lesson.

When that timer is running, don't do anything else.

Do what you can. Make *Pattern Practice* a regular part of your regimen. If twenty minutes feels overwhelming, do one round of ten minutes. Maybe later in the overall practice session, you will be ready for another ten minutes.

You can also use otherwise lost time, like waiting for a bus, for mental practice. You don't need a bass in your hand to play through *Connection Exercises*. In fact, I found mental-only practice to be very powerful.

If you hit a wall — schedule a break. Do a few improvisation exercises and enjoy experiencing the result of your hard work.

Practice Tips for Good Tone

Play all notes legato (smoothly connected). I don't mean as hammer-ons. Rather, pluck every note with the right hand, but don't allow any spaces between the notes.

This necessitates that your right and left hands work precisely in concert. You will get them to coordinate with each other if you listen carefully how you proceed from one note to the next. Try putting your focus into both hands at the same time. While mildly entrancing, this exercise will bring all the subtle movements that need to happen in a coordinated and well-timed fashion to your awareness to produce a smooth transition between notes.

- Let your ear be your guide.
- Allow your fingers to be your tools.
- Permit your bass to become an extension of your body.

Even if you are "just" playing patterns, play them in a musical fashion. For example, you could imagine playing a lovely melody consisting only of scalar motions. Put emotion into it!

- Listen for consistent volume; work on minimizing fret buzz.
- Watch your fingering — both conceptually (one-finger-per-fret) and literally. Watch yourself in a mirror — mirrors are great visual feedback devices.
- Stay relaxed (drop your hand if you cramp up; feel the blood rushing into your fingertips as you sense gravity taking over your arm).
- Make the practice deliberate. Be mentally present.
- Track in your mind's eye and ear what your fingers are doing.
- Listen to your playing and your body. Observe your breathing.

Scalar Studies

Interval Study in Thirds (Combined)

In *Chapters 4* and *5*, I showed you how to practice the patterns "in thirds."

You did two versions:

- Ascending/up (and descending/down on the reverse)
- Descending/up (and ascending/down on the reverse)

In this chapter I have more variations for practicing diatonic thirds for you.

But first, here is a recap of the previously presented ways.

Key of C: *Pattern V, Area 1*

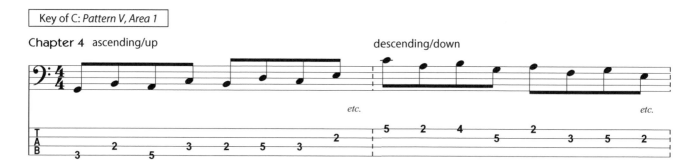

Now, we combine the two. Imagine we take the two eighth notes of **beat 1** of the *Chapter 4* version and the two eighth notes of **beat 2** from the *Chapter 5* version and combine them. Sounds hip and ingrains the patterns deeply! I call them *Mixed Motion Interval Studies*.

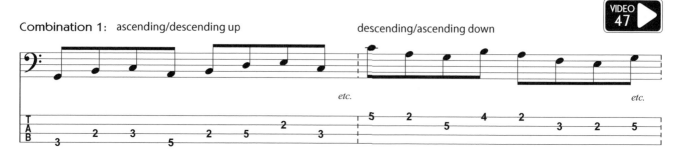

What about starting on the "other foot," meaning with the **beat 1 notes** of *Chapter 5* and the **beat 2 notes** of *Chapter 4?* Also hip!

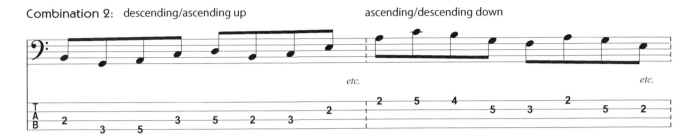

Notice that the figure is sequenced at the interval of a third (meaning the four-note figure repeats a third up or down respectively. I marked the thirds with stars.).

Interval Study with Other Intervals (Combined)

- What works for diatonic thirds also works for all other intervals. Below I start you off on all these exercises.
- Remember to always stay within the key — some intervals will turn out major, some minor, some diminished.
- The bigger the interval gets, the fewer repeats you can fit into one pattern.
- Your fingers will thank you. Within the pattern, you will execute some mighty finger acrobatics here! Keep it one-finger-per-fret and aim for smooth string crossing!
- Say note names, scale degrees, or nothing at all while you practice these.

If you struggle — write them out. Remember that in these interval exercises (the simple versions, not the mixed motion variants), you are "braiding" together two scales:

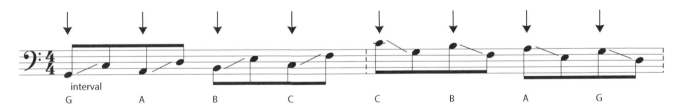

For the *Mixed Motion* exercises, use the strategy described at their introduction in this chapter. Alternatively, you can also use the above diagram and think about turning every other group on its head:

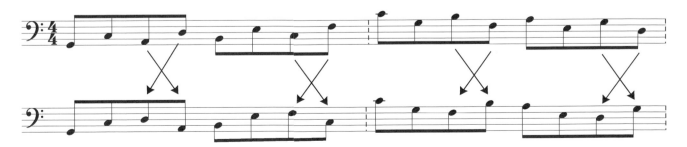

Interval Study Fourths

Key of C: *Pattern V, Area 1*

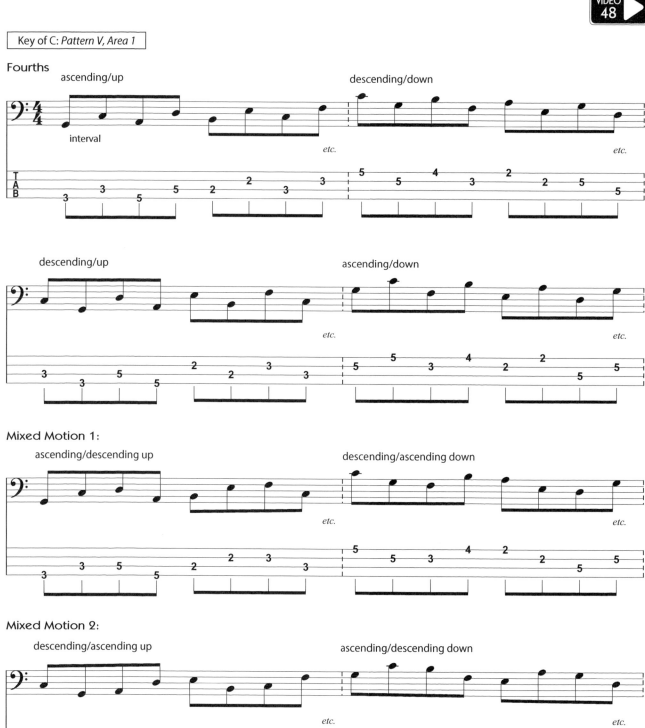

Interval Study in Fifths

Key of C: *Pattern V, Area 1*

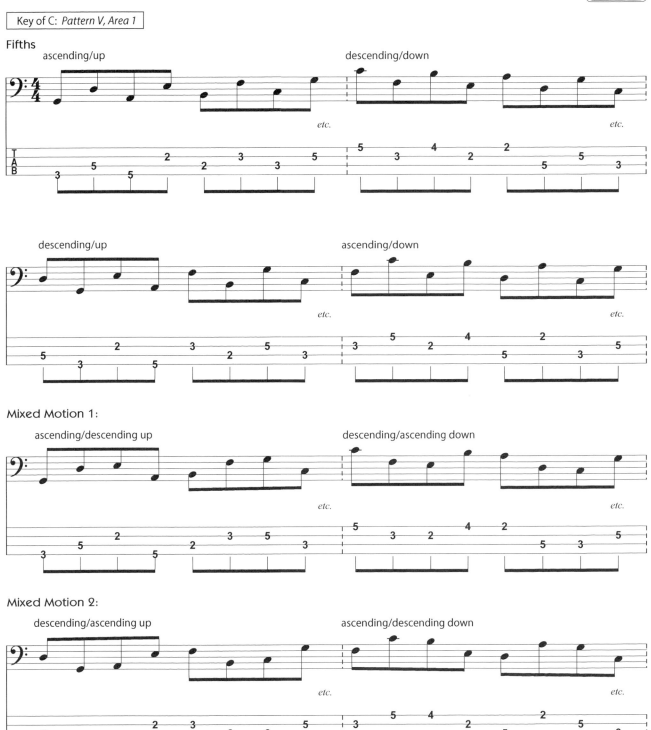

Interval Study Sixths

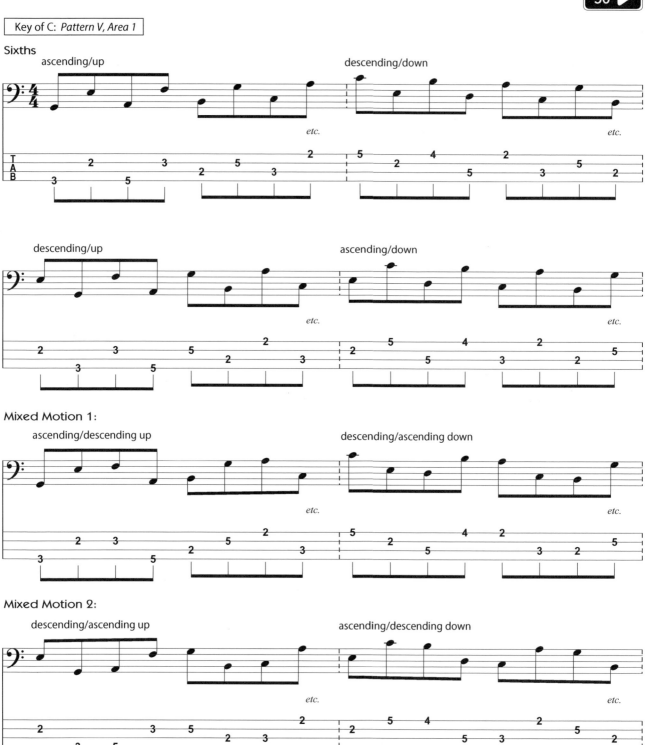

Interval Study Sevenths

A very large interval, you can only go for a few rounds with sevenths. I wrote them out in their entirety.

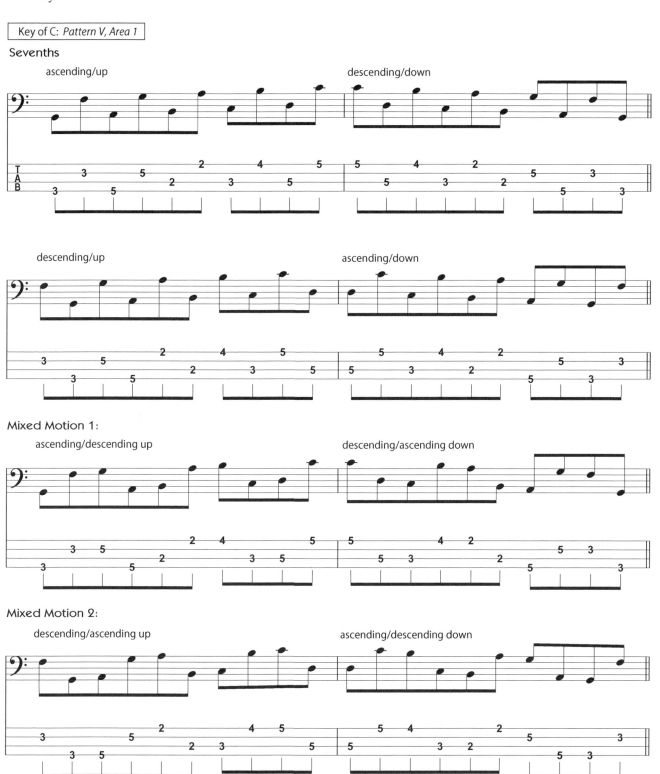

Interval Study Octaves

Even shorter (but very cool!) — here they are:

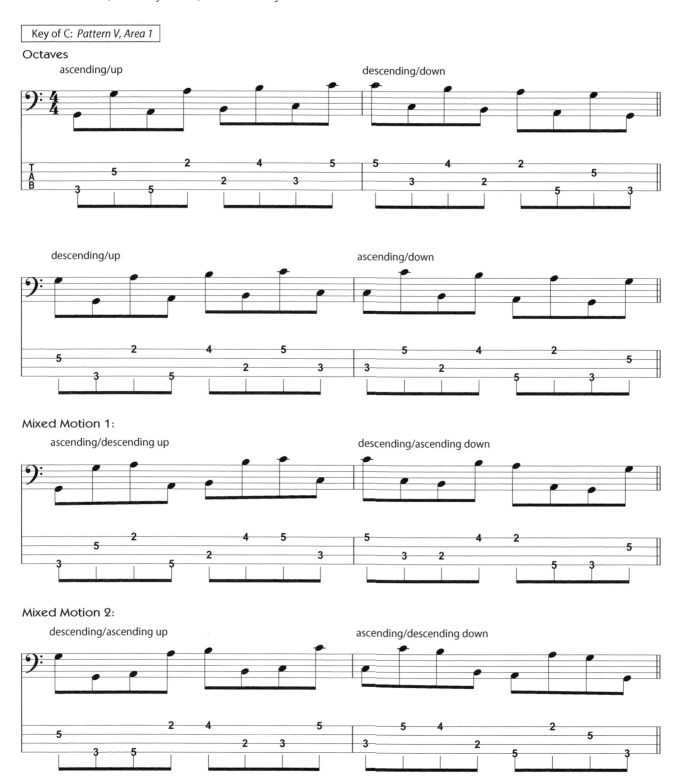

Over the next few chapters, you will continue to work on all of these in your blueprints for practice. These combinations sound hip in musical contexts!

Major Third Sequence Improvisation

John Coltrane's tunes "Giant Steps" or "Countdown" are famously hard to solo over because their key centers shift in major thirds. Let's practice such a chord progression. The actual tunes also include ii–V's. Once we have included diatonic progressions into *The Pattern System* (*Chapters 8* and up), you can include those as well.

This improvisation drill displays beautifully how you can use *The Pattern System* for practicing tunes. Use the patterns (major scales) to improvise over the "cycle of major thirds."

The setup:

- 4/4 meter

- Each scale/key gets two measures.

- Play a short motif for 2 to 3 beats (up to one measure maximum. Use the rhythmic template to start you off).

- Then use the remainder of the first measure and the entire second measure to improvise using excerpts from the pattern!

- Aim to eventually use all the notes from each pattern/key (not necessarily within each round, but as you keep looping through three keys, make sure to get to all the notes of each pattern/ key eventually!).

- Initially, start each new key with the tonic. This means — start your motif on the tonic. Become freer and pick other starting notes as you get more comfortable with the idea and patterns.

- Aim to connect to the next tonic via a half or a whole step (that makes for a smooth transition!)

- Repeat for each key. Feel free to expand on the template and create your own motifs and rhythms once you have the hang of it.

- Stick to the pattern fingerings!

VIDEO 53

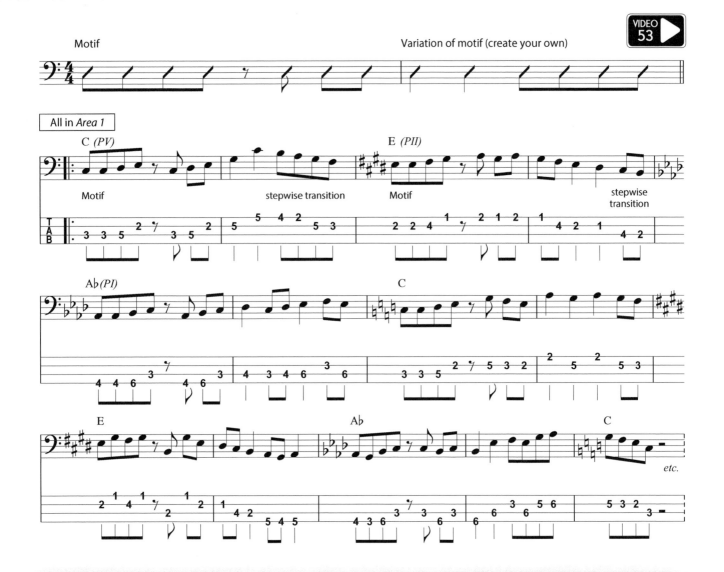

Motif   Variation of motif (create your own)

All in *Area 1*

TEST YOUR UNDERSTANDING #6

1. Continue the sequence of keys: C D E F♯ ___ ___ ___

2. Continue the sequence of keys: A F D♭ ___

3. Continue the sequence of keys: D F A♭ ___ ___

4. Continue the sequence of keys: F♯ D ___ ___

5. If you practice in the sequence of minor thirds, you need to do ___ rounds to play through all keys.

6. If you practice in the sequence of major seconds, you need to do ___ rounds to play through all keys.

7. If you practice in the sequence of major thirds, you need to do ___ rounds to play through all keys.

8. Thirds, ascending and up. Finish the sequence (*Open Area*, two flats):

   F A, G B♭, _____

9. Fourths, ascending and up. Finish the sequence (*Open Area*, four sharps):

   E A, F♯ B, _____

10. Fifths, ascending and up. Finish the sequence (*Open Area*, four sharps):

   E B, F♯ C♯, _____

BLUEPRINT FOR PRACTICE #6

1. **PP:** *Connection Exercises, Area 2,* for 8 beats; cycle to the left and right; say scale degrees/note names/nothing **pp. 106–109** · **Videos 37 and 38**

2. **PP:** Ascending/descending; descending/ascending; all ascending; all descending; one key ascending, next key descending; then: *Connection Exercises* for 8 beats; *Area 2*; Cycles of major seconds to the right; for all sequences: **p. 126**

3. **SS:** Interval studies in fourths; various combinations as shown in *Chapter 6; Areas 1* and *2*; practice several keys (suggesting B♭ D F♯) **pp. 136–142** · **Videos 47 to 52**

4. **IE:** *Chapter 6* improvisation exercises in all major third sequences **pp. 143–144** · **Video 53** for all sequences: **p. 126**

The "Area Matrix"

THE "AREA MATRIX"

Review of Areas 1 and 2

The *Open Area*, *Area 1* and *Area 2* have hopefully become easier and easier with practice. In this chapter, I have you finish up the entire neck. You will continue to practice area by area, one by one, in order, while continuing to repeat the earlier areas. For an overview of this, please fill in the table below:

Area 1	Area 2	Area 3	Area 4	Area 5
I	II	III	V	VI
II	III		VI	
III	V	VI		
V	VI			
VI	I			

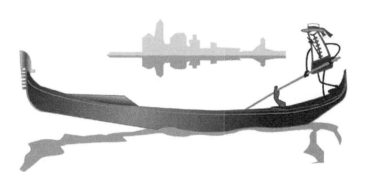

Trust Skippy to safely navigate you through the labyrinth of Area canals!

Take your time over the next few days filling in the *Area Maps* for each of the missing areas. I recommend writing just dots, scale degrees or note names below. I left space for one version below — feel free to do note names in one area, scale degrees in another — switch things up. At this point, you will be very fast. For additional practice, download pattern paper from my blog, and complete some more.

Square the tonics. Name the pattern. Fill in the header below whether you are doing dots, note names or scale degrees. As always, find the correct answers (as black dots) in our resources to check yourself.

Area 3 Diagrams

Area 3 – Area Map – _____

C   *Pattern* _____

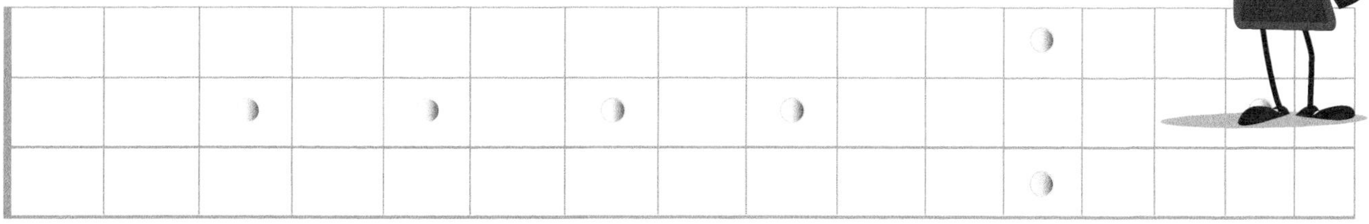

F   *Pattern* _____

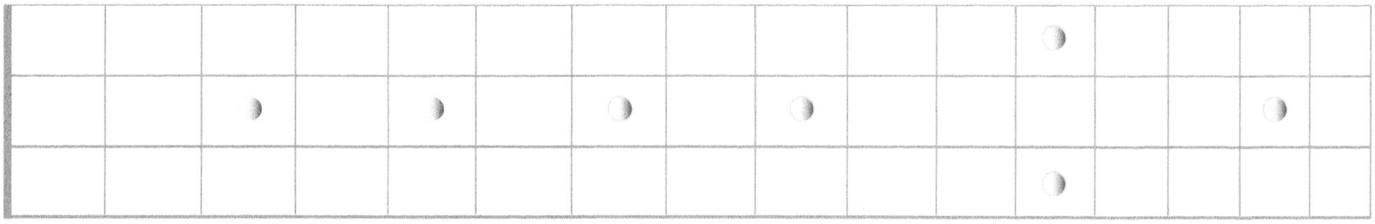

B♭   *Pattern* _____

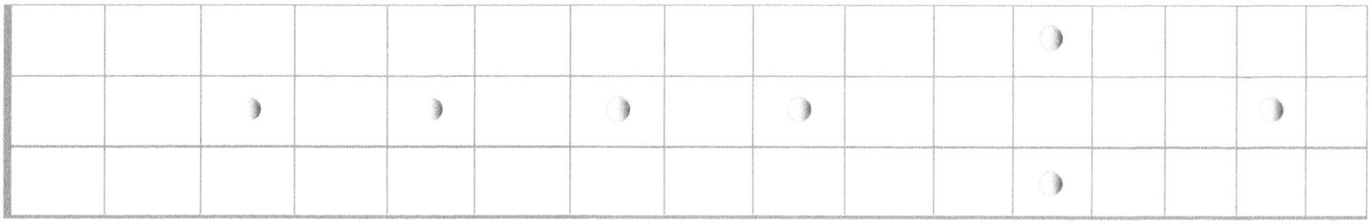

E♭   *Pattern* _____

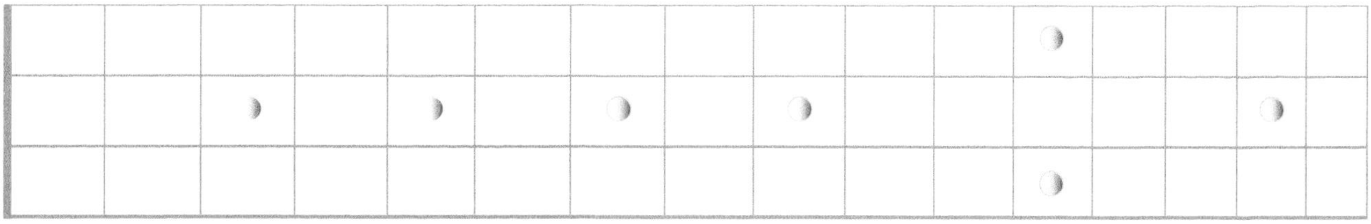

A♭   *Pattern* _____

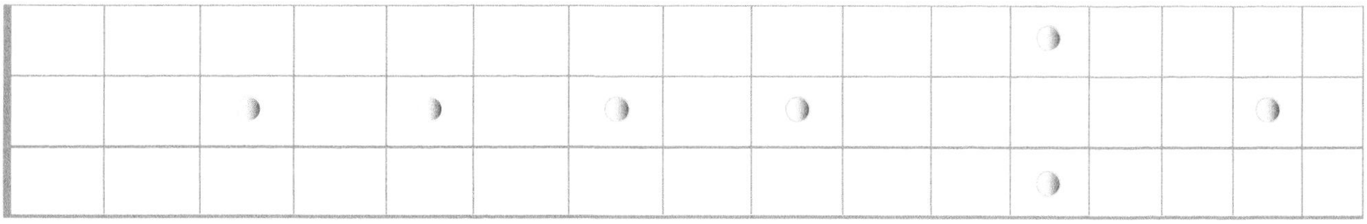

Db *Pattern* _____

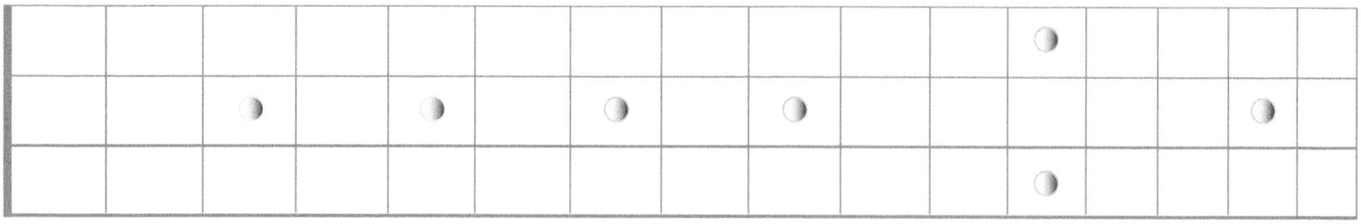

Gb *Pattern* _____

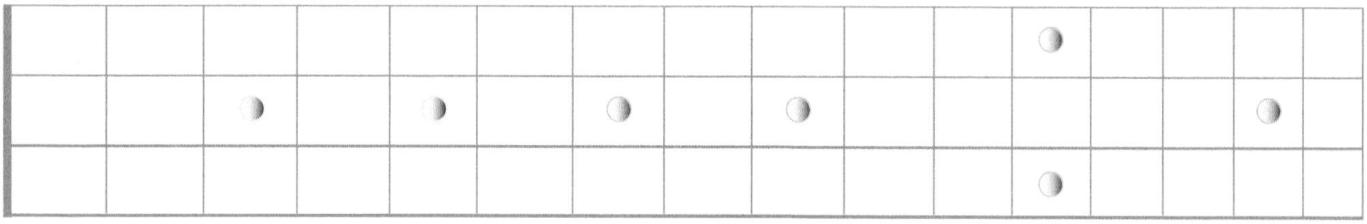

B   *Pattern* _____

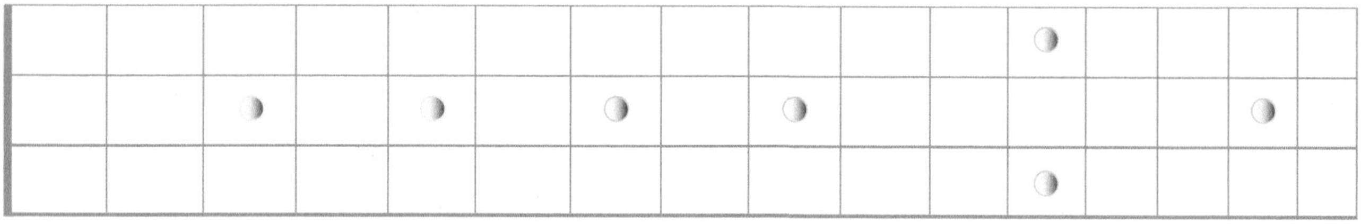

E   *Pattern* _____

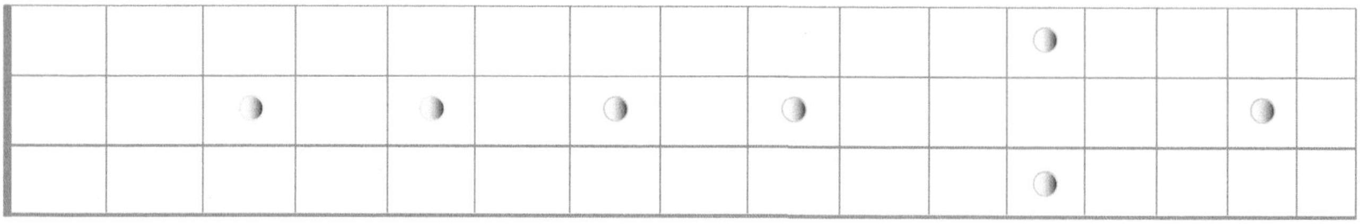

A   *Pattern* _____

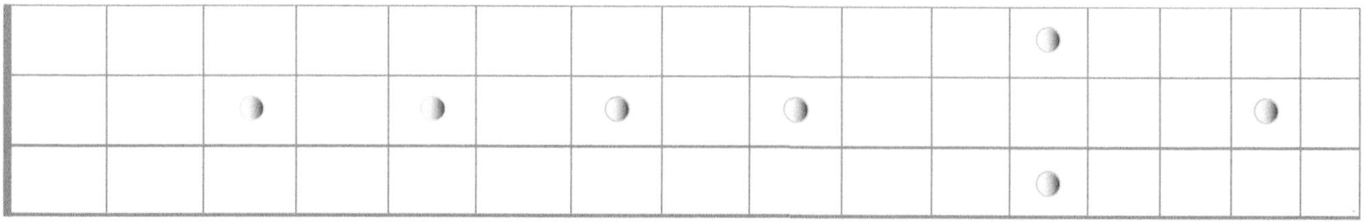

D   Pattern _____

G   Pattern _____

F# Pattern _____

C# Pattern _____

C♭ Pattern _____

Area 4 Diagrams

Area 4 – Area Map – _____

C   *Pattern* _____

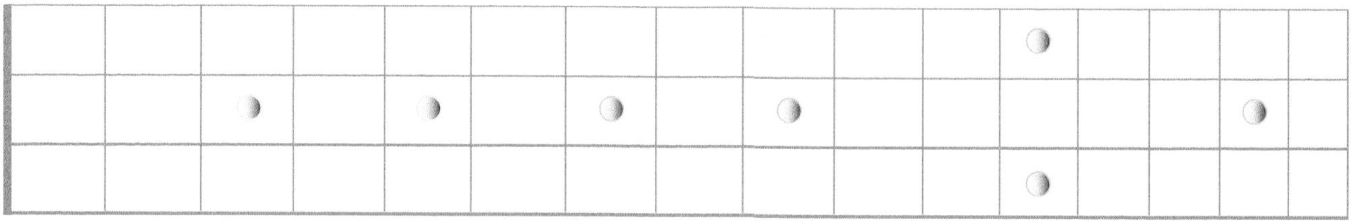

F   *Pattern* _____

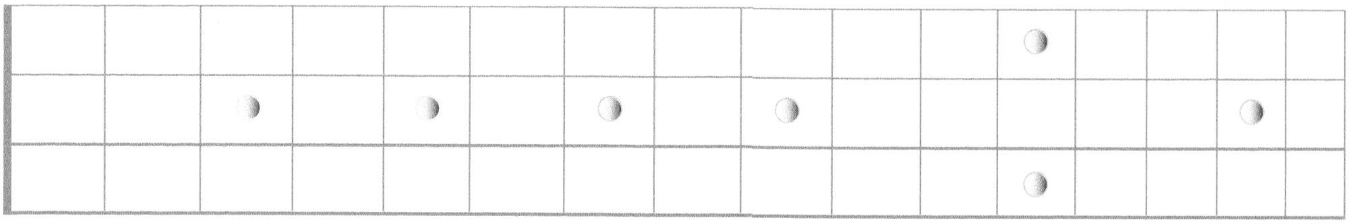

B♭   *Pattern* _____

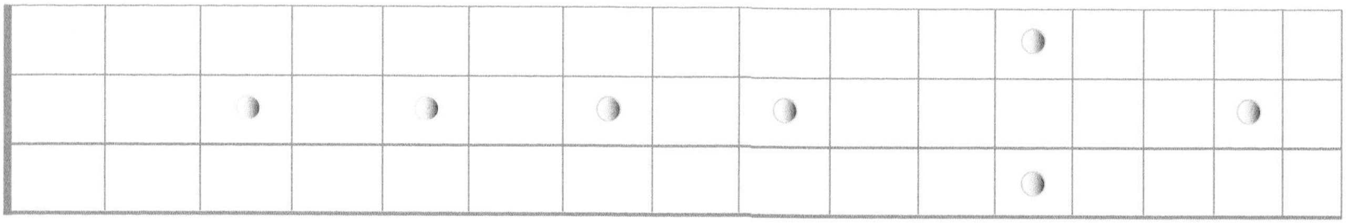

E♭   *Pattern* _____

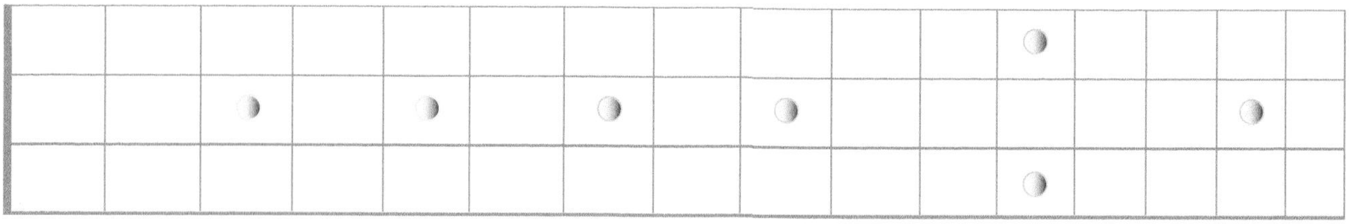

A♭   *Pattern* _____

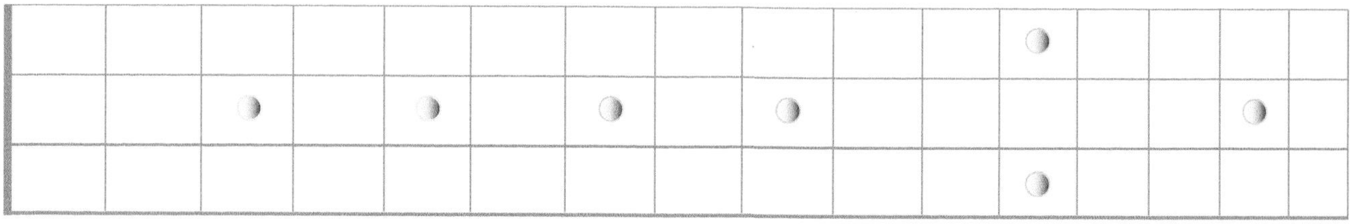

Db *Pattern* _____

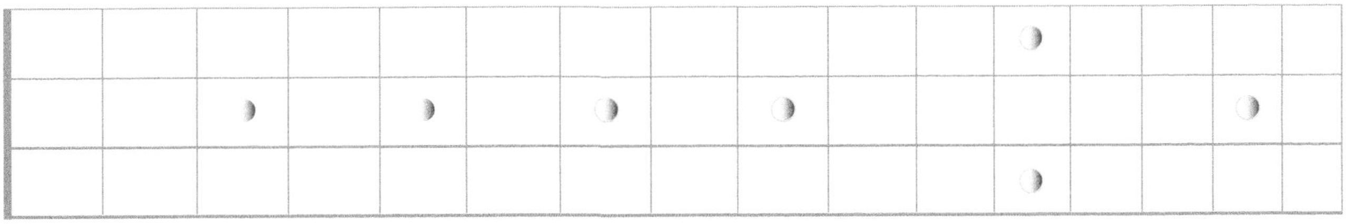

Gb *Pattern* _____

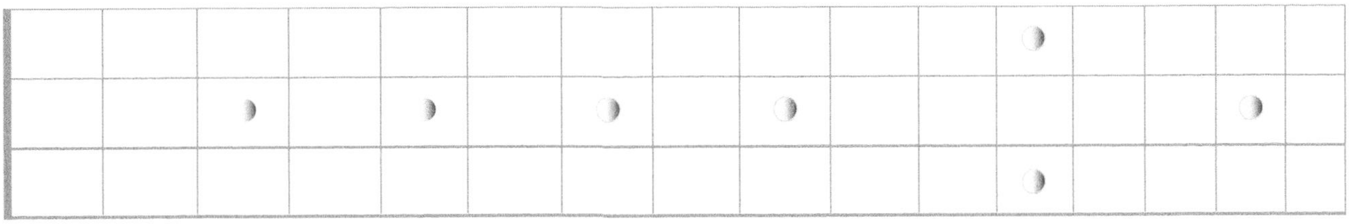

B   *Pattern* _____

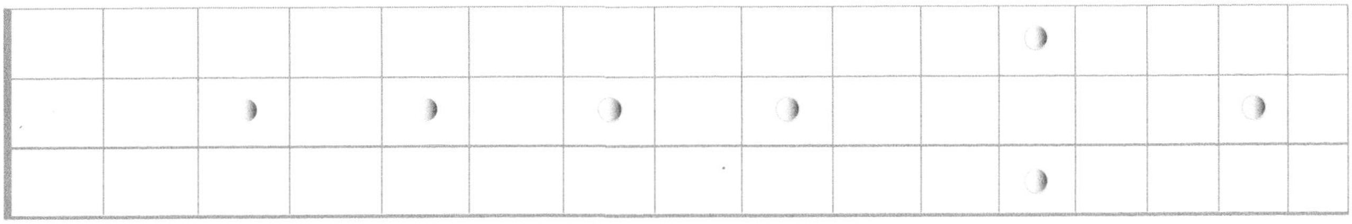

E   *Pattern* _____

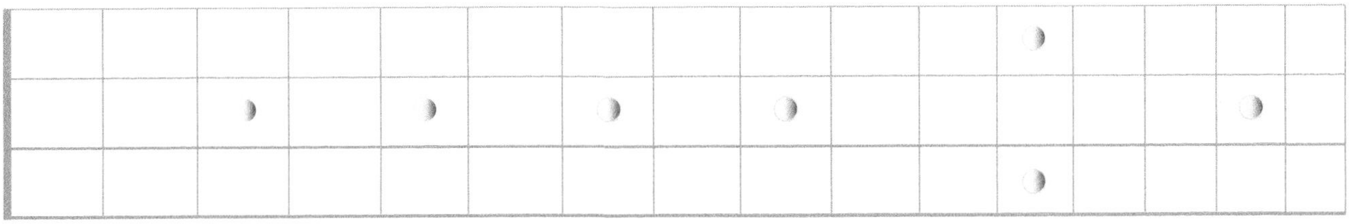

A   *Pattern* _____

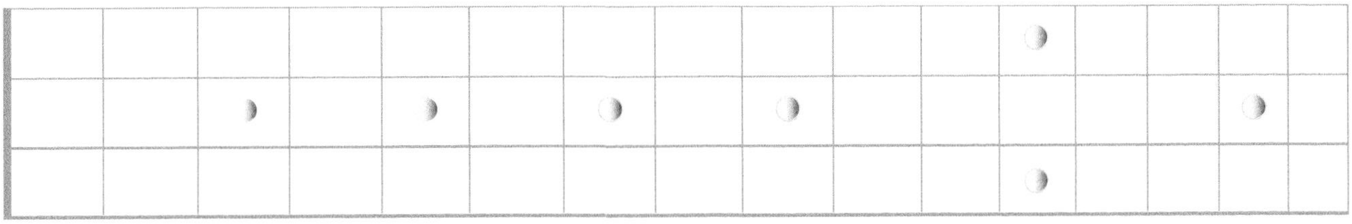

D   Pattern _____

G   Pattern _____

F#   Pattern _____

C#   Pattern _____

C♭   Pattern _____

Area 5 Diagrams

Area 5 – Area Map – _____

C   Pattern _____

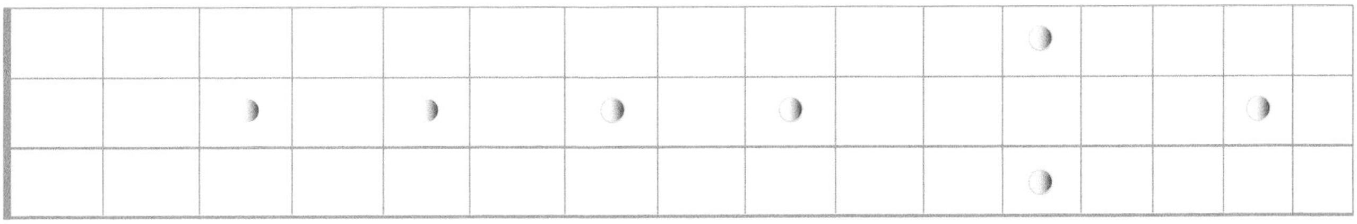

F   Pattern _____

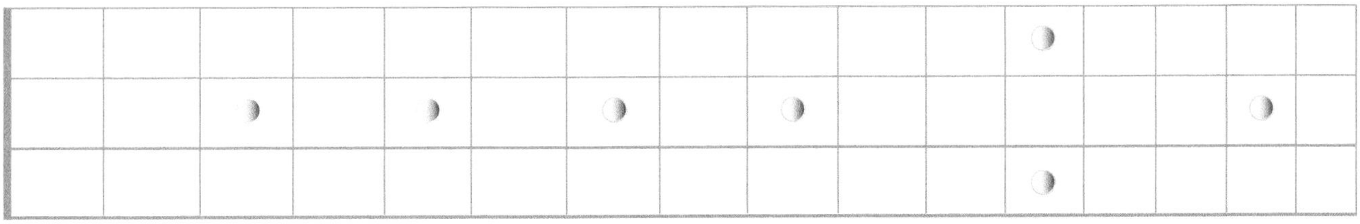

B♭ Pattern _____

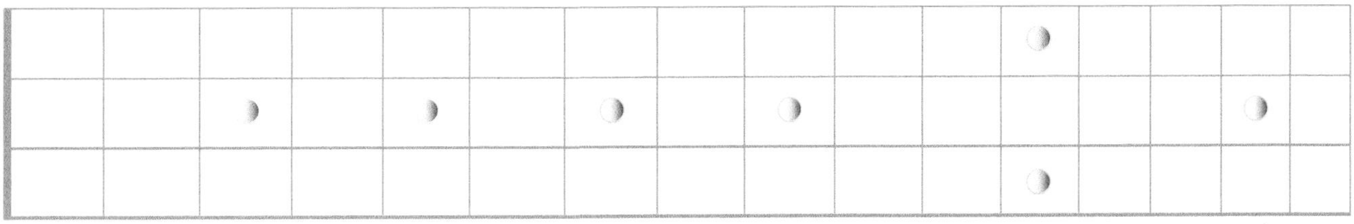

E♭ Pattern _____

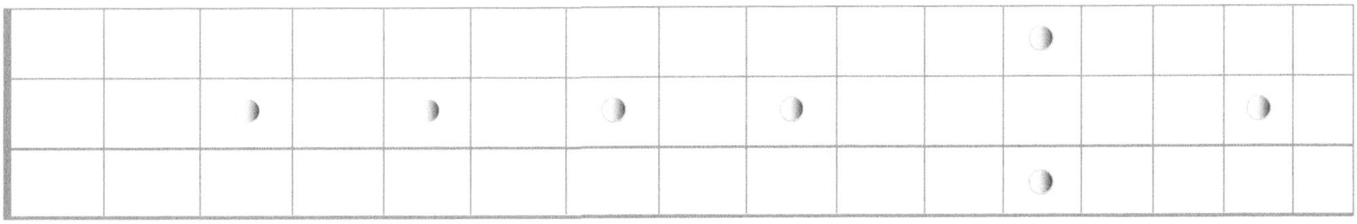

A♭ Pattern _____

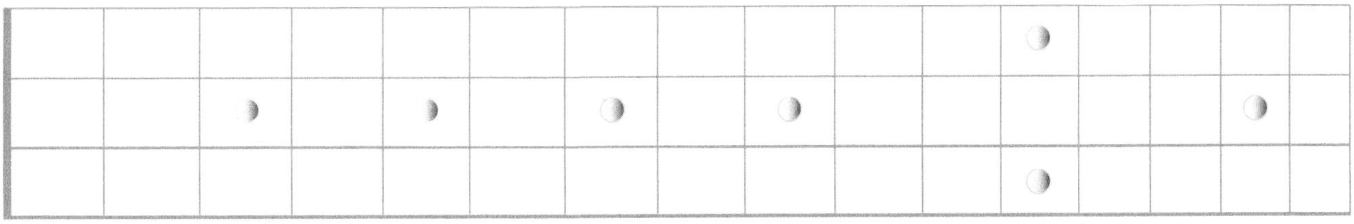

D♭ *Pattern* ____

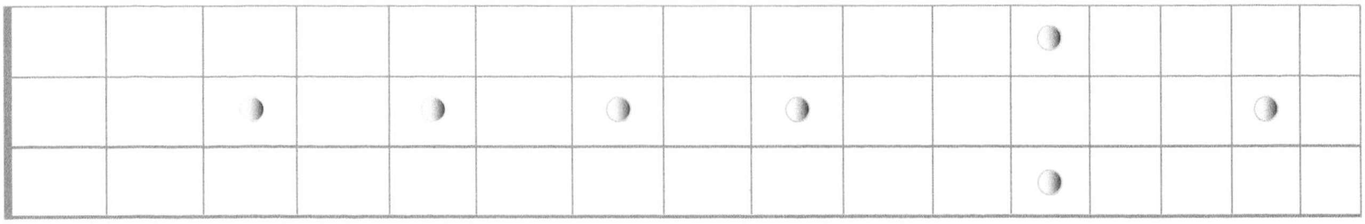

G♭ *Pattern* ____

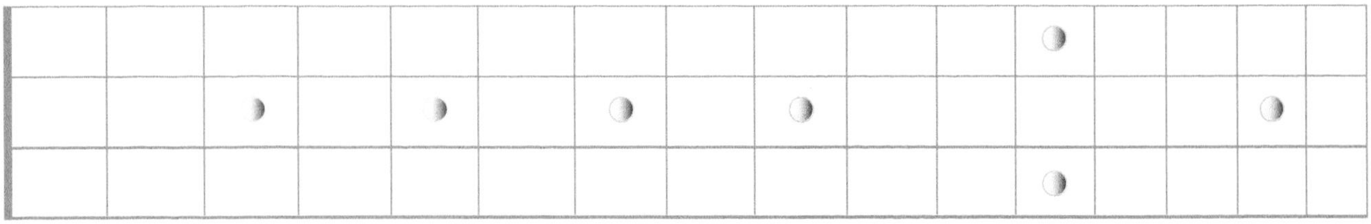

B *Pattern* ____

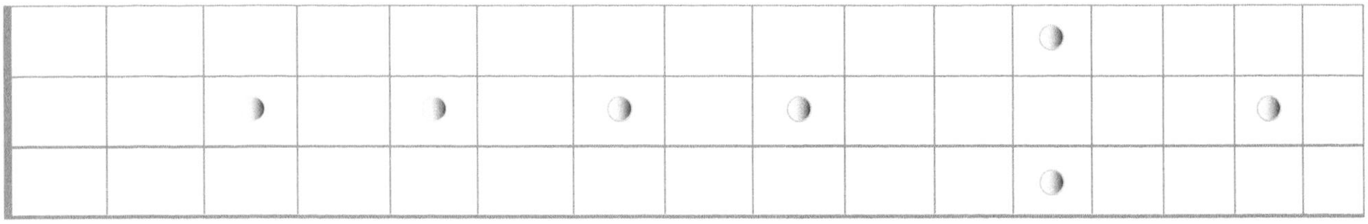

E *Pattern* ____

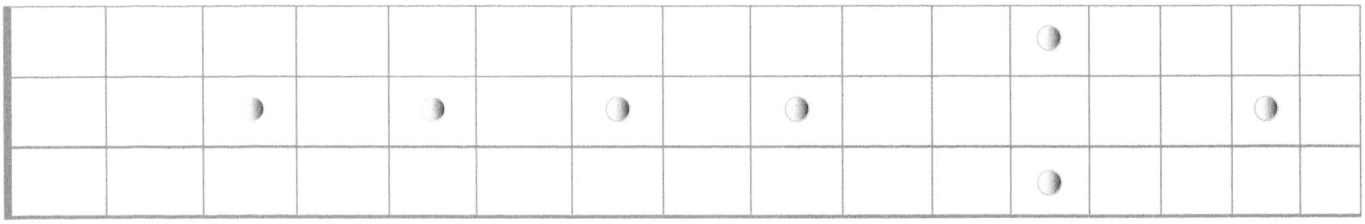

A *Pattern* ____

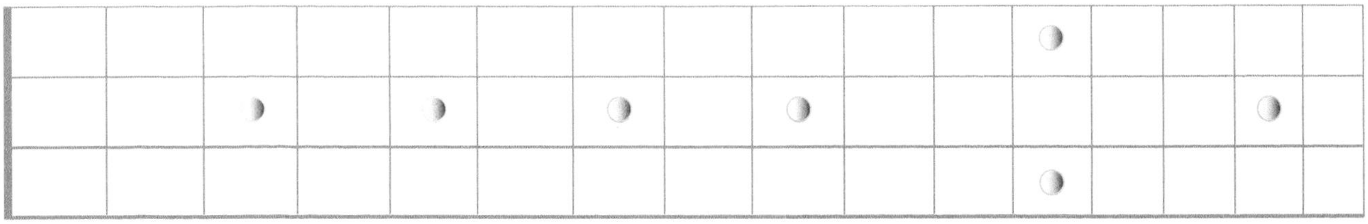

D   *Pattern* _____

G   *Pattern* _____

F#   *Pattern* _____

C#   *Pattern* _____

C♭   *Pattern* _____

The Area Matrix

> **Quick Overview:**
>
> 6 *Areas*: Open, 1 through 5
>
> 5 *Patterns* (*I II III V VI*) plus the *Open Area Patterns* unique to each key

Next, I want you to create the *"Area Matrix,"* a quick reference guide containing pattern numbers per area.

Fill in the table below (including how many frets each area spans — sometimes six frets, sometimes seven).

Fret span — while interesting to know and count out — it is not necessary to know this by heart. What is helpful, however, is to memorize the starting notes (lowest note on the E-string of the pattern). I left a row for you to fill in those notes — all areas have three notes as possible starting notes, except for *Area 4*, which has four. Various enharmonic spellings exist for these starting notes; you are welcome to keep things simple here and just write one enharmonic spelling.

Your turn:

The *Area Matrix* for *The Pattern System*

	AREA 1 Frets 1 – 6	AREA 2 Frets 3 – 9	AREA 3 Frets 5 – 11	AREA 4 Frets 8 – 13	AREA 5 Frets 10 – 16
C					
F					
B♭					
E♭					
A♭					
D♭/C♯					
G♭/F♯					
B/C♭					
E					
A					
D					
G					
Starting Notes (E string)					

Focus on knowing which pattern corresponds to which area — mainly so that your practice is comprehensive and systematic.

TIP: A good way to find your keys when you are away from the *Area Map* is to know the five Patterns in the key of G (*Patterns I, II* and *III* correspond to *Areas 1, 2* and *3, Pattern V* to *Area 4, VI* to *Area 5*). Some keys always share the same pattern in each area; this observation will help you when you practice in one area!

Including the enharmonic keys: Without the enharmonic keys:

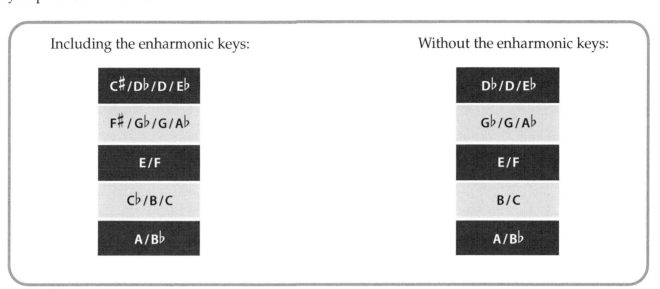

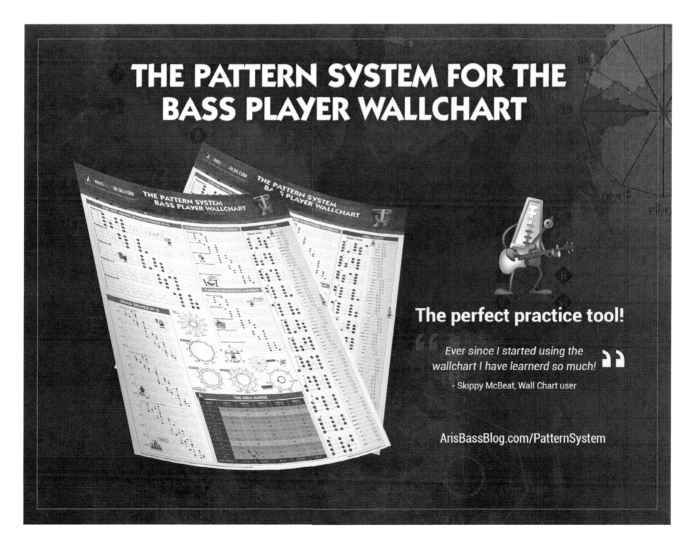

Here is the *Area Matrix* with keys that share the same patterns per area marked in the same color:

C: PV! F: PII! B♭: PVI …

THE AREA MATRIX

* = enharmonically simplified for space reasons
** = frets

KEYS	AREA 1 1 - 6**	AREA 2 3 - 9	AREA 3 5 - 11	AREA 4 8 - 13	AREA 5 10 - 16
C	V	VI	I	II	III
F	II	III	V	VI	I
B♭	VI	I	II	III	V
E♭	III	V	VI	I	II
A♭	I	II	III	V	VI
D♭/C♯	III	V	VI	I	II
G♭/F♯	I	II	III	V	VI
C♭/B	V	VI	I	II	III
E	II	III	V	VI	I
A	VI	I	II	III	V
D	III	V	VI	I	II
G	I	II	III	V	VI
Lowest Notes*	F F♯ G	G♯ A B♭	B♭ B C	C C♯ D E♭	E♭ E F

▌▌▌ TIP: I highly recommend you keep this reference handy on your music stand. Or get the wall chart that goes with this book, which puts this and many other key elements and elements of the *Pattern System* on display. Info at: *ArisBassBlog.com/PatternSystem*.

POWERFUL PRACTICE

I sometimes hear people say that "knowing theory takes the magic out of playing music." I believe the opposite to be true — the more you know, the deeper the magic becomes. And most importantly, as the fretboard and the theory "rules" become ingrained and automatic, you will play with more confidence and freedom. Tension will fall by the wayside and the music will flow. *The Pattern System* bridges theory, technique and fretboard knowledge in a unique way with musical expression. To get the most out of it, it's very helpful if you understand more about how learning works.

Fine Tuning Your Training

When studying an instrument, many often assume it takes:

- Rote learning (imitation and repetition)
- "Talent"
- Assimilation (copying and intuiting)
- "Just playing a lot"

…and *somehow* the learning will take place.

A lot of learning *can* happen this way, especially for young children. However, for the motivated learner who looks for fast results and a clear trajectory with defined benchmarks and measurable milestones, there are much more powerful strategies we can employ. Not only through specific drills (such as the *Connection Exercises* above, for example), but also in terms of where specifically we put our attention when doing the drills.

Amazing musicians who are also passionate teachers can sometimes feel helpless here. This happens because they may have forgotten what it was like to struggle at certain junctures, such as not being able to play a melody, or trouble improvising and connecting the dots of chord progressions. Some teachers, though well-intentioned and wanting to help — may simply not know how to convey certain skills or thought processes. Typically, these skills have become second nature to them, and they'd have to ask themselves: "How am I actually doing what I am doing?" This phenomenon is known as "Unconscious Competence" in the highly useful model of learning by Gordon Training International.

I will show you shortly how *The Pattern System* specifically addresses the various channels of learning. First, let's walk through a quick refresher on Gordon Training International's *Competence Model*, which I introduced in *Music Theory for the Bass Player*.

Here I apply it to *The Pattern System.*

The Four Stages of Competence

(basic idea inspired by Gordon Trainings International)

STAGE 1

UNCONSCIOUS COMPETENCE – You don't even know what you don't know.

Example: You have learned a few basslines and can play them by heart. It doesn't occur to you that there could be more to know about playing bass. You got what you need at the moment and you have not thought about what else you might need or miss.

STAGE 2

CONSCIOUS INCOMPETENCE – You become aware of what you don't know.

Example: You learn a bit of theory. You begin to understand musical shapes and learn how notes relate to each other. You realize the benefit of consistent fingering and good technique. You are beginning to wrap your mind around how the fretboard works, how it all connects.

STAGE 3

CONSCIOUS COMPETENCE – You know what you know in a particular subject matter.

Example: You are practicing the Patterns and it shows. You know which areas and keys you know well and which ones you still want to work on some more. Your knowledge is becoming more and more solid.

STAGE 4

UNCONSCIOUS COMPETENCE –
You know what you know so well that you "have forgotten about it."

Example: Your knowledge of the fretboard feels effortless. You know the patterns so well that you don't have to think about them anymore. Recalling them seems instant. Your musical mind is free to pay attention to other things, like performing expressively, your bandmates, and the interaction with the audience — all the finer points of your playing.

This last stage is, of course, the goal of *The Pattern System*.

As for *The Pattern System* right now, you are likely finding yourself between the slightly uncomfortable Stage 2 and the very exciting Stage 3. When doing the *Improvisation Exercises*, you may even see or feel glimpses of Stage 4. It certainly is out there on the horizon and you are getting closer every time you practice!

Keep your eye on the prize, Skippy!
It will all come into focus very soon!

Music is a very wide field. Learning stages can overlap. You may enjoy the benefits of Stage 4 competency in some areas, yet still have many Stage 1 fields of knowledge waiting to be discovered. The wheel keeps turning.

The Channels of Learning

Rather than hoping for the best by "just playing a lot," you can train your mind to pay attention to very specific streams of information while practicing. Learning, for one, happens through a variety of different channels. Below, I describe the channels that I have found to be most practical for learning music. You may discover a favorite one or two. The goal, however, is to integrate and practice them all deliberately.

I like to distinguish these six channels of learning:

- **Visual:** This can mean seeing fingers on the fretboard or reading music from a lead sheet. When the visual channel is predominant, we access information by visualizing the fretboard or shapes on the fretboard, or by seeing a chart, or notes on a staff with our eyes, or within our mind's eye.

- **Auditory:** The ear guides us to the notes and provides feedback about how our playing sounds. An important aspect of auditory information is what's called Relative Pitch — hearing notes in relation to each other. When you play a scale, for example, you can focus on the sounds themselves and also hear them as relationships to the tonic. You can either play against a drone (or an open string) as the tonic or hear the tonic in your mind's ear (excellent training!).

- **Kinesthetic:** This is the channel based on the feeling of muscle movement. "Kinesthetic" means sensing the hand, the shapes that your fingers make, and feeling the vibrations of the bass. This sense also informs us of where our limbs are in relation to the body — our posture. I like to include the spatial sense here: The distances as felt by our body — between frets or strings, for example — as well as where we are in relation to the room and others around us.

  Attention to good technique is largely guided by kinesthetic exercises such as focusing on the index/middle alternating or keeping your fingers close to the fretboard. When you practice the patterns, you ingrain them into your muscle memory to "get them under your fingers." When you know a scale or arpeggio by the movements of your fingers with correct fingering, then you have learned it kinesthetically.

Also, our sense of rhythm is largely kinesthetic — a cool groove makes us want to move! We feel rhythm in our body! When you do an improvisation exercise in this book and lose the downbeat, for example, let your body sway in the rhythm and sense a "refresh" after four beats or four bars. Counting happens in the head, feeling the beats happens in the body.

- **Conceptual**: The thinking mind! It consists of abstractions of the world that we use to navigate and make sense of things. Words, music theory, patterns are all abstractions with very real practical applications. In fact, they are derived from the sensory world around us. When we extract a concept from what we perceive (or when we invent one in our minds), we can apply it to new situations, combine it with other concepts and come up with new combinations of all sorts of things. This is an important aspect of creativity.

  Saying note names, scale degrees, knowing music theory or memorizing a tune by analysis makes up this learning channel. Counting out rhythm is conceptual. The conceptual channel brings the auditory, visual and conceptual channels together. It can guide them and receive feedback from them.

- **Musicality**: The music accomplishes what it sets out to do: it serves the song and enhances the lyrics/melody/story. Here is where I place experiences we have gained from transcribing and assimilating material through listening to our heroes. This channel also concerns itself with the interaction between musicians — with deep listening, with being open to where the song takes you, and the big mystery question: Where does the inspiration come from? (See the next Channel…)

- **Spiritual**: Being aware of ourselves beyond the physical senses. The sense that we are here now and connected to everything.

  Undoubtedly when we are truly in the flow of the music, there are powers at work that seem quite elusive, to say the least. I offer this channel as an open question. We can practice it by not only practicing our patterns and tunes, but also through physical and spiritual disciplines, from meditation or spiritual practices to physical exercise and choosing healthy foods, cultivating friendships and love, "goodness" and more. This channel is nourished by carefully tending to all the previous channels and at the same time, it feeds them. For example, the deeper we listen, the more we discover in the music and the more our soul feels enriched by the musical experience.

Do you recognize these channels? Maybe you picked your preferred one as you were reading or noticed that you retrieve information mostly one way or another. You could also observe that the last two defy description a bit. Have you ever felt those last two channels? My guess is — likely yes, you have.

When you do, your mind tends to get very quiet and everything else seems to disappear. The sense of flow, bliss and satisfaction that comes from being wrapped up in these channels keeps us practicing. Like Skippy eyeing that horizon earlier, we sense that this is where we want to be as much as possible!

Channeling Your Practice Results

Knowing how to use each channel effectively when practicing this system multiplies your results, not only for the *Pattern Practice* itself, but for all the practice you do.

In *The Pattern System*, we actively work on these channels:

Visual – Visualizing the pattern diagrams! With practice, this becomes very fast! When doing *Connection Exercises*, visualize the entire shape before you play it!

Auditory – Hearing pitch is the most obvious aspect. As mentioned, hearing the notes in relationship to the tonic is extremely useful, as is hearing them in your mind before you play them! Connecting sounds with saying scale degrees enhances this!

And there is so much more you can hear — actively listen for: buzz-free tone, even note length and volume, etc.

Kinesthetic – Be able to run these patterns without having to think about them conceptually. Your fingers know them. You can feel where to go. You sense the tonic under certain fingers, and the patterns just unfold. This channel can become lightning fast, certainly faster than saying note names. This is the power of muscle memory! Once you have accomplished this, your mind has free capacity to focus on other aspects like phrasing, musical context, etc. That is why I say, "Learn each pattern so well that you can forget about it." This simply means your conceptual mind is no longer needed extensively to recall the pattern — your muscles know it instantly. This is an extremely important aspect of this training.

Conceptual – Saying note names or scale degrees when practicing the patterns engages this channel. It will also help you learn songs, transpose, understand how chord progressions work together, etc. You'll start to recognize many kinds of patterns in music — we just started with scales here. This leads to scale groupings, intervallic playing, chords, chord progressions, melodies, and so on. We will be employing this channel quite a bit, and for good reason. It is, however, quite slow compared to the other channels. Saying note names will slow you down, as will thinking scale degrees. Use it to strengthen your understanding and help ingrain the information in the other channels. Once you "got it," use it only when needed (for example, when reading or writing music, or when communicating with others).

Mental Practice (Away From the Bass!)

Practicing these patterns "mentally" by visualizing them in your mind is the most powerful practice of all.

I know this firsthand:

When I first learned *The Pattern System*, I used the kinesthetic channel intuitively as my leading one — and because I knew my theory and key signatures very well, the conceptual channel as a close second. Nobody at the school paid attention to how we learned or why we were able to pass our tests, as long as we were able to present the various drills at a reasonable tempo. I was able to play the assignments and say the note names too, so I thought I had maximized my learning potential and was quite happy with that.

Later, I was shown by my teacher Wolf Wein, that I hadn't utilized the potential of visualization in connection with *Pattern Practice*. By training the shapes visually — only in the mind — they get ingrained on a powerful level. I had no idea that there was a whole other level of "knowing" these shapes. Seeing the entire fretboard light up according to the shapes in all areas enables an entirely different level of freedom! This taught me to do the *Pattern Practice* — especially the *Connection Exercises* — without a bass, only in "my mind's eye." This mental practice blows actual finger-moving practice out of the water!

A Most Powerful Visualization Exercise

Look at *Pattern I* in G major and take note of the shape of the pattern. Close your eyes and see the pattern in your mind's eye. It does not matter how clear your inner picture is. It's different for everybody and will get more distinct with practice. See it as one snapshot.

If this is too challenging at first, start with the lowest string and see the pattern there, in this case, a circle, then square, then circle, with distances of one or two frets, respectively. Then, internally see the pattern for the next string. Next, work on seeing both strings together. Continue in that vein until you have all of *Pattern I* memorized visually and can recall the image quickly.

Pick the next pattern, *Pattern V* in C (I am in *Area 1*, stepping through the cycle to the left), and visualize it in the same way. After a few moments of working on this shape, recall *Pattern I* again. Switch back and forth between the two patterns a few times. Then add *Pattern II* (F) and follow the same process.

After doing a few minutes of this mental-only work, play the shapes on the bass. Keep your eyes closed and keep visualizing the mental snapshot as you play the shapes. If you feel your mental picture needs further re-imprinting, switch back and forth between playing the pattern and looking at your fingers (or the pattern diagram paper) and seeing it in your mind's eye.

Also, see your fingers on the fretboard in your mind's eye. Connect the sensation of the finger movements and positions to your image of the pattern.

To become even more familiar with the patterns, look for notable features of each.

As an example, look at *Pattern I:* its outer notes form a rectangle. It has three notes on each string and is the only pattern with this characteristic. The fingering pattern is either 1-2-4 or 1-3-4; they appear in sets of two, on strings next to each other. Roots are contained in the first set of each pair.

Find your own recognizable characteristics for each pattern. Also, build associations with shapes you are familiar with (Tetris pieces, for example). Later, when doing *Pentatonic Shapes*, I will go all the way with this idea by naming the patterns according to the shapes they make on the fretboard. Mnemonics work!

▌▌▌ TIP: Do this exercise whether you consider yourself a "visual learner" or not. Even if visualization is hard or feels unnatural for you, approach it with playfulness and curiosity, and give it your best shot.

Daily Visualization Practice

Throughout this book, I have encouraged you to use visualization for *Pattern Practice*. Start slowly and ramp up your routine from there. Aim to do a bit of mental practice throughout the day. If you do *Pattern Practice* with the bass at one point and just mentally at another point during the day, you increase the effectiveness of your practice exponentially!

Mental Exercise Using Multiple Channels

Pick a Pattern. Let's say *Pattern VI* in *Area 2* in C.

- Close your eyes and see the pattern in your mind's eye. (If you need help, look at the diagram.)

- Then hear it in your inner ear. Similar to the visual exercise above, the goal is to do this internally, without actually referencing the pattern first by playing it. If you struggle or are not sure, just play the pattern (or parts of it) and listen. Then immediately "play back internally" what you just heard. Switch back and forth until your inner hearing becomes more refined.

- Now play through the pattern in your mind only. Internally feel your fingers move, the sensation of touching the strings, the bass under your fingers, etc. You can move your fingers in the shape ("air guitar" style). If this is tricky at first, do the same thing you did for visualizing and hearing — **switch back and forth between the physical doing and the mental-only representation. Soon you will be able to practice without needing the bass.**

- Also, think or say note names or scale degrees just from imagining the patterns.

In relation to the pattern, attempt to answer these questions:

- Which note is the highest?
- Which finger plays it?
- What scale degree is it?

Improvising in Your Mind

Now imagine you want to improvise using this pattern. This can be the start of an incredible journey where you learn to connect the music in your mind to your bass. You hear music internally and know how to translate it to your instrument. I can't emphasize enough how important and rewarding this skill is. The exercises above, combined with the improvisation explorations in this book that relate to the patterns present a great way to get started on this path.

The Gold Standard of the *Pattern Practice: Connection Exercises* in Your Mind

If you do these for just minutes a day, the payoff will be huge. Can you do them with a metronome? Very slowly is fine. Skippy demonstrates a great way to do this (best to say it out loud to the click to make it even more real):

See each pattern in its entirety as you say just the keys and patterns. In addition, run *Connection Exercises* in your mind. I like moving my fingers on an imaginary fretboard while I execute this.

More Tips for Mental Practice

- Set a timer and spend two sets of three minutes each (with a short break in between) on mental practice. You can also start with just one minute. Switch up which pattern you use and revisit those that you have already covered. Is it getting easier with time? If it isn't, focus on just one pattern for a few days before adding others.

- See the fret markers of your bass in your mind's eye. Visualize the patterns in relationship to the fret markers. It is indeed helpful to have a bass that has markers not just on the side but on top of the fretboard. You can have a luthier place real mother-of-pearl markers, or you can purchase fret stickers for about ten dollars on Amazon (links at *ArisbassBlog.com/Resources*).

- See the various patterns in your mind's eye and visualize the highest and lowest notes of them on the fretboard, as well as the finger you would play them with. Skippy is demonstrating the D scale in *Area 2 (Pattern V)*.

Scalar Studies

Four-Note Groupings

Below I show you four versions (playing the notes ascending/up as well as descending/up and their respective reversals) in a few sample keys. I have written out just the beginnings to give you a jump start. Continue to write them out on your own until you can play them from recalling the patterns alone.

Let's start out in *Area 1,* in the sample keys of G♭ and C. Find the pattern first and play it in its entirety. It will lock your mind into the shape. Then start playing groups of four ascending consecutive scale notes, with each group starting one note higher than the previous one. For many, this is the easiest configuration to start with.

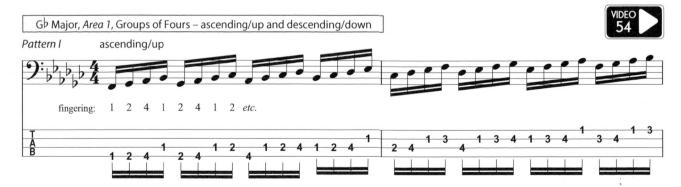

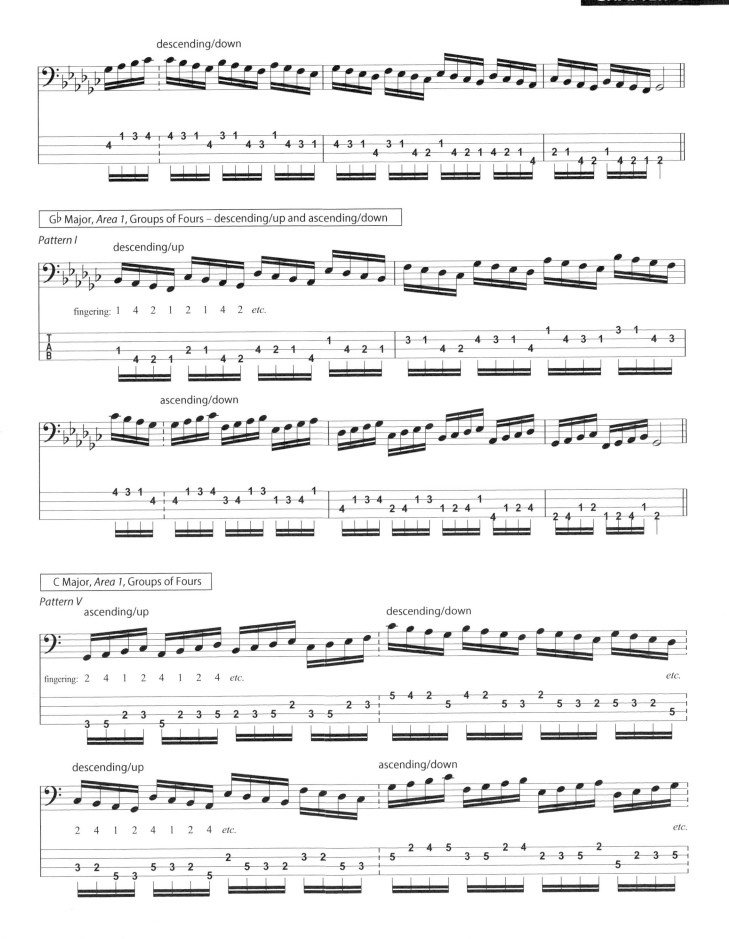

descending/down

Gb Major, *Area 1*, Groups of Fours – descending/up and ascending/down

Pattern I

descending/up

fingering: 1 4 2 1 2 1 4 2 *etc.*

ascending/down

C Major, *Area 1*, Groups of Fours

Pattern V

ascending/up   descending/down

fingering: 2 4 1 2 4 1 2 4 *etc.*   *etc.*

descending/up   ascending/down

2 4 1 2 4 1 2 4 *etc.*   *etc.*

To switch it up with a few more examples, move on to Area 2, key of G. Find the pattern first and play it in its entirety, then do the exercise!

G Major, *Area 2*, Groups of Fours

Pattern II

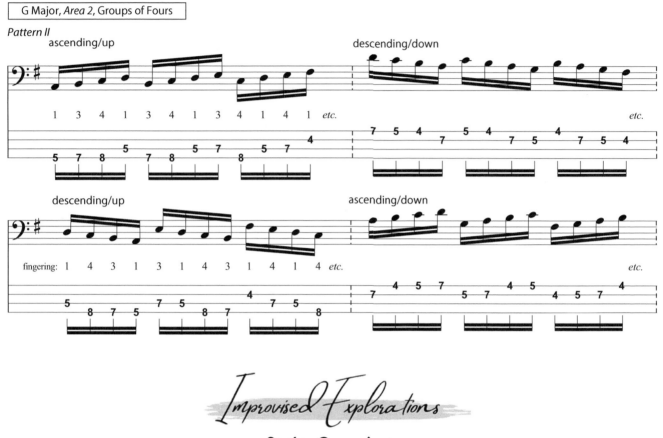

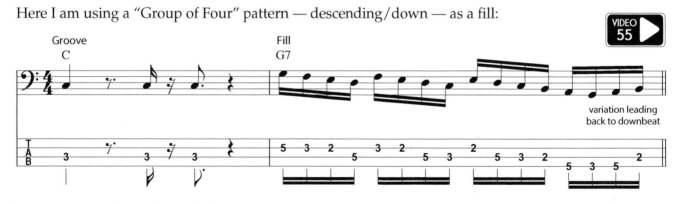

Improvised Explorations

Scalar Groupings

I mentioned that groups of threes or fours work great in a variety of musical contexts. Let's put this idea to work in an exercise using these new four-note groupings. The following chord progression — C to G7 and back — keeps you in *one* pattern. G Mixolydian — the fifth mode of C major and the scale to use over the G7* — is the pattern for C major, of course, as is C major itself. In this example, I am in *Area 1*, where C major is *Pattern V*. Program a bar of C and a bar of G7 into iReal Pro, your looper, Band-in-a-Box®, or use our free jam tracks and have fun improvising using four-note-groupings in the rhythmic variations below!

Here I am using a "Group of Four" pattern — descending/down — as a fill:

---

* If you have any holes in your theory knowledge, check out *Music Theory for the Bass Player*, which explains all types of triads and chords, extensions, alterations, the diatonic cycle and modes.

Now I move the fill over by one sixteenth note — this creates a cool variation:

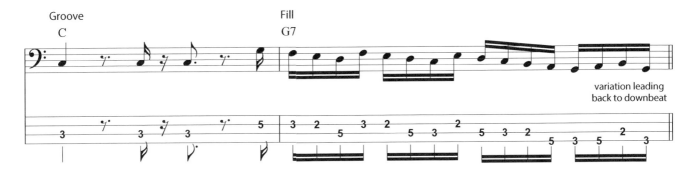

You can continue to move the four-note groupings over by a sixteenth note.

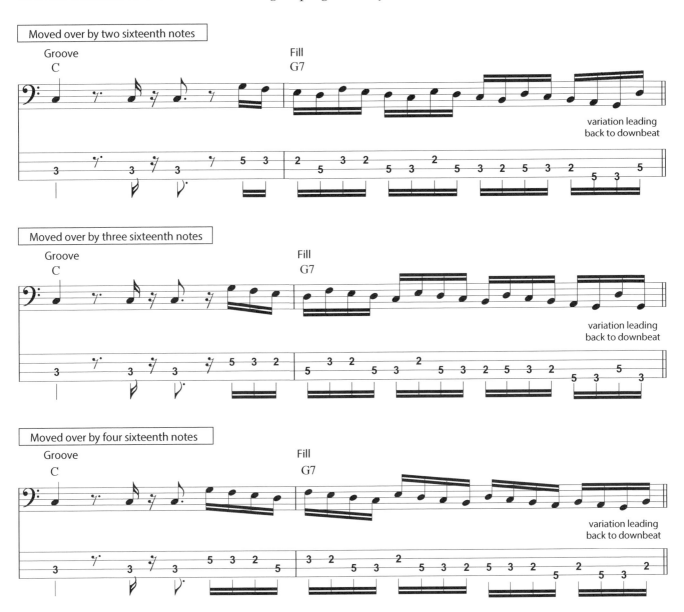

Practice
LIKE THIS

- Pick a pattern in an area.

- Determine the I and V7 chords.

- Use this rhythmic template to come up with your own four-note grouping idea.

Then move the four-note grouping over by one, two, three, or four sixteenth notes, as shown above. Remember you can use any of the ascending/descending up/down combinations! Have fun!

 What About the Upright? Does *The Pattern System* come into play here?

When I started learning upright and dove into the study of Simandl, Streicher, Drew, and Montag, I already had a solid understanding of the location of the notes on the electric bass fretboard from using the patterns and a one-finger-per-fret approach. I could very easily adapt this to upright fingering using that same four-fret grid for orientation that I had in my mind's eye from the electric. The shapes still unfolded in four-fret spans, even though, of course, I had to use proper classical upright fingering to execute them (the technical learning curve was still there, including the need to train the muscles in the fingers in new ways). The organization and note finding, however, map across to the upright bass perfectly — it turned out to be very easy for me to translate my knowledge to the upright fretboard!

 What about using upright fingering on the electric?

Paradoxically, players who started on upright often argue against a one-finger-per-fret approach on the electric and favor the traditional upright fingering they are used to for the electric. Upright bass fingering, however, does not constitute a valid model for electric bass because:

- The ergonomics of the bass neck are entirely different.

- Distances are larger on upright.

- The force needed to press down a string properly on the electric is less than on the upright. On the electric bass, even the pinky finger has enough strength to do this on its own. On the upright, other fingers support the pinky.

- Tempos of scale runs (and similar figures) are severely limited (or much harder to execute) when using upright fingering on the electric.

- Upright fingering does not use the ring finger in lower positions (only as support for the pinky) — I see no reason to do the same on electric. The ring finger is strong enough and can stretch easily to create a four-fret span with the first finger. If you struggle with this, make a small shift — still better than upright fingering!

 FACT: *The Pattern System* will be a very helpful guide for the location of notes on the upright. Also, the aspects of training your musical mind translate directly — not just to upright, but to any aspect of music-making. When playing upright, access the patterns in your mind's eye, and play them using proper upright fingering. Use classical upright fingering on the upright as your starting point and use one-finger-per fret on the electric.

FAQ   How Can I Get Myself to Practice Consistently?

- Keep track of your practice sessions. Some students thrive on marking an X on a wall calendar for every day they practiced according to their plan. Set a doable minimum amount of time to count for an X. Aim to never interrupt your run streak. Daily is great, but one day of rest per week is entirely fine, and you may want to place a special X for that one day off…

- Do not underestimate the power of the visualization exercises. Practice away from your instrument should make up about 25% of your practice time. If you are traveling without your bass, use it as an opportunity to do more mental practice. Mental practice counts for your run streak!

- Schedule your practice time. Reserve time in the day and strive to minimize potential distractions.

- Whenever you have completed a practice session, make a point to congratulate yourself in some physical way. This can be as simple as high-fiving yourself or telling yourself: "Good job following through." Research has shown these small acts of self-encouragement make the difference!

TEST YOUR UNDERSTANDING #7

1. True or False: You should know what your favorite learning channel is and mostly cater to that channel, ignoring all others. ☐ True ☐ False

2. The kinesthetic learning channel concerns itself with (select the best answer):
   ☐ a. Muscle memory
   ☐ b. Fingerings
   ☐ c. Feeling distances
   ☐ d. All of the above and more
   ☐ e. None of the above. It is a trick question.

3. The fastest route of memory recall is:
   ☐ a. The visual channel
   ☐ b. The kinesthetic channel
   ☐ c. The conceptual channel
   ☐ d. The auditory channel
   ☐ e. All of them equally
   ☐ f. Visual and kinesthetic can become very fast with practice

4. Since we are learning music, the most important channel is:
   ☐ a. The auditory channel
   ☐ b. Muscle memory, such as the kinesthetic channel. (This is a book on "Patterns" after all.)
   ☐ c. All learning channels are important. The most effective learning strategy will use all of them.

5. You are in *Area 3*. Which pattern do you play for the following scales? Answer without consulting the *Area Map*.
   a. G major – *Pattern* _____
   b. D♭ major – *Pattern* _____
   c. F major – *Pattern* _____
   d. C♯ major – *Pattern* _____
   e. E major – *Pattern* _____
   f. A major – *Pattern* _____

6. As for the upright bass…
   ☐ a. Do not use this book.
   ☐ b. Use upright fingering but utilize the knowledge of the patterns.
   ☐ c. Upright bass fingering should be used on the electric for reasons of tradition.

~~~~~ **BLUEPRINT FOR PRACTICE #7** ~~~~~

Written Assignment: Write out *Area 3, 4* and *5* diagrams into the book (choose note names or scale degrees, switch it up). **pp. 147–155**

Fill in the *Area Matrix* **p. 156**

1. **PP:** *Connection Exercises,* 8 beats, *Area 3;* cycle to the left and right; say scale degrees/note names/nothing

2. **PP:** *Connection Exercises,* 8 beats, *Areas 2* and *3;* minor third sequence to the right and left; say scale degrees/note names/nothing
   for all sequences: **p. 126**

3. **SS:** Interval studies in fourths; various combinations as shown in *Chapter 6; Areas 3* and *4;* practice several keys (suggesting E A C) **pp. 136–142** • **Videos 47 to 52**

4. **SS:** *Chapter 7* Scalar Studies in a variety of keys **pp. 166–168**

5. **IE:** *Chapter 7* improvisation , scalar groupings, pick various areas; **pp. 168–170** • **Video 53**
   for all sequences: **p. 126**

SHAPES WITHIN SHAPES — THE MAJOR TRIADS

Introduction

Inside the scalar patterns reside:

- All modes of the major scale
- Diatonic triads and chords
- The common pentatonic scales

Another helpful feature of the *Pattern System* unveils itself when diving into these shapes and then extending them to common chord progressions.

Major Triads

Practicing scales will get you a myriad of benefits. Adding triad arpeggios will provide an even bigger payoff because:

- Chord progressions consist of chords — they form the foundation of basslines for many styles.
- They are highly relevant musically for the creation of grooves and fills.
- They provide guideposts for several frequently employed soloing strategies, such as guide-tone lines, chromatic approaches to chord tones, and the like.

You will start with major triads on the tonic.

Then you will also add the diatonic triads on all steps of the scale.

This has several benefits that will pay off in many musical applications:

- You will understand how modes and chords fit together in diatonic and modal contexts.
- You will become proficient at recognizing chord progressions within any key (called "diatonic chord progressions") and consequently will also be able to quickly identify chords that expand or leave the key.
- You will be able to instantly transpose many chord progressions to any other key.
- The scale determines the diatonic seventh and all extensions (9,11,13) the chord will use.

Open Area Triad Maps (Tonic)

Open Area – Triads on the Tonic

Do this in the order of the cycle to the left — write the scale pattern in light grey or pencil, then fill the circles and squares with a solid color for the triad notes, like this:

C major triad in the *Open Position*

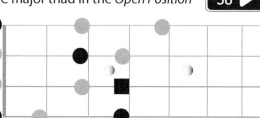

Open Area Triad Maps (I Chord)

C

F

B♭

E♭

A♭

Db

Gb

B

E

A

D

G

F#

C#

C♭

Practice
LIKE THIS

- Play the scale pattern from lowest to highest note and back. Recall it in your mind.

- Then play the triad only.

- Sense the *"Shape within a Shape."* Visualize the triad shape only, as well as the triad shape within the scale shape.

- Start with the cycle to the left, then right, then also go through the other sequences (major seconds, minor thirds, major thirds, minor seconds).

- Once you are familiar with the above exercises, omit the scale pattern and play just the triads:

  - All ascending only

  - All descending only

  - One key ascending, next key descending

  - *Connection Exercises*

Bring in Skippy when you are ready. Use cheater beats, if needed, but aim to have a rhythmic flow without pauses in between.

Say the new key out loud as you start a new shape.

Areas 1 Through 5 – The Five Major Triad Shapes

In the previous section, you wrote out the major triads on the tonic of every key in the *Open Area*. You got a different shape for almost every key (C♯/D♭, F♯/G♭, C♭/B were, of course, identical, but all others were unique).

Moving to *Areas 1* through *5*, you will appreciate that just like the major scales, only five shapes exist.

First, find these five shapes in the key of G, paying close attention to:

- The shape itself

- The location of the chord root within the shape (square it in the diagrams)

- In regards to fingering, notice how all major triad shapes have their roots either under finger #2 or finger #4 (just like the major scales!), with the exception of *Pattern VI* — because the way the triad shape falls within the pattern you can forego "the crab" movement and finger the top root with the first finger. Similarly, *Pattern II* (the other "crab pattern") relinquishes the shift and stays in one position. The tonic, however, stays on finger #2.

In the following diagrams, I wrote out the G major scale patterns in light grey for you. Find the triad notes of the tonic (G major: G B D) and fill them in. Square the root. This will provide you with the five shapes for triads.

Major Triad Map in G Major

Pattern I

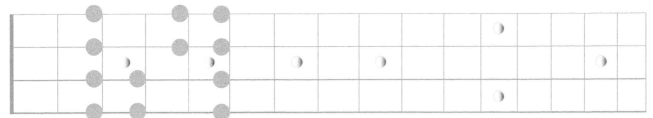

Pattern II

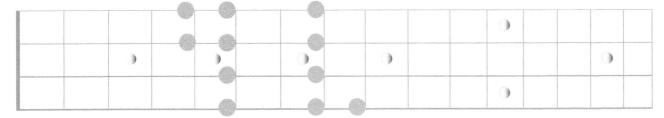

Pattern III

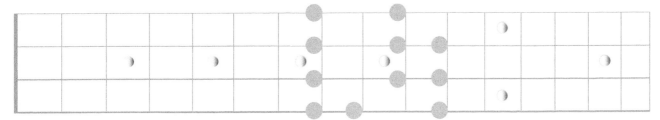

Pattern V

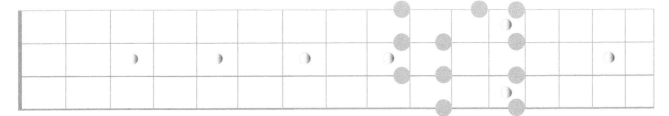

Pattern VI

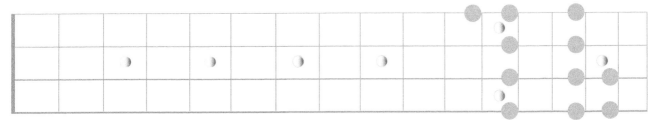

Make sure to check the appendix to ensure you filled these in correctly.

What you are learning here is that five triad shapes exist. When you play triads within a key, i.e., diatonic triads, you will encounter (or find) three major triads, namely the I, IV and V chords. As you find the chords within the patterns of the various keys, all these shapes will already feel familiar.

For now, focus on getting the shapes under your fingers. Start from the root and play all the way up, back down to the lowest note in the shape, and then back up to the root.

Also, play the *five triad shapes* over the whole fretboard, for now in the key of G. Play *Pattern I* ascending — switch to the next pattern: *Pattern II* — play it descending — next *Pattern III* ascending, etc. Take note of the shapes of neighboring patterns and which notes they have in common. Visualize both at the same time if possible or shift between them in your mind.

Major Triad Area Maps

Area 1 – Triads in All Keys on the I Chord (the Tonic)

Write the scale pattern in light grey or pencil, then fill the circles with a solid color for the triad notes, like my example of the C major tonic triad. As always, write down the pattern number and key, and square the chord root, which in this case coincides with the tonic:

C – *Area 1, Pattern V*

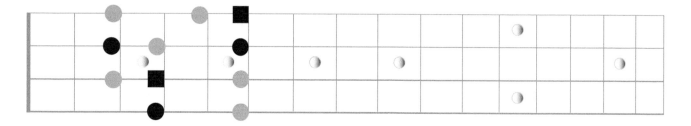

C   Pattern _____

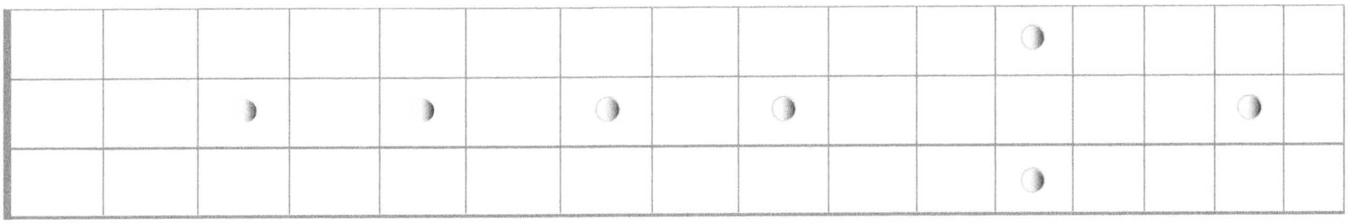

F   Pattern _____

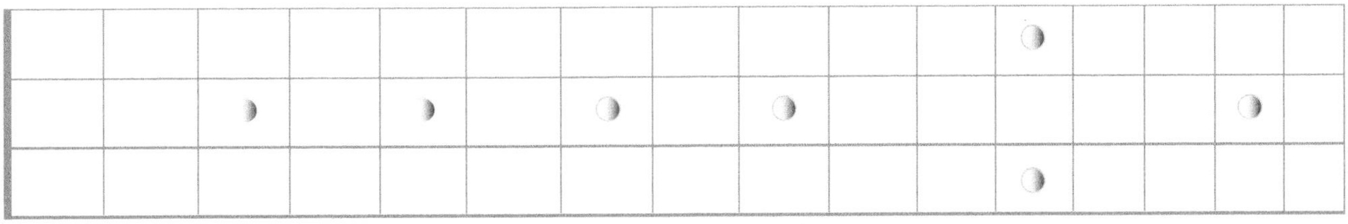

B♭   Pattern _____

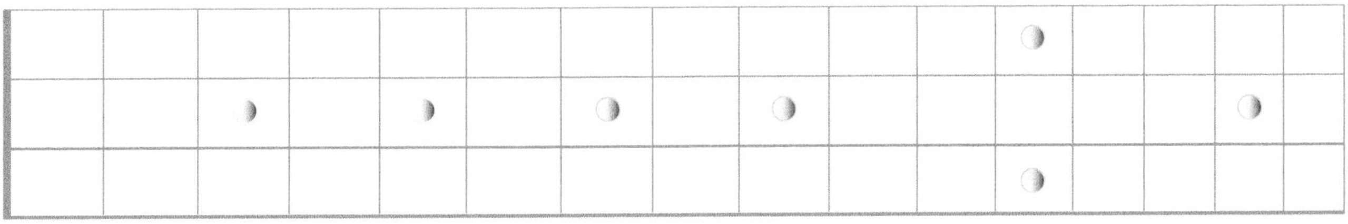

E♭   Pattern _____

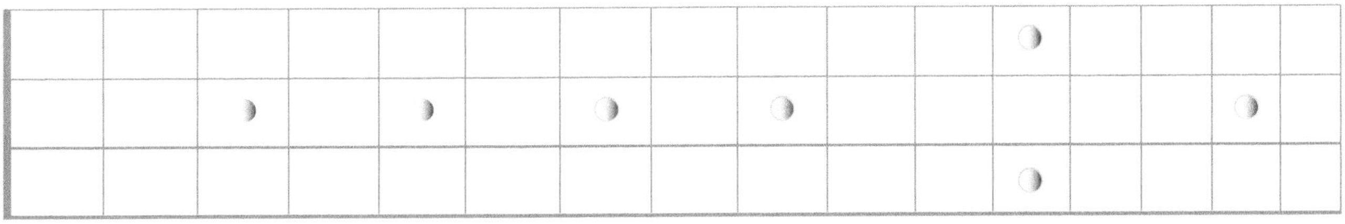

A♭   Pattern _____

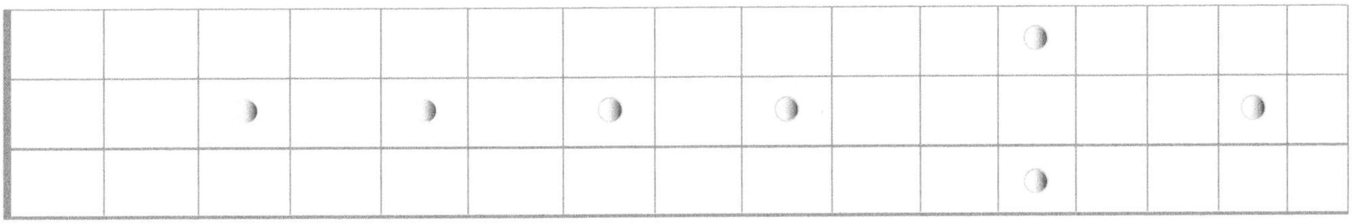

Db *Pattern* ____

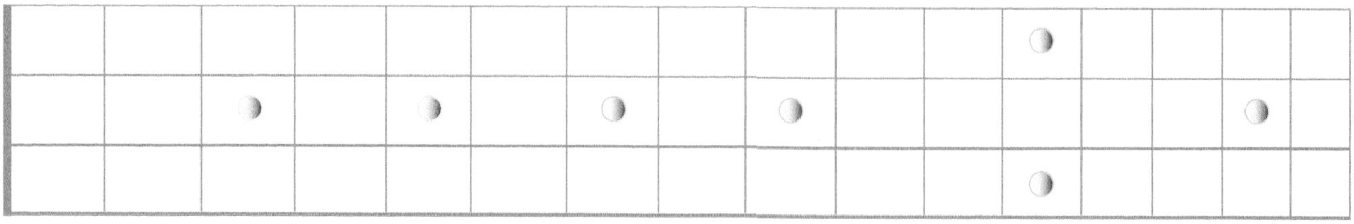

Gb *Pattern* ____

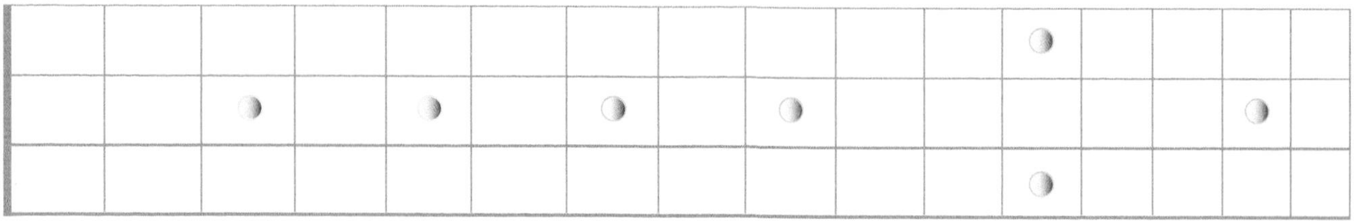

B *Pattern* ____

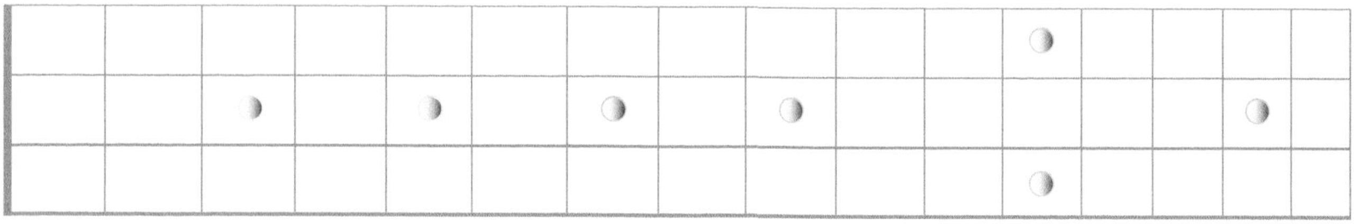

E *Pattern* ____

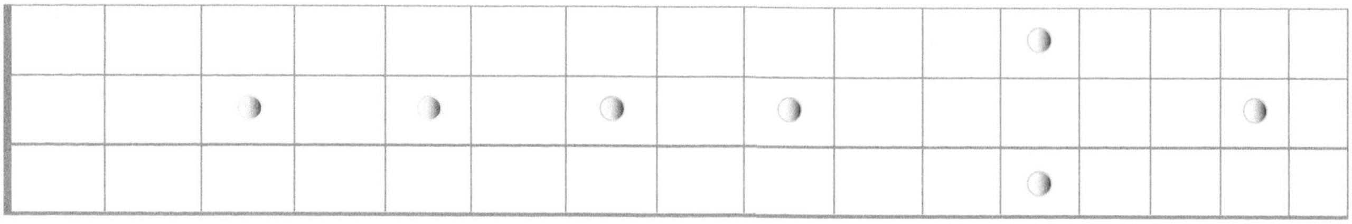

A *Pattern* ____

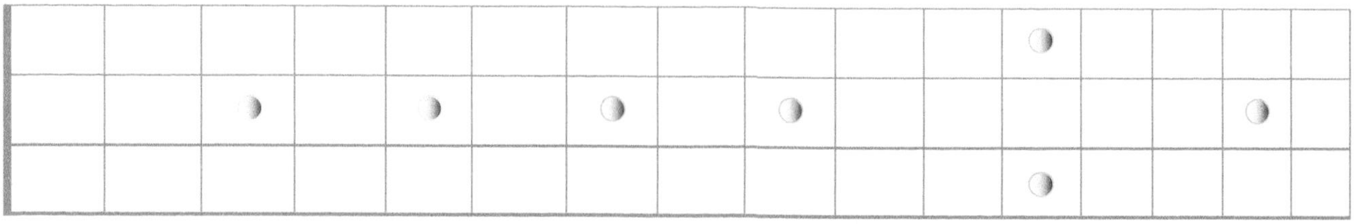

D *Pattern* ____

G *Pattern* ____

F# *Pattern* ____

C# *Pattern* ____

C♭ *Pattern* ____

Area 2 – Triads in All Keys on the I Chord (the Tonic)

Write out all triads on the I chord (the tonic) in *Area 2*.

Write out all *Area 2* major triads:

C   Pattern _____

F   Pattern _____

B♭   Pattern _____

E♭   Pattern _____

A♭   Pattern _____

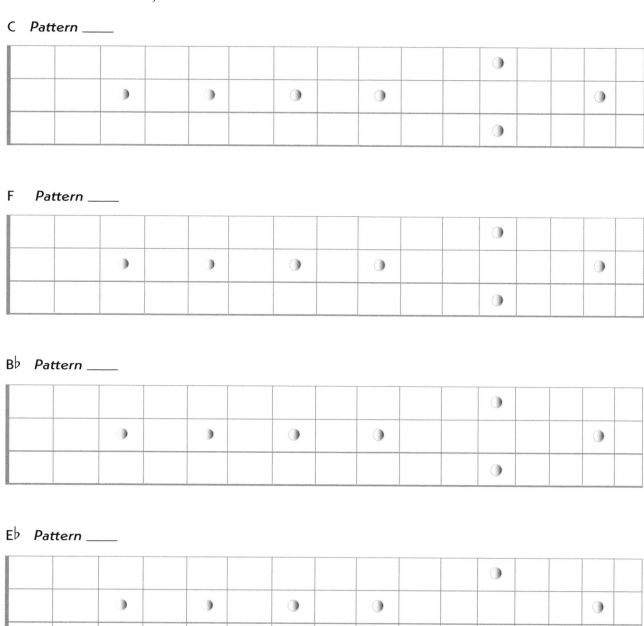
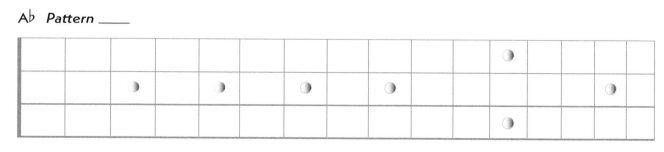

Db *Pattern* ____

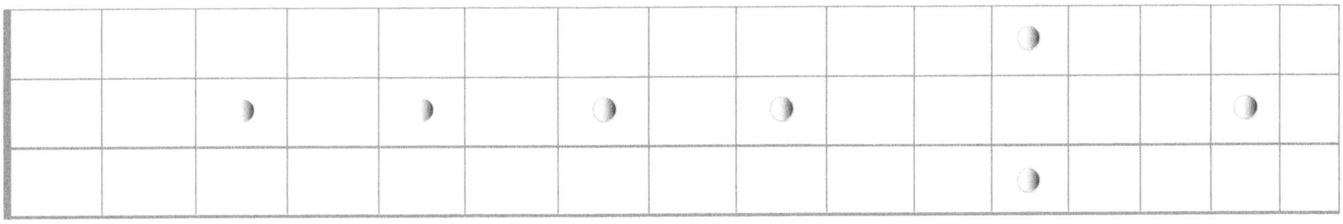

G♭ *Pattern* ____

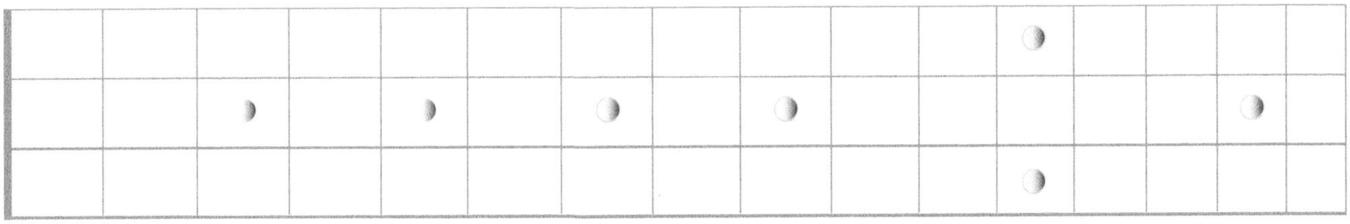

B   *Pattern* ____

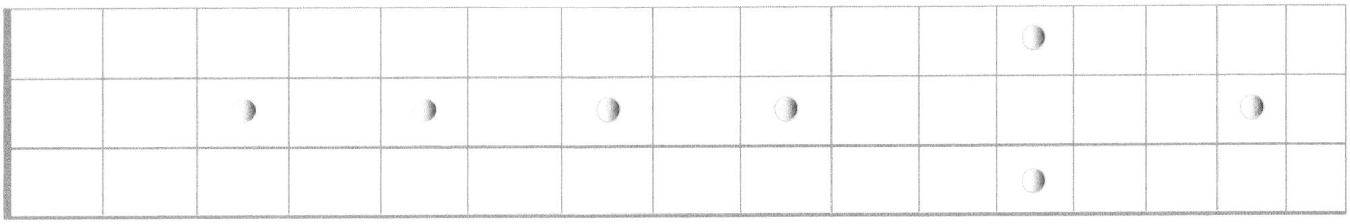

E   *Pattern* ____

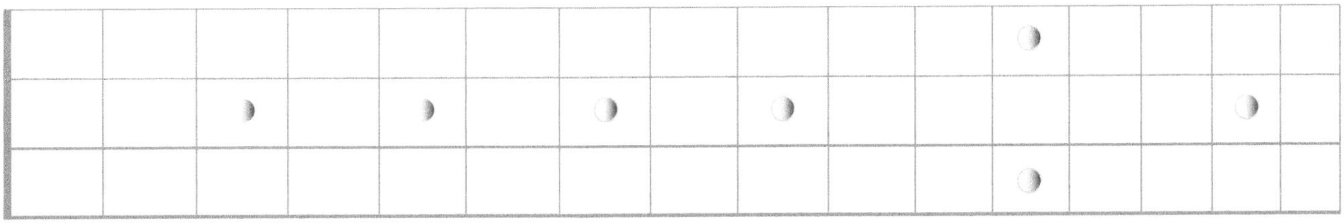

A   *Pattern* ____

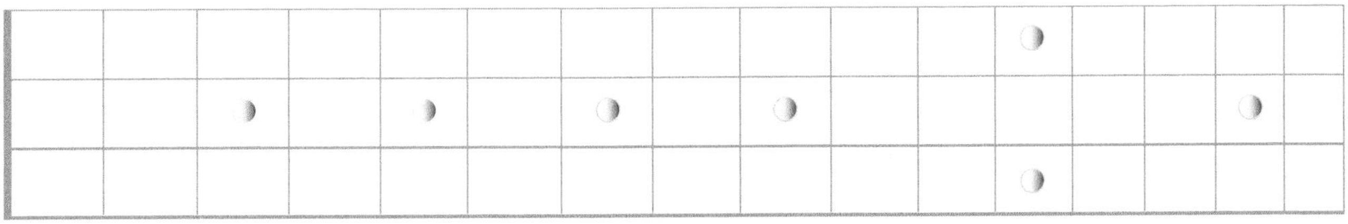

D   *Pattern* _____

G   *Pattern* _____

F♯   *Pattern* _____

C♯   *Pattern* _____

C♭   *Pattern* _____

Areas 3 to 5 — Triads in All Keys on the I Chord (the Tonic)

If you'd like, you can write them out, however, at this point you may begin to notice that you no longer need to write out every single exercise in every single area.

Here is how you know whether you should write them out or not: Can you visualize the triads in *Area 3*? Think of the major scale patterns and see the major triad in your mind's eye. If you can play through the triads in your mind, you most likely will be able to actually play them. Try playing through the major triads in *Area 3* after some practice of *Areas 1* and *2* and see if you can do it by just playing and visualizing. Likely you will be able to! If not, or if you simply prefer to write out the three missing areas (I still highly recommend it to deepen your learning), go for it!

Practice
LIKE THIS

- Practice these triads through each area and in various sequences, as discussed above.

- Say the new key out loud as you start a new shape.

- Play the *Connection Exercises* and keep switching things up.

▌▌▌ **TIP:** Try doing *Connection Exercises* with six or seven beats rather than eight. Especially with triads, this makes for more interesting *Connection Exercises;* and the slightly quicker key changes add a nice challenge. Remember to also switch up starting points and sequences of keys (cycle to the left, to the right, whole steps, etc.).

All the Major Triads in the Major Scale: I–IV–V

Remember, only five distinct major triad shapes exist within this system. (At this stage, you could also combine patterns and move diagonally. Stay within an area for now!) You first learned them by writing them out in the key of G major.

Keep in mind that you can find major and minor triads *(Chapter 9)*, as well as a diminished triad *(Chapter 10)* within a major scale. And that the major triads are built on the first, fourth and fifth scale degrees of the major scale.

Roots of the I–IV–V

First, find the roots.

It's extremely helpful to draw out the diagram of the root notes of these chords within each pattern. I don't think there is a need to do this for every key, but since you're learning to play in every key with equal ease — practice them in each key just like every other pattern you study in this system. The I, IV, and V triads form a very widely used chord progression that shows up in many variations and musical styles. Being able to instantly recall these and other chord progressions (which I will soon introduce) is a vital skill and immediately applicable to many styles of music.

There are two versions of this shape that stand out for me:

1) I – IV – V on the next highest string

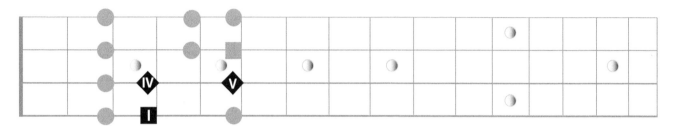

2) I – IV – V on the next lowest string

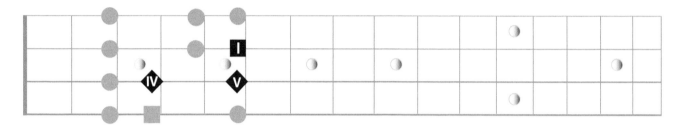

Here is a diagram of all the root notes in all five patterns, again in G major. I squared the tonic to make the visual patterns more obvious. The roots of the IV and V chords are drawn as diamonds.

Pattern I, Area 1 (G)

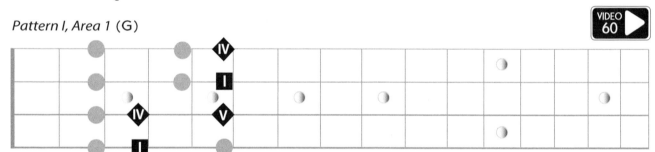

Pattern II, Area 2 (G)

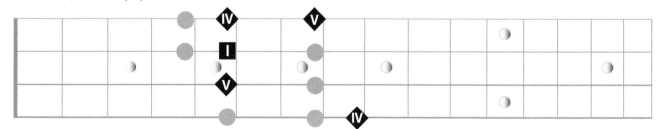

Pattern III, Area 3 (G)

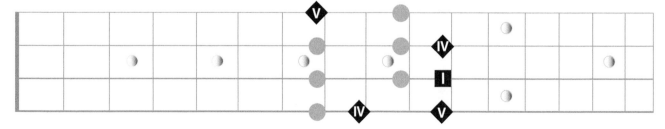

Pattern V, Area 4 (G)

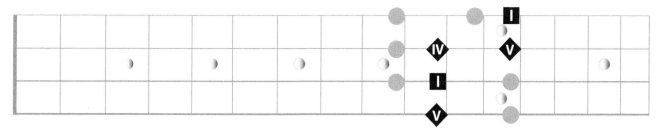

Pattern VI, Area 5 (G)

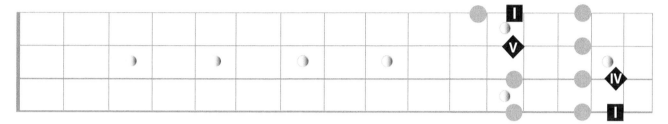

Roots on I, IV, V

Practice this progression of root notes — I, IV, V, I — in all keys, similar to how you practiced scales and triads.

Say the note names out loud while you visualize the shape the roots form.

Great Variation:

Once you have achieved basic familiarity with the root shapes, apply a groove to them. This can be in any style, any meter or tempo. Improvise as if you were creating a bassline.

VIDEO 61

Triads on I, IV, V

Now we add the triads on top of the triad roots (diamonds). Take care to stay within one key (scale pattern) and find the major triad shapes on the I, IV and V within it. First, draw up a couple of sample keys and practice them.

I don't think it is necessary to draw up all these triads in all the keys. Do it for a few select ones until the triad patterns within the five scale patterns become familiar to you. You will find rather quickly every single triad pattern represented that you drew up in the *"Major Triad Map in G Major"* above.

NOTE: Practicing chords as *Shapes within Shapes* gives you confidence playing within each key (and eventually all over the fretboard).

I–IV–V in G (Pattern I)

Here I am demonstrating *Patterns I, IV,* and *V* in *Area 1* in the key of G major.

G major *Pattern I, Area 1* – I chord (G major)

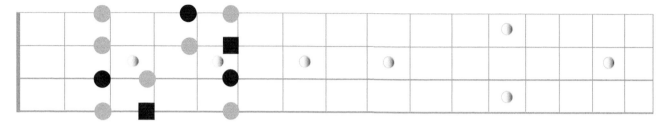

G major *Pattern I, Area 1* – IV chord (C major)

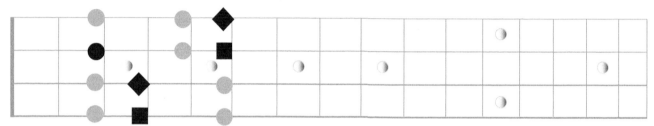

G major *Pattern I, Area 1* – V chord (D major)

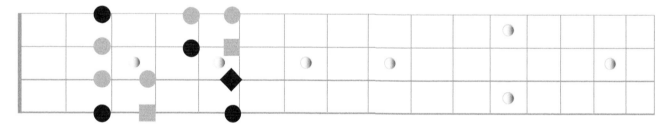

The grey dots and squares, of course, show *Pattern I* of the G major scale (we are in *Area 1* here). Since I, IV and V chords are shapes within the G major shape, all you need to do is identify the triad notes and mark the identified triad notes black.

The resulting shapes will be one of the five triad shapes you created at the beginning of this chapter. The C major triad, for example, is the same shape you drew for G major as *Pattern V* – just transposed to C. Can you find which triad shape in your G major triad matrix correlates with D major?

The answer to the above question is, of course, *Pattern III* — the triad shape that D (the V chord of G) forms inside the G major scale shape looks exactly like the triad shape you drew up inside *Pattern III* in *Area 3* of G major.

In all practicality, there is no need for you to name these triad shapes. Just get them under your fingers with attention to where the root(s) is/are. Your fingers will catch on quickly. Remember, five shapes are all it takes!

Diamonds and Squares

Here's a more detailed explanation of why I use squares for the tonic but diamonds for the diatonic chord roots. Using the G major matrix all across the bass, you'd mark every G as a square because it's the tonic. Then staying within one area (and one pattern!), you'd draw up three different chords (I, IV, V), keeping the tonic (the I) of the key in mind as the central note that everything else relates to. But rather than using squares for the roots of the IV chord (C) or the V chord (D), you'd use diamond shapes. Why? You are no longer just learning the shapes; you are relating shapes within a pattern to the tonic of the key they are occurring in (in this case, G). And that is critically important! When playing music that largely uses diatonic harmony, it is essential to keep the reference of the tonic in your mind. In other words, you are training yourself to see (and hear!) the relationship of the diamonds to the square(s).

Fill in the shapes for the I, IV, and V chords below. Remember to make diamonds for the roots of the IV and V chords. I marked the major scale shapes very lightly so you can place the diamonds above the dots. Mark the triad notes and diamonds in black.

I–IV–V in C (Pattern V)

C major scale, *Area 1, Pattern V*

I chord: C

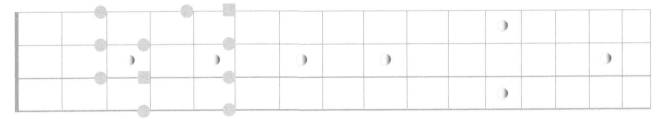

IV chord: F

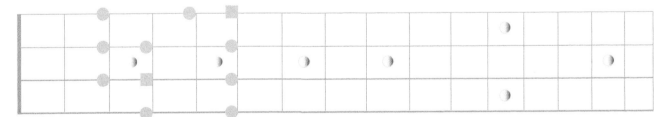

V chord: G

I–IV–V in B♭ (Pattern VI)

B♭ major *Area 1, Pattern VI*
I chord: B♭

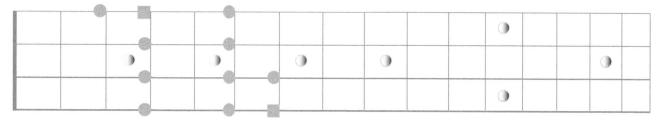

IV chord: E♭

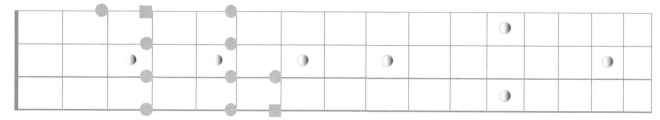

V chord: F

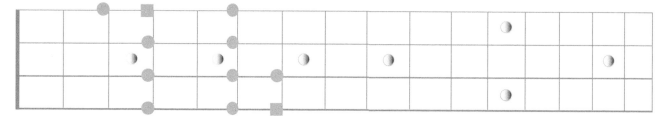

I–IV–V in E (Pattern II)

E major *Area 1, Pattern II*
I chord: E

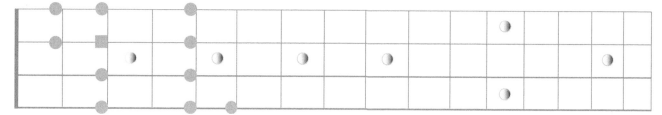

IV chord: A

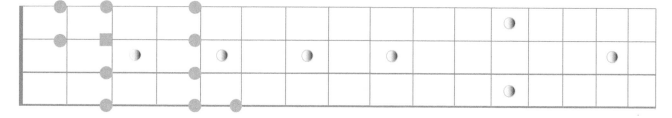

V chord: B

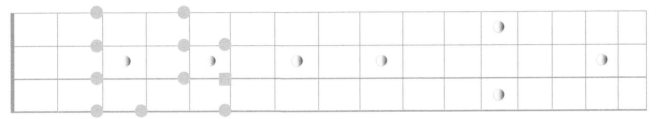

I–IV–V in D (Pattern III)

D major *Area 1, Pattern III*

I chord: D

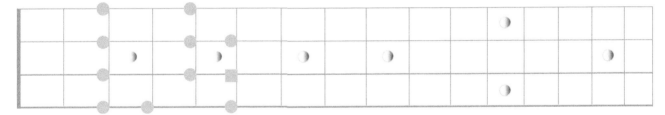

IV chord: G

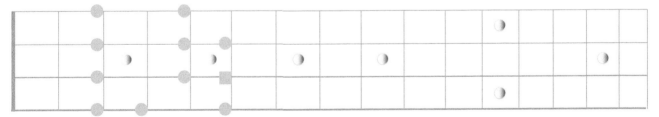

V chord: A

Practice
LIKE THIS   Triads on I, IV, V

a) First play I – IV – V – I. No meter (meaning do not worry how to fit this into a 4/4 — or other — context). Just play all the notes as outlined above.

b) Start the triads on their root, then ascend all the way to the upper end of the pattern, descend to the lower end of the pattern, then back up to the root.

c) Start the triads on their root, then descend all the way to the lower end of the pattern, ascend to the upper end of the pattern, then back down to the root.

d) Start the triad with the lowest possible note in the area, ascend all the way to the upper end of the pattern, then descend.

e) Start the triad with the highest possible note in the area, descend all the way to the lower end of the pattern, then ascend.

f) Alternate playing the triads ascending and descending. Play the I triad ascending (starting from the lowest note in the pattern). When you reach the highest note in the pattern, play the next triad descending, in this case: IV. Then V ascending — I descending, etc. Aim to go through this without any pauses when switching triads — if you need to, use cheater beats until you can eliminate the pauses!

g) Play *Connection Exercises* through the chord changes. I suggest starting with six beats per triad because using eight beats (or two bars of 4/4) too often results in switching chords exactly at the end of the shape.

The Powerful Take-Aways:

Consistent with all practice in *The Pattern System*, you play triad shapes not just from root to root, but **including all notes of the given pattern (or area)** in your routine. Always be aware of **where the roots of the triads are**, as well as the **tonic(s) of the parent key**.

Unlock the fretboard by practicing the five major triad shapes and by practicing I, IV, V within each key. Since there are only five triad shapes and five scale patterns containing those triad shapes in the I, IV, and V chords, you cover an immense amount of ground here. Even if you have not yet practiced all areas, you will likely learn these rather quickly.

▌▌ **TIP:** Get these shapes under your fingers. If you have a hard time wrapping your mind around these concepts, look forward to the improvisation exercise in this Chapter. **Integrating this within a musical context will be satisfying and instructive.**

Also, don't forget your mental practice, away from the bass, like Skippy is demonstrating here…

Is there something wrong with me for needing to practice this quite a bit to get it?

No, not at all.

This method requires intense and focused work — and contrary to what some may think, this can actually be very satisfying and motivating. We thrive on challenges as long as they are manageable. And this is why we carefully structured the path for you. You may never have practiced in such an intense and focused way. Give yourself the chance to get used to these new practice processes!

One of the biggest mistakes often made is to disregard or at least vastly underappreciate the importance of step-by-step and comprehensive practice and — most importantly — practice that includes creative application! The assumption is that just by knowing something in theory (such as a scale from root to root!), it will magically be accessible to you when you play a groove, fill or solo. Or, that by sightreading exercises in all keys, the fretboard will reveal itself.

And while this can happen to a degree, that is a slow and unreliable process – one that makes it very hard to gauge progress. *The Pattern System* accurately fills this gap and gives you immediate feedback every step of the process. It is precise and incredibly focused and invariably puts your creativity, memorization, visualization, and technical skills to the test. The good news is that learning occurs reliably and faster than via any other way I know. Getting the hang of some of the drills can take a moment, however. This is entirely normal as the system is designed to constantly challenge you in new ways.

You are likely encountering a lot that is new to you here as in this system you are:

- Practicing comprehensively and step by step
- Employing mental techniques, writing and visualization
- Using improvisation
- Keeping track of multiple streams of information
- Applying the click to ensure you are thinking ahead yet staying in the groove

Allow yourself to get used to the structure of this approach. The good news is that this is 100% doable with a bit of patience and perserverance. I have droves of students of all levels, ages and walks of life who can attest that the results are well worth the effort, even though the learning curve may be steep.

So, there is nothing at all "wrong with you." Deep knowing takes a step-by-step approach and consistent practice. Heed the advice of throttling back the dials of your *Connection Exercises* cockpit if things get too hard — slower tempo, cheater beats, easier sequence, working your way up to *Connection Exercises* as described. Most importantly, stay in the zone of learning. Be your own coach!

Follow the system as laid out here and **trust the process.** The rewards will come swiftly!

Why do you sometimes use the word "tonic" and other times "root"?
Is there a difference?

The tonic is the central note of a piece of music and most often coincides with the I — the first note of the key/scale the piece is in. Within a scale, there are other points of reference, such as diatonic triads, modes, etc. Those shapes have roots. There are seven roots in a scale, but only one tonic. The tonic gives the pattern its letter name, and you mark it with a square. You will mark other relevant roots with diamonds. This helps you to visualize the relationship between the squares (tonics) and diamonds (roots)!

▌▌ NOTE: For practical reasons, we focus on the major tonic triad of the major scale, but the music could also be in natural/Aeolian minor, relating all notes of a shape to the minor tonic. The shapes of the Five Patterns will remain the same.

 Why do you teach triads and not four-note chords?

Triads form the basis of harmony. Always start with triads and add the seventh (or ninth, eleventh, thirteenth) to complete all notes of the scale as needed. Triads are foundational for many styles of music and, therefore, important to study in-depth. Once you know them well, all other chords will become much quicker and easier to learn.

I also start with triads because they present more of a technical challenge; they often have only one note per string and therefore require more string crossings.

Scalar Studies

Major Triad Arpeggios Over Two Octaves

Practice two-octave triads through the cycle! Many good fingerings for this exist. Because no pattern extends over more than an octave-and-a-half, we have to use more than one pattern. In my example below, I use a combination of *Patterns I* and *V* of each key.

Practically speaking, do this:

> **VIDEO 64** ▶

- Ascending:
    - Play the first triad in *Pattern I*, whatever area of the bass that may fall into (aim for lowest possible). The root will be on the E-string.
    - For the second octave, switch to *Pattern V* — practically speaking, move the root to the A-string. Finish the triad all the way to the top octave in that position.
- Descending:
    - Without shifting (still in *Pattern V!*), descend the triad down one octave.
    - Then, aim for the *fifth of the triad* on the A-string, which will bring you back home into *Pattern I*.

▌▌▌ **NOTE:** If you have a 20-fret bass, you will need to use open strings for the keys of E and F. If you have a 24-fret bass, you can avoid the *Open Area* for the keys of F and E and just move those keys above the 12th fret to start.

▌▌▌ **TIP:** Always think ahead and aim your eyes on the fret your fingers will go to next. One goal is to not just find the notes by ear, which means you have to play and hear them first to know if they are correct. Instead, identify the correct string and fret before you play the note! Go slow, think ahead — for as many notes as you can.

Many other good fingerings exist. Discover your favorite ones. Consistent fingering is key to playing these fast!

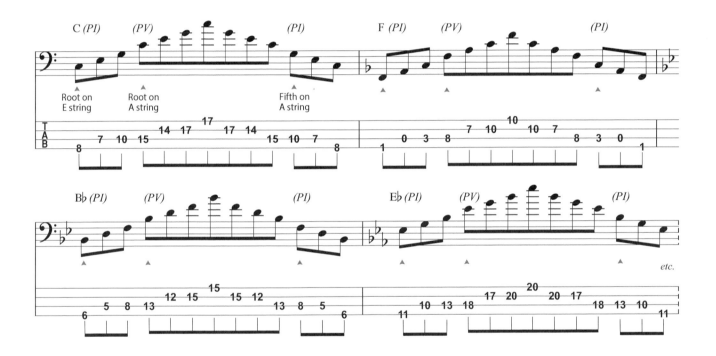

Major Triad Improvisation

This improvisation using triads will drive home the power of the triad drills we did earlier in this chapter.

Jam along with a ‖ I │IV│ V │ I ‖ track. (Complimentary tracks at *ArisBassBlog.com/PatternSystem*)

Jam like this:

Play the root of each chord on the downbeat and then improvise using only triad notes. Stay within a pattern and use all available notes of the triad!

A few ideas:

- Form groove figures using triad notes.
- Play melodies or solos using only triad notes.
- Play a basic groove on the root and use triad notes for groove variations or fills (see example below).

Practice this in the keys of F and E♭ in *Area 1* and A, D, C in *Area 2*. That way, you hit every one of the five patterns. Add the key of F♯ to the mix, and you will have covered every triad at least once. For the purpose of this exercise, stay within the pattern, and resist the temptation to play non-triad notes. You can go strictly in order, or make jumps; you can repeat notes, or not… Observe the musical effects of various strategies!

Have fun!

TIP: This type of playing — which is usually too busy as a groove under a melody — sounds great as a "groove solo"!

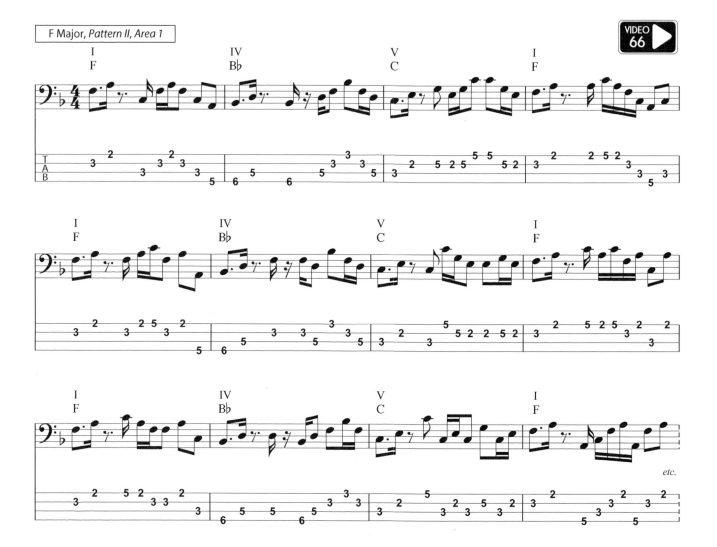

Definition

What is a triad? What is a chord?

In the context of this system, think of diatonic triads and chords as *"Shapes within Shapes."*

If you need a refresher on the theory behind chords, triads and arpeggios, consult *Music Theory for the Bass Player* for more information.

Framing Your Practice

Start your practice session by affirming what you will work on and come up with a defined goal of what you will accomplish. Don't worry if you aim too high or too low at first. Simply observe your progress and results and adjust accordingly. In general, aim for just a little more than what you think you can do. You grow best by making consistent small improvements.

End your session by doing a quick review of the material you worked on, what went well and what you want to focus on next time. Do this mentally and jot down a few quick notes. This should take only a minute or two but makes a huge difference.

Skippy recommends taking a quick snapshot of your practice progress!

TIP: To enhance and deepen the learning effect, take a minute before going to sleep to recall your practice session. You'll be sending a signal to your mind: "This is important to me — I want to remember this."

TEST YOUR UNDERSTANDING #8

1. How many distinct shapes/patterns are there for the major triads? _____

2. Which finger plays the chord root in a major chord?
   - ❑ a. The second finger or the fourth finger
   - ❑ b. The first, second or fourth finger
   - ❑ c. It is best to use any random finger for maximum flexibility
   - ❑ d. The pinky should not work so hard. Avoid it.

3. Why are you learning triads within the context of the major scales?
   - ❑ a. Because that way you can think of them as *"Shapes within Shapes"*
   - ❑ b. Because these chord progressions show up in music all the time
   - ❑ c. Because it trains our ears
   - ❑ d. All of the above

4. How many notes per string do you play when playing major triads within the five patterns you studied?
   - ❑ a. Either one or two
   - ❑ b. Three (they are triads!)
   - ❑ c. Stop trying to learn these things by heart; just make them up on the fly!

5. The major triads in the major scale are on the following scale degrees:
   - ❑ a. I, II, III
   - ❑ b. All of them. It is the major scale, after all!
   - ❑ c. I, IV, V

BLUEPRINT FOR PRACTICE #8

Written Assignment: Major triads in the *Open Area* **pp. 175 to 177**
Fill in the *Major Triad Map* in G major **p. 179**
Triads on the I chord *Area 1, 2* (or more) **pp. 181–186**
Various I IV V chord sequences **p. 191 to 193**

1. **PP:** *Up/down* variations, then *Connection Exercises*, 8 beats, *Area 4*; cycle to the left and right; say scale degrees/note names/nothing

2. **PP:** *Up/down* variations, then *Connection Exercises*, 8 beats, *Areas 3* and *4*, sequence of major thirds to the right and left
   for all sequences: **p. 126**

3. **Triad PP:** Major Triads on tonic through the cycle to the left and right, *Area 1*; *up/down* variations, then *Connection Exercises* (experiment with number of beats other than 8) **p. 178 • Video 57 and p. 187 • Video 59**

4. **Triad PP:** Diatonic major triads, roots only. *Area 2*, cycle to the left or pick various keys and improvise **p. 189 • Video 61**

5. **Triad PP:** Diatonic major triads, play the triads. *Area 1*; *up/down* variations, then *Connection Exercises* **p. 194 • Video 63**

6. **SS:** Interval studies in fourths; various combinations as shown in *Chapter 6*; *Area 5*; practice several keys (suggesting G E♭ B) **pp. 136–142 • Videos 47 to 52**

7. **SS:** Interval studies in sevenths; various combinations as shown in *Chapter 6*; *Area 5*; practice several keys (suggesting G E♭ B) **pp. 136–142 • Videos 47 to 52**

8. **SS:** Major triad arpeggios over two octaves **pp. 196–197 • Videos 64 and 65**

9. **IE:** Triad improvisation *Area 1* in F and E♭; *Area 2* A D C; *any area:* F♯ **pp. 197–198 • Video 66**

Minor Triads

MORE SHAPES WITHIN SHAPES – THE MINOR TRIADS

The Minor Triads

Minor chords occur on these scale degrees: Second, Third and Sixth (the root of the relative minor scale).

Because of its frequent occurrence and the fact that it can be the key of a tune, we will focus on the minor chord at the sixth scale degree first.

You will soon realize that all your hard work on the major triads will pay off as we work through the minor triads — they will be yours with minor effort (pun intended!).

Reminders:

- When writing out the cycle in the minor keys, always be aware of the relative major. And remember, no key of D♭ minor exists. It should be called C♯ minor, as it is the relative minor of E major (not F♭ major, a key that does not exist in the cycle!)

At right are the relative minor keys within the cycle of fifths for your reference:

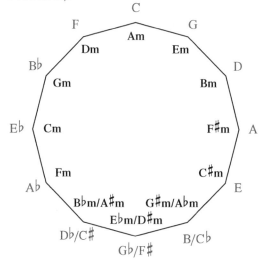

Open Area Minor Triad Maps

Write out the *Open Area* minor triads. Again, start with the pattern — in this case, the relative major pattern in grey, then fill in the relative minor triad, built on the sixth scale degree in black. That way, you can clearly see the *"Shape within the Shape."* Write the name of both the major and minor keys, square the major root, and make a diamond for the relative minor.

VIDEO 67 ▶

Open Area (C major / Amin)

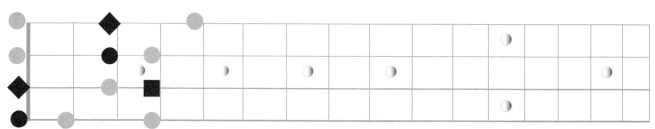

TIP: When you practice these minor triads, also practice playing the whole scale while saying out loud the scale degrees in relation to the minor root (instead of relating all scale degrees to the relative major). The note names stay the same, but the numbers change.

Open Area Minor Triad Maps

C • Amin

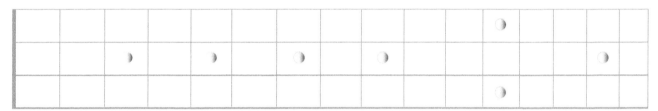

F • Dmin

B♭ • Gmin

E♭ • Cmin

A♭ • Fmin

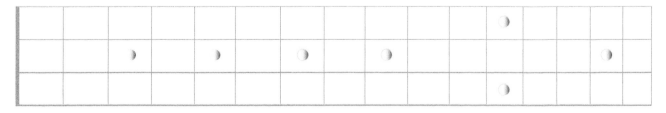

D♭ • **B♭min**

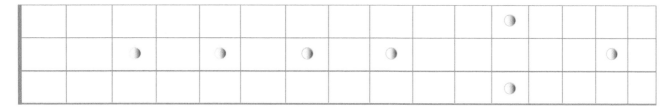

G♭ • **E♭min**

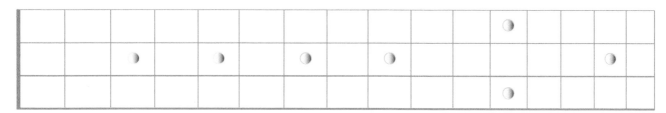

B • **G♯min**

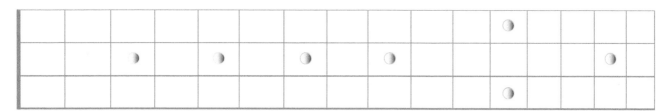

E • **C♯min**

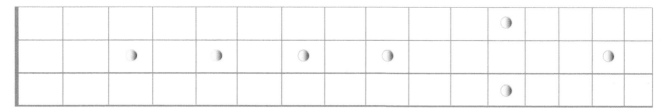

A • **F♯min**

D • **Bmin**

G • **Emin**

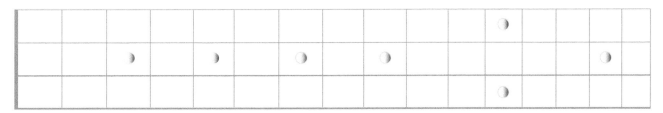

F♯ • **D♯min**

C♯ • **A♯min**

C♭ • **A♭min**

Areas 1 through 5: The Five Minor Triad Shapes

In *Chapter 8*, you started your triad exploration by finding the five possible shapes for the major triads by writing out the G major triads within the five G major scale shapes.

Now do the same with the E minor triad within the five G major scale shapes.

Remember, these are *"Shapes Within a Shape."* Diatonic chord progressions operate in reference to a key center (= tonic); therefore, keeping both the tonic and the chords in your mind simultaneously is a gigantic shortcut to master playing over common chord progressions.

Just as before, focus your attention on:

- The shape itself

- The location of the root of the minor triad

- How the minor triad relates to the relative major tonic (mark the minor root as a diamond and the major tonic as a square)

- The fingering. Notice how all minor triad shapes start with either finger #1 or finger #4. Similar to the major triad shapes; however, *Pattern VI* presents an exception: Finger #3 gets the root in this pattern in addition to the first finger.

- The fact that these triads are *"Shapes within Shapes."* Be aware of the scale shape "wrapping around" the triad. You have already practiced those shapes extensively; use them to help you find the minor triads within those shapes now.

  - In the following diagrams, I wrote out the G major scale patterns in light grey for you. Find the triad notes of E minor triads (E G B) and fill them in. Mark a diamond for the relative minor root and a square for the major tonic.

- This will provide you with the five minor shapes for triads.

Minor Triad Map in E Minor

Pattern I Root on ____ &____

Pattern II Root on ____

Pattern III Roots on ____ &____

Pattern V Roots on ____ &____

Pattern VI Roots on ____ &____

Minor Triad Area Maps

Now fill in the *Area Maps* for the relative minor triads.

Area 1 – Relative Minor Triads

C • **Amin**

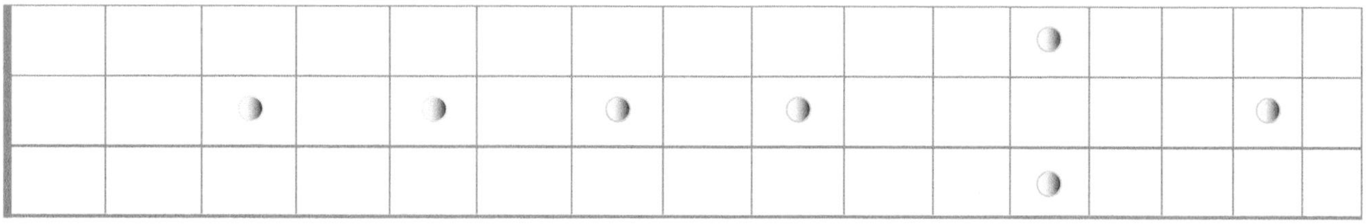

F • **Dmin**

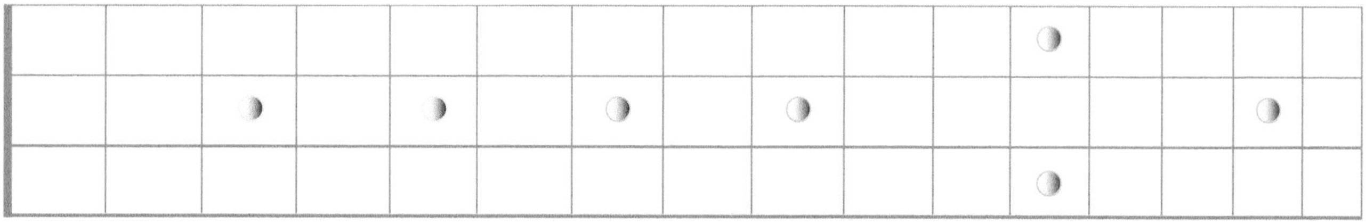

B♭ • **Gmin**

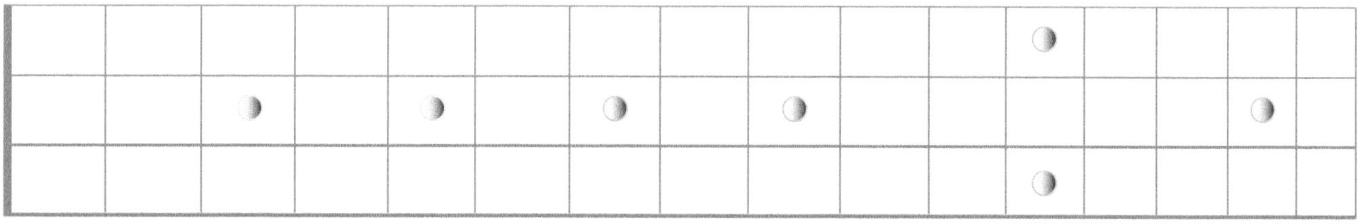

E♭ • **Cmin**

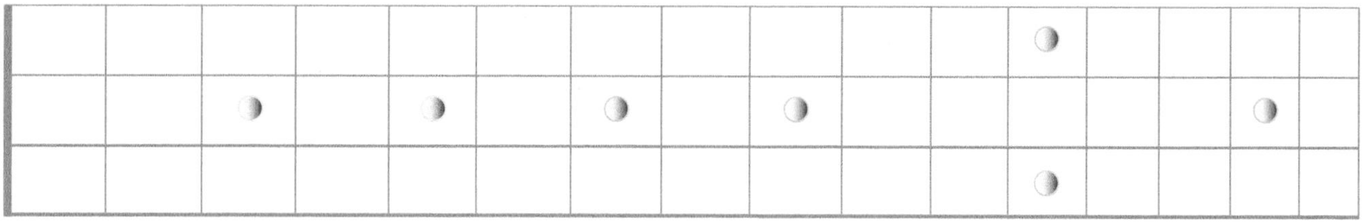

A♭ • **Fmin**

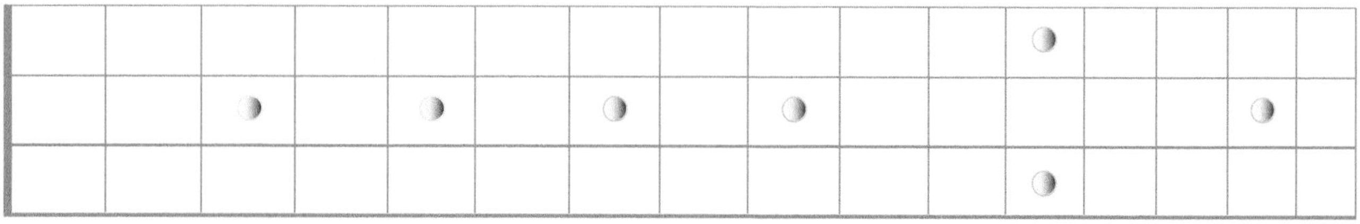

Db • B♭min

Gb • E♭min

B • G♯min

E • C♯min

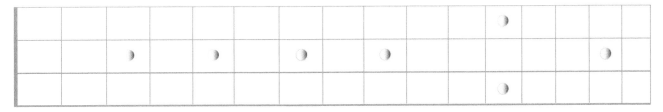

A • F♯min

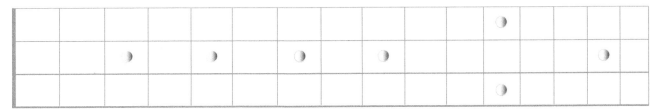

D • Bmin

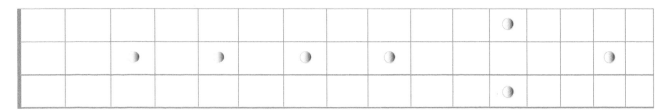

G • Emin

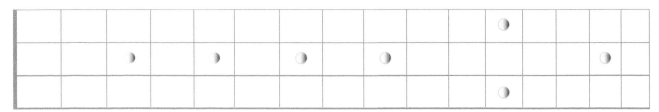

F# • D#min

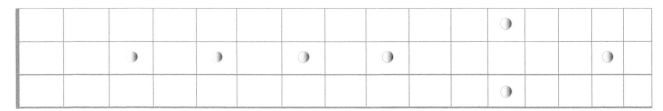

C# • A#min

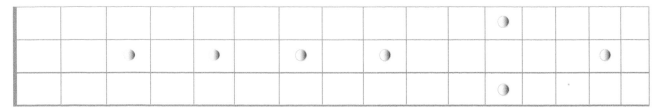

Cb • Abmin

Area 2 – Relative Minor Triads

Now — to switch it up — I suggest you write all VI minor triads for *Area 2*. As always, I encourage you to eventually write out the minor triads in all areas.

C • **Amin**

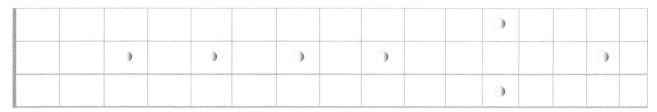

F • **Dmin**

B♭ • **Gmin**

E♭ • **Cmin**

A♭ • **Fmin**

Db • Bbmin

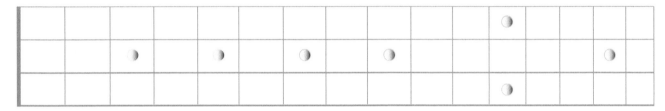

Gb • Ebmin

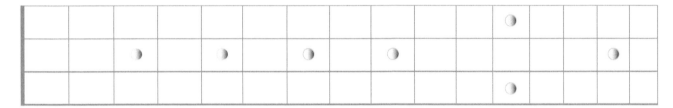

B • G#min

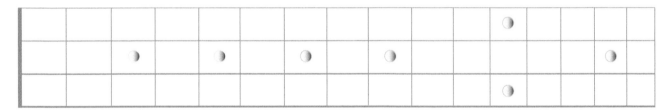

E • C#min

A • F#min

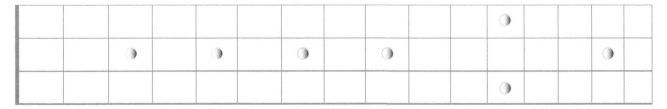

D • **Bmin**

G • **Emin**

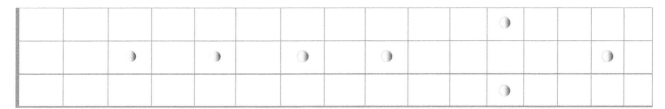

F# • **D#min**

C# • **A#min**

C♭ • **A♭min**

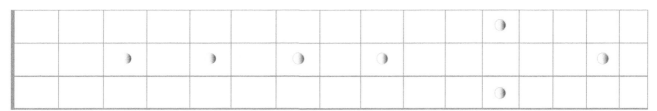

All the Minor Triads in the Minor Scale: IIIm, VIm, IIm

The minor triads on these scale degrees are part of many common chord progressions. In the upcoming pages, you will learn more about the significance of this particular order.

Just like with the major chords, it's extremely helpful to draw out the diagram of the root notes of these chords within each pattern. Here are all five shapes of G major with their IIIm, VIm and IIm roots marked out:

Roots of the Minor Triads

VIDEO 69

Pattern I, Area 1 (G)

Pattern II, Area 2 (G)

Pattern III, Area 3 (G)

Pattern V, Area 4 (G)

Pattern VI, Area 5 (G)

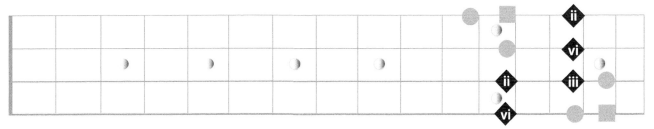

Practice

LIKE THIS

Practice this progression of root notes — IIIm, VIm, IIm — in all keys the same way you practiced scales and triads. Keep the tonic in your ear!

Say the note names out loud while you visualize the shape the roots form.

> Great Variation:
>
> Once you have achieved basic familiarity with the root shapes, apply a groove to them. This can be in any style, any meter or tempo. Improvise as if you were creating a bassline. (Grab a jam track at *ArisBassBlog.com/PatternSystem.)* Also see *Improvised Explorations* in this chapter.
>
> Add the V chord to make it a common chord progression: IIImin–VImin–IImin–V.

Make an X!

It's worth pointing out the shapes the roots make within the patterns in this very common chord progression:

I–VImin–IImin–V — as featured in the beginning of "Rhythm Changes" and many other songs — forms an "X" on the fretboard in some patterns:

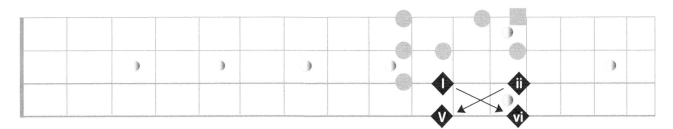

Often, the song then goes on to continue with this common turnaround (IIImin–VImin–IImin–V), which creates an easy to remember shape on the fretboard (like a backwards "N" — as far as the roots are concerned!):

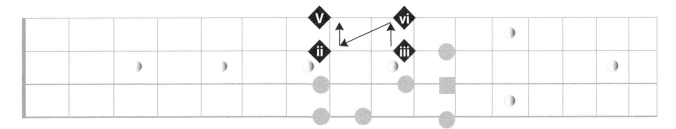

▌▌▌ **TIP:** Find the patterns that the roots of common chord progressions involving major and minor triads make on the fretboard.

Triads on IIImin–VImin–IImin

This segment further explores the triads of the IIImin–VImin–IImin–V chord progression. This progression includes all three minor triads and the V chord. Notice that even though the tonic chord is not included, you still hear the tonal center without a doubt!

Within *Pattern I/Area 1* in G major, I wrote out the IIImin, VImin and IImin chords as well as the V to complete this common "turnaround":

IIImin–VImin–IImin–V in G (Pattern I)

G major *Pattern I, Area 1* – IIImin chord (B minor)

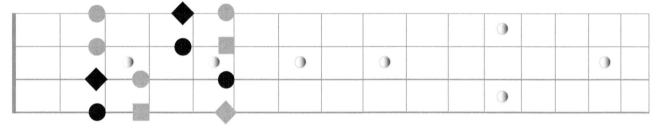

G major *Pattern I, Area 1* – VImin chord (E minor)

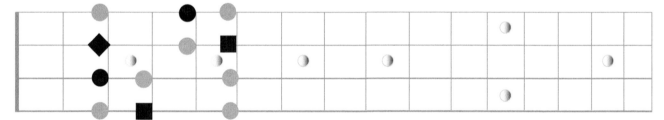

G major *Pattern I, Area 1* – IImin chord (A minor)

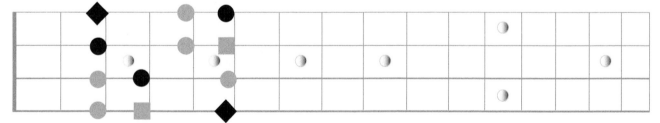

G major *Pattern I, Area 1* – V chord (D major)

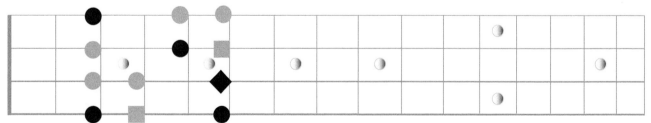

Finish the diagrams below by filling in the IIImin, VImin, IImin, V chords. Remember, the main purpose of this exercise is to recognize common shapes (in this case, triads) within the scale patterns. Diamonds remind you of the crucial relationship to the tonic (the square). Once you start improvising using these shapes, you will undoubtedly realize its practical application.

IIImin–VImin–IImin–V in C (Pattern V)

C major *Pattern V, Area 1* – IIImin chord (E minor)

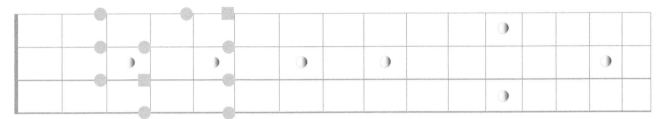

C major *Pattern V, Area 1* – VImin chord (_____ minor)

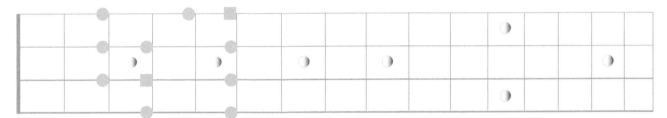

C major *Pattern I, Area 1* – IImin chord (_____ minor)

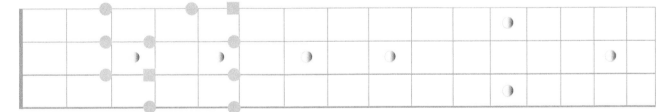

C major *Pattern V, Area 1* – V chord (_____ major)

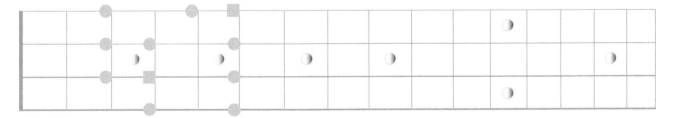

IImin–VImin–IImin–V in B♭ (Pattern VI)

B♭ major *Pattern VI, Area 1 –* IIImin chord (D minor)

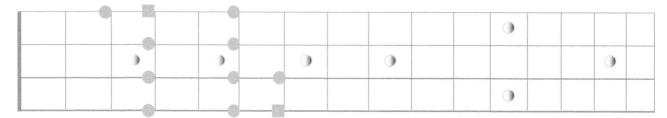

B♭ major *Pattern VI, Area 1 –* VImin chord (_____ minor)

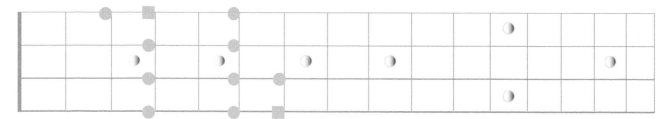

B♭ major *Pattern VI, Area 1 –* IImin chord (_____ minor)

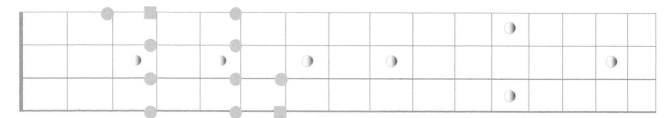

B♭ major *Pattern VI, Area 1 –* V chord (_____ major)

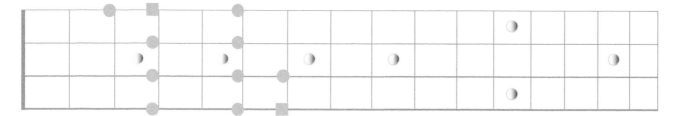

IIImin–VImin–IImin–V in E (Pattern II)

E major *Pattern II, Area 1* – IIImin chord (G♯ minor)

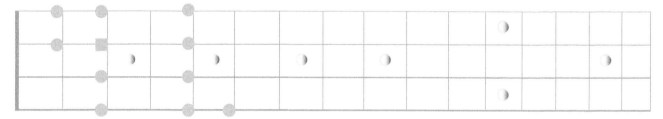

E major *Pattern II, Area 1* – VImin chord (_____ minor)

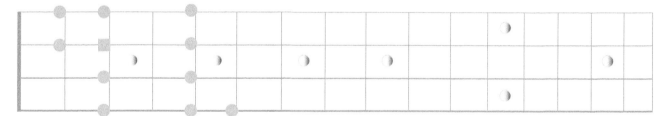

E major *Pattern II, Area 1* – IImin chord (_____ minor)

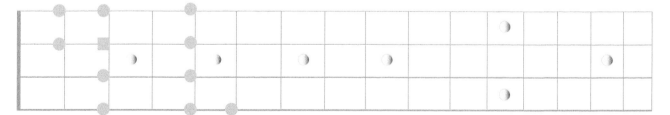

E major *Pattern II, Area 1* – V chord (_____ major)

IIImin–VImin–IImin–V in D (Pattern III)

D major *Pattern III, Area 1* – IIImin chord (_____ minor)

D major *Pattern III, Area 1* – VImin chord (_____ minor)

D major *Pattern III, Area 1* – IImin chord (_____ minor)

D major *Pattern III, Area 1* – V chord (_____ major)

Practice
LIKE THIS

Revisit the Practice tips in the previous chapter on major triads and practice the minor triads in the same way!

Scalar Studies

Scalar Studies: Minor Triad Arpeggios Over Two Octaves

Practice two-octave minor triads through the cycle of fifths! Several good options exist. Similar to what we did with the two-octave major triads, in my example I place the lowest root on the E-string, play the first triad, and then switch to the top root on the A-string. In major, this puts me into *Patterns I* and *V*. In minor, it puts me into *Patterns VI* and *III* of the relative major scale.

When descending, you will need to do one jump — aiming for the fifth to finish up the triad like you began it with the minor root on the E-string.

NOTE: If you have a 20-fret bass, you will need to adapt the fingering of D♯ minor (and E♭ minor). For E minor, use the open E.

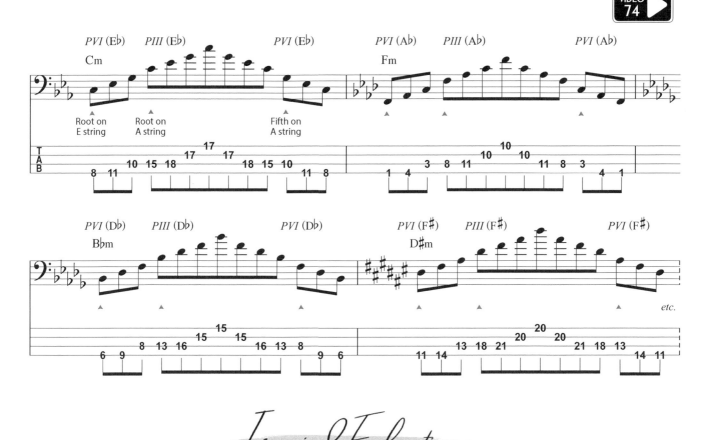

Major and Minor Triad Improvisation

This improvisation using triads will drive home the power of the triad drills:

- Pick an area.
- Pick a key.
- Find the pattern.
- Find the roots of all the triads (sequence below) within the pattern.

- Find the triads of all the chords of the sequence within the pattern (double-check that you are staying within the pattern, no shifts, unless you picked a key that forms *Pattern II* or *VI* in that Area!).
- Jam along with these chords using roots on the downbeat and triads and scalar runs as transitions.

▌▌▌ NOTE: You are staying in one pattern! All the diatonic triads and chords are accessible to you without any shifts. Think about the benefit this provides to sight-reading by not having to take your eyes off the paper. (We will talk about shifting between areas effortlessly in a later chapter).

Progression I:

‖ IIImin ‖ VImin ‖ IImin ‖ V ‖

You don't play the tonic as an actual chord change, but you will hear it internally; and make sure to think of the tonic's pattern! Remember, you are only playing *Shapes within the Scale Shape!*

My example here is in the Key of E♭, *Pattern I, Area 4*

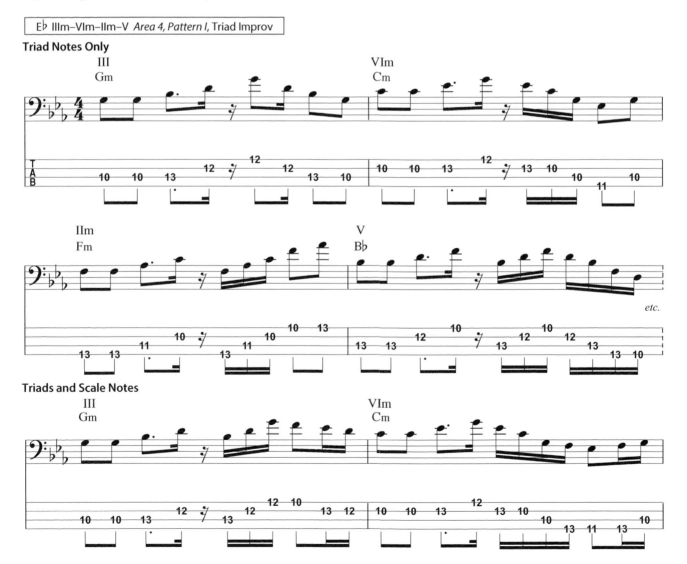

E♭ IIIm–VIm–IIm–V *Area 4, Pattern I*, Triad Improv Example 2

VIDEO 76

Triad Notes Only

Triads and Scales

Progression II:

```
‖ IImin │ V │ I │ VI │
│ IImin │ V │ I │ I ‖
```

The VI chord in the progression above is non-diatonic. Frequently used as a "secondary dominant" to the IIm chord, the third of the VI chord will take you outside of the pattern. Find the VI (major) triad before you start and notice how it relates to the pattern at hand. Notice that only one note has changed: the third is major instead of minor. In relation to the key, the changed note is the **tonic raised by a half step**. In the example below in the key of Eb, the note Eb changes to E for the VI major triad (Cmaj). This note becomes the leading tone to the root of the next chord in the progression (which is the IImin chord, Fmin, with E leading into F by a half step), thereby giving the chord progression a stronger forward motion. Another effect of this secondary dominant is that it temporarily brightens the sound due to the raised note. Listen for this effect as you play through the progression.

VIDEO 77

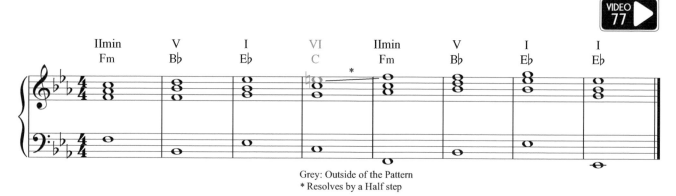

Grey: Outside of the Pattern
* Resolves by a Half step

When practicing the chords of this and similar chord progressions, locate the changed note in relation to the key. In this case, locate the raised 1 (♯1) – E♮. In some patterns, this note will be outside the regular shape and necessitate a shift. Decide on how you will include this note (location, fingering) and visualize this expanded pattern. Then follow the same practice procedures you have learned for triads and scales:

- Play just the roots and say/think the chord names.
- Play each triad from the root ascending, then descending such that you play each chord note in the pattern.
- Play *Connection Exercises*. Use various meters and starting points.

Once you're comfortable with these exercises, you are ready to start improvising.

Here are two examples of improvisation. Notice how they start with a short motif that is then repeated and varied with freely improvised connections between the chords.

Eb IIm–V–I–VI–IIm–V–I–I *Area 4, Pattern I*, Triad Improv

Triad Notes Only

Triads and Scale Notes

Practice this in a variety of keys and areas. Pick different ones each time. Have fun!

The Power of Celebrating Small Achievements

Break free from the shackles of energy robbers and negative voices!

Many of us are quick to judge ourselves, hasty to berate our shortcomings, and swift to put ourselves down. Others flee into denial and skillfully "un-hear" any mistakes they might have made, certain they are beyond the need to practice anything.

Mix in some old — but still echoing — "well-meaning" voices of the past from parents, teachers or bandmates, and the internal dialogue can become quite a toxic cocktail that works against us and keeps us from progressing.

With so much negativity under the surface, is it any wonder that we begin to dread playing altogether at times?

How can I break this pattern?

Aim for a small achievement. Then celebrate it with a good feeling.

Is a Small Achievement enough?

It is. Don't fall into the trap of asking mountains of yourself. Exactly the opposite! See this as more of an exercise in attitude rather than in practicing patterns. Pick something very small, for example, one from this list:

- Practicing two minutes in one area.
- Doing one improvisation exercise through the cycle.
- Executing a scalar drill in one key.

For this to work, make it a small assignment. Do it first thing when you pick up your bass. And practice feeling great about yourself when you have finished your small assignment. Pat yourself on the back. Strike a victory pose! Pump your fists! You can exaggerate a little (or a lot!) with that good feeling… even if at first it feels odd, unnatural, or like you don't deserve it — it will still work!

The sequence goes like this:

- Plug in your bass
- Play (for example) D major in *Area 2*.
- Celebrate — enjoy a moment of good feelings!

Skippy demonstrates how to appropriately celebrate a small assignment done well.

What will this do for you, and why does it work?

These small, frequent celebrations establish this routine as a habit. Contrary to popular belief, habits are *not* created through mere repetition — no teenager ever needed the famed "21 days" to get addicted to their new smart phone or PlayStation. Rather, the habit formed instantly. Why? Because habits are created by good feelings!

Imagine the kind of havoc negative self-talk can wreak as you try to build a positive practicing experience. I have observed how fighting the negative voices directly does not work very well because that tends to just ramp up their resistance. What does work, however, is to create and practice a short and reliable positive routine and celebrate that because this creates good feelings.

To learn about a scientifically studied method of behavior design and read about the magic of creating habits effortlessly and joyfully, I recommend Professor BJ Fogg's wonderful book, *Tiny Habits — The Small Changes That Change Everything.*

 Why do you write IImin? Shouldn't it be ii?

Classical music theorists like to write lower case letters to distinguish minor from major chords. In modern styles of music — typically the types of music electric bassists play — this has slowly changed. I prefer to go with the capital numeral and the addition "min" for minor (could also be m or -) to stay closer to what modern chord symbols look like.

Another reason is that in handwritten charts, the size difference between capital and lower-case Roman numerals, or the dots on the i's, can get lost or be hard to see. Generally, the simpler and more obvious the notation method is, the better.

In some diagrams, I may use "IIm" or "ii" simply for reasons of space.

 Why do you never do Area "X" in interval sequence "Y" in direction "Z" in this book?

Two reasons:

1. Because after working through the materials in this system, you can do it on your own, whenever you choose to. I have given you all the tools. Go for it! If you want more guidance and ideas, check out our corresponding course, where we explore many ways to get creative with the materials presented here. We show you how to invent your own variations, apply it all to songs, create your own etudes, etc.

2. I have found that after a certain point, you no longer need to systematically practice every option, in every sequence, in every area. You will have reached this point when you can do any exercise you choose in any area at will. Test yourself randomly, and you will know immediately whether you "got it down" or whether (and what) you need to practice a bit more!

What is important though, is to switch your practice routine up as much as possible — vary starting points, directions, sequences of keys. That way, you never practice the exact same thing twice, and you continually stretch your mind.

Keep track of your progress, come up with your own drills, and put your full focus into it. If you need more help, we have it for you at *ArisBassBlog.com/PatternSystem.*

And don't forget the mental practice…

What *Area* is Skippy in here?

It seems in each chapter there are so many different concepts we are working on at the same time. Can't I just do the scales everywhere first, then return to the lowest area for the triads and so on?

I don't recommend it. The way I designed the system, it works on several levels at the same time. For example, the triads are a *"Shape-within-the-Scale"* shape. So, when you practice the diatonic triads, you reinforce your recall of the scale patterns since each triad is seen as part of its corresponding parent scale.

What you suggest will work, but the results will be less integrated, and your mental training will not be as deep. Overall, it will take you longer.

TEST YOUR UNDERSTANDING #9

1. Which finger plays the chord root in a minor chord?

   ❑ a. The first, third or fourth finger

   ❑ b. The first finger or the fourth finger

   ❑ c. It is best to use a random finger for maximum flexibility.

   ❑ d. Only the first finger

2. Strictly diatonically speaking, minor triads are on the following scale degrees:

   ❑ a. 3, 6, 7 (as seen from a major root)

   ❑ b. 1, 4, 5 (as seen from the minor root)

   ❑ c. 2, 3, 4 (as seen from the major root)

3. It is important to celebrate after you practiced, even if just after completing a small assignment, because research has shown that…

   ❑ a. Celebrating leads to better sleep.

   ❑ b. This will help create a practice habit.

   ❑ c. It helps you to believe that you are amazing, and that is super important for a good practice outcome!

BLUEPRINT FOR PRACTICE #9

Written Assignment: Minor triads in the *Open Area* **pp. 203–205**
     Fill in the *Minor Triad Map* in E minor **p. 207**
     Relative minor triads *Area 1, 2* (or more) **pp. 208–213**
     Various IIIm–VIm–IIm chord sequences **pp. 227–220**

---

1. **PP:** *Up/down* variations, then *Connection Exercises*, 8 beats, *Area 5*; cycle to the left and right; say scale degrees/note names/nothing

---

2. **PP:** *Up/down* variations, then *Connection Exercises*, 8 beats, *Area 5* and *Open Area*, sequence of major seconds to the right and left
for all sequences: **p. 126**

---

3. **Triad PP:** Major Triads on tonic through the cycle to the left and right, *Area 1*; *Up/down* variations, then *Connection Exercises* (experiment with number of beats other than 8) **p. 187** • **Video 59**

---

4. **Triad PP:** Minor Triads on the minor tonic through the cycle in minor to the left and right, *Open Area*; *Up/down* variations, then *Connection Exercises* (experiment with number of beats other than 8)
p. 187 • **Video 59**

---

5. **SS:** Interval studies in sixths; various combinations as shown in *Chapter 6; Area 3*; practice several keys (suggesting G♭) **pp. 136–142** • **Videos 47 to 52**

---

6. **SS:** Interval studies in octaves; various combinations as shown in *Chapter 6; Open Area*; practice several keys (suggesting D) **pp. 136–142** • **Videos 47 to 52**

---

7. **SS:** Minor triad arpeggios over two octaves **p. 221** • **Video 74**

---

8. **IE:** IIIm – VIm – IIm - V Improvisations; pick a few keys (suggesting A and E♭) and do them in *Area 3*.
pp. 221–225 • **Videos 75 to 78**

The Diatonic Cycle

10

THE DIATONIC CYCLE IN THE PATTERN SYSTEM

As readers of *Music Theory for the Bass Player* know well, I consider grasping the diatonic cycle an important milestone because it is the master template as far as diatonic chord progressions are concerned: it includes all diatonic triads! Its chord progressions are ubiquitous in songs, sometimes in its entirety, and many times just in parts. To master a key in my book means to know its diatonic cycle.

With the Pattern System, you can achieve this beautifully while staying within one pattern. So far, you have learned the diatonic major and minor triads. To round out all the diatonic triads, however, we need to tackle one more — the diminished triad, the triad on the seventh scale degree.

MORE SHAPES WITHIN SHAPES: THE DIMINISHED TRIADS

The diminished triad is built on the seventh scale degree of the major scale. With its minor third and flatted fifth, it has a very tense sound. Another way to describe it is to state that it is built from two minor thirds stacked on top of each other.

In order to play chords successfully through the entire diatonic cycle, we need three major and three minor triads, as well as one diminished one. You have already learned about and written out the first two, so now comes the time to tackle the diminished triad.

Open Area Diminished Triad Map

Write out the *Open Area* diminished triads. Since the diminished triad is built on the seventh scale degree, look for the tonic in the pattern of the parent scale, and find the seventh, second and fourth scale degrees. They will form a diminished triad. *Peculiar to this triad is that some patterns skip a string.* Don't be alarmed; that is part of the nature of this shape.

Again, start with the pattern and fill in the diminished triad in black. Mark the tonic of the parent scale as a square and the root of the triad as a diamond.

VIDEO
79 ▶

Open Area (C major / Bdim)

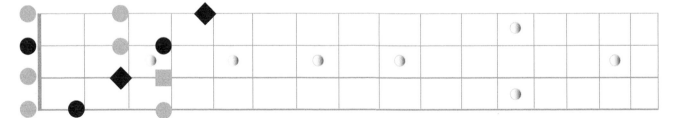

OPEN AREA Diminished Triads

C • **Bdim** Root(s) on _____

F • **Edim** Root(s) on _____

B♭ • **Adim** Root(s) on _____

E♭ • **Ddim** Root(s) on _____

A♭ • **Gdim** Root(s) on _____

D♭ • **Cdim** Root(s) on _____

E • **D♯dim** Root(s) on _____

G♭ • **Fdim** Root(s) on _____

B • **A♯dim** Root(s) on _____

A • **G♯dim** Root(s) on _____

D • **C♯dim** Root(s) on _____

G • **F♯dim** Root(s) on _____

F♯ • **E♯dim** Root(s) on _____

C♯ • **B♯dim** Root(s) on _____

C♭ • **B♭dim** Root(s) on _____

Areas 1 through 5: The Five Diminished Triad Shapes

Find the five possible shapes for any diminished triad by writing out the F♯ diminished triads within the five G major shapes.

Relevant as always are:

- The shape itself
- Where the roots of the diminished triads are (you may also notice if a string is not used at all!)
- How the diminished triad relates to the major tonic (mark the diminished root as a diamond and the major tonic as a square – sevenths and first scale degrees are a half step apart)
- The fingering. Notice how all diminished triad shapes start with either **finger #1** or **finger #3**
- Notice the patterns that skip a string!

In the following diagrams, you again already have the G major template prefilled. Mark the F♯ diminished triads (F♯ A C). Mark the F♯ root as a diamond and note on which strings the roots are.

Diminished Triad Map in F♯ Diminished

VIDEO 80 ▶

Pattern I Root on ___ & ___

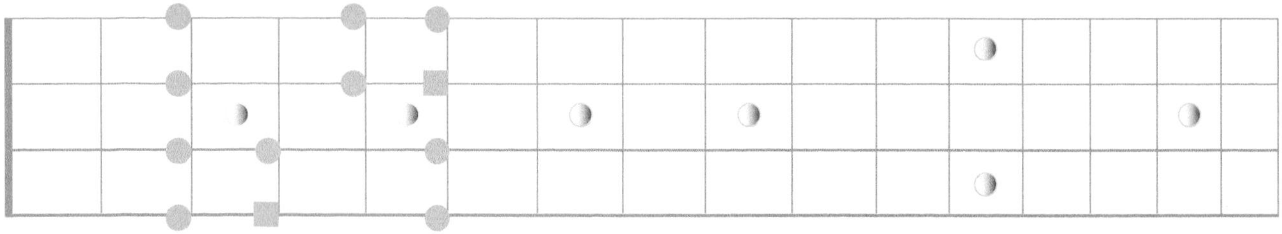

Pattern II Root on ___

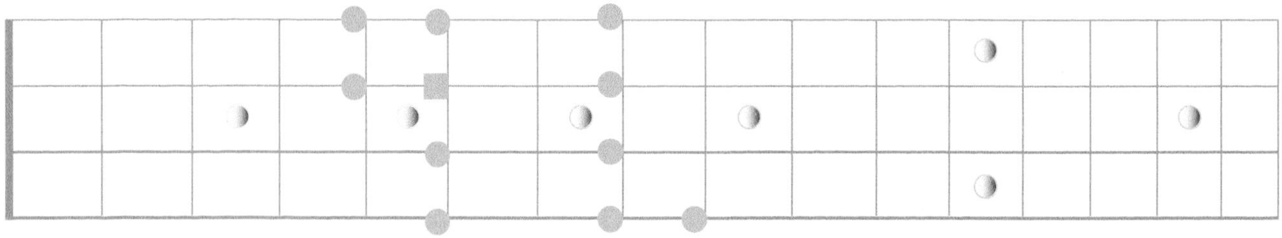

Pattern III Root on ___

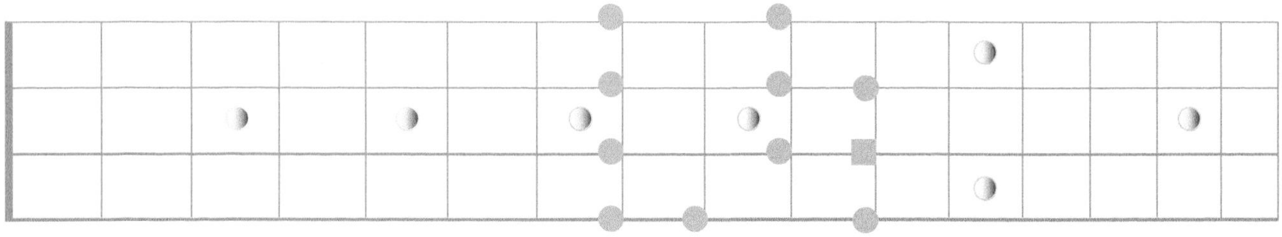

Pattern V Roots on ___ &___

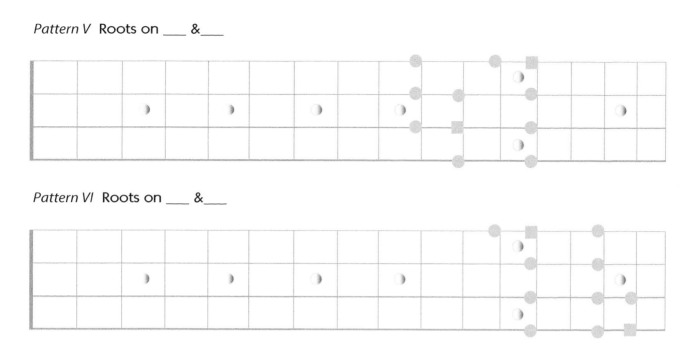

Pattern VI Roots on ___ &___

▌▌▌ NOTE:

- *Pattern I:* the only pattern featuring a note of the diminished triad on every string
- *Pattern V:* no note on the E-string
- *Pattern II:* no note on the A-string
- *Pattern VI:* no note on the D-string
- *Pattern III:* no note on the G-string

▌▌▌ **NOTE:** Wherever a pattern features a whole step (either fingered 2-4, 1-3 or as a "crab," 1-4), the diminished triad will have no note at all on that string.

CHAPTER 10

Diminished Triad Area Maps

Area 1 Diminished Triads

A reminder that the diminished triad occurs on the seventh scale degree. Find the parent pattern and the diminished triad within it. Unlike with major and minor triads, only one diminished triad per major scale exists, namely on the seventh scale degree.

C • **Bdim** Root(s) on _____

F • **Edim** Root(s) on _____

B♭ • **Adim** Root(s) on _____

E♭ • **Ddim** Root(s) on _____

A♭ • **Gdim** Root(s) on _____

Db • **Cdim** Root(s) on _____

Gb • **Fdim** Root(s) on _____

B • **A#dim** Root(s) on _____

E • **D#dim** Root(s) on _____

A • **G#dim** Root(s) on _____

D • **C♯dim** Root(s) on _____

G • **F♯dim** Root(s) on _____

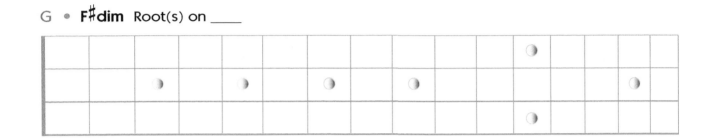

F♯ • **E♯dim** Root(s) on _____

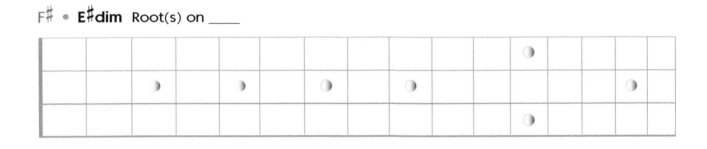

C♯ • **B♯dim** Root(s) on _____

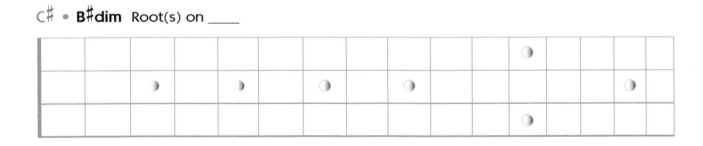

C♭ • **B♭dim** Root(s) on _____

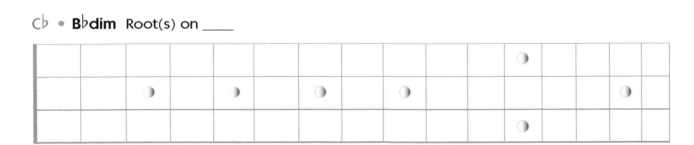

Area 4 Diminished Triads

Again, I am switching things up a bit. Write a higher area for practice! If you feel reasonably fit in *Area 4*, go for it. If not, make it *Area 2* or *3*.

C • **Bdim** Root(s) on _____

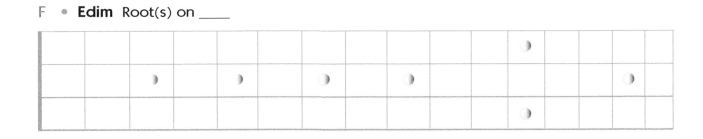

F • **Edim** Root(s) on _____

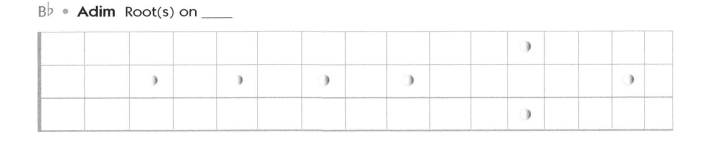

B♭ • **Adim** Root(s) on _____

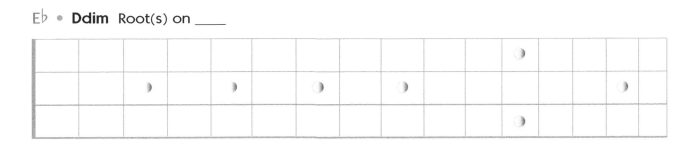

E♭ • **Ddim** Root(s) on _____

A♭ • **Gdim** Root(s) on _____

D♭ • **Cdim** Root(s) on _____

G♭ • **Fdim** Root(s) on _____

B • **A♯dim** Root(s) on _____

E • **D♯dim** Root(s) on _____

A • **G♯dim** Root(s) on _____

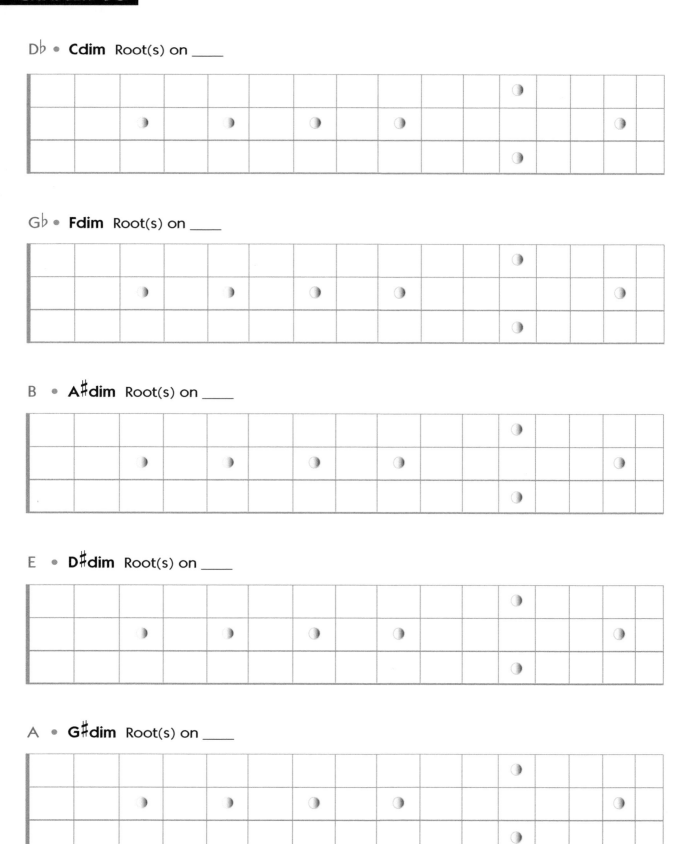

D • **C♯dim** Root(s) on _____

G • **F♯dim** Root(s) on _____

F♯ • **E♯dim** Root(s) on _____

C♯ • **B♯dim** Root(s) on _____

C♭ • **B♭dim** Root(s) on _____

Scalar Studies

Diminished Triad Arpeggios Over Two Octaves

With the major and minor triads under your belt, practicing the diminished triads over two octaves completes these types of diatonic triad drills. In my example, I am sticking with the same idea as with the major and minor versions in that I place the lowest root of the diminished triad on the E-string, play the first diminished triad, and then switch to the top root on the A-string to finish out the octaves. Since the originating scale degree of the diminished triad sits just a half step below the major root, you can use the same patterns for the comparable exercise of the major triads (using *Patterns I* and *V*). Remember to relate the diminished triad to the pattern (and key signature) of the parent scale. When descending, *aim for the flat fifth with the second finger.*

▌▌▌ **NOTE:** If you have a 20-fret bass, you need to adapt the fingering of D♯ diminished (E major): place the F♯ in the upper octave on the D-string 16th fret (instead of the A-string).

This example is in *Area 4*. Starting with C diminished puts you into *Pattern I* of the key of D♭, then *V* in G♭, etc.

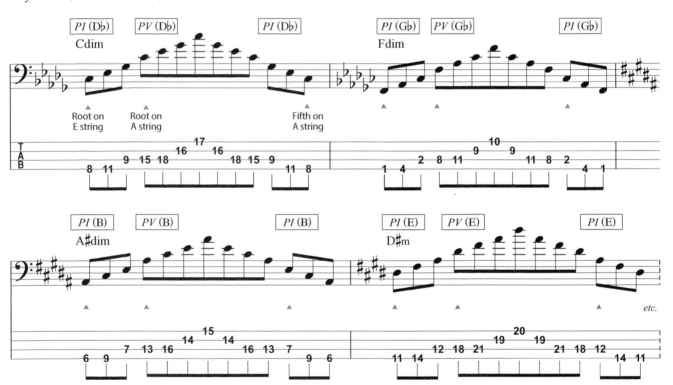

MORE ON THE DIATONIC CYCLE

To review, the diatonic cycle features:

- Chords built on scale degrees using (mostly) diatonic material — the "diatonic" in the diatonic cycle

- Chords that are set in the order of descending fifths/ascending fourths/the cycle to the left — the "cycle" in the diatonic cycle

Here is the diatonic cycle in the key of G, triads only. Go counterclockwise:

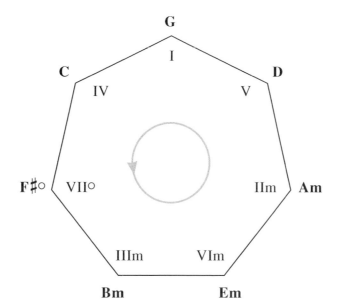

Snippets of the diatonic cycle show up everywhere in music, in almost all styles!

Notice that:

- The snippets out of the cycle can start anywhere and typically end with either the I or the V7 before looping back around.

- Minor chords often get turned into dominant chords for stronger resolution ("Secondary Dominants").

- Most tunes go to the left ("descending fifths" — a strong V → I bass resolution!).

- Again — remember the feeling of falling down a hill without being able to stop? We recognized that with the counterclockwise (chromatic) Cycle of Fifths as well. That's what you get again here, but you stay inside one key throughout.

- Chord progressions going to the right (ascending fifths) also occur, although less frequently.

- Often, (shorter) chord progressions that use the cycle of fifths and don't constitute a whole song, don't start with the I, but rather lead to the I:

Here are a few examples. Look for them in the tunes you play (leaving out major/minor here):

Skippy is still rolling down that hill; he hasn't stopped since *Chapter 3!*

			V	I
		II	V	I
	VI	II	V	I
III	VI	II	V	I

etc.

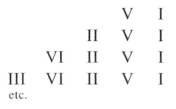

If you find these progressions quickly, you will have a leg up on learning tunes and having the shapes under your fingers immediately for grooving and improvising! You can remember these segments of the cycle as one chunk of information, which makes recalling the changes much faster.

The trick to recognizing such cycle progressions is to listen for their characteristic "rolling down the hill" sound. You can also see them plainly on the fretboard: **Does the root movement of the progression move in ascending fourths (inverted descending fifths?)** If you see the movement from fret to fret (with the one correction of a half step between the fourth and seventh scale degrees), you are likely dealing with a diatonic cycle snippet. Here are just the roots on the fretboard in the key of C to demonstrate this characteristic root movement; for your actual practice, I prefer you stay within one pattern for now, but this view helps see the theory in action on the fretboard (tuned in fourths!):

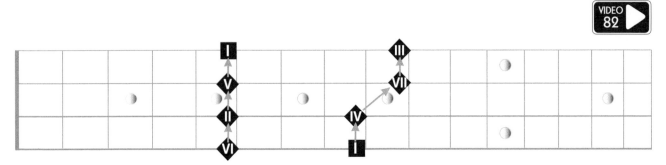

Four-note Chords

Once you are confident that you can play the diatonic cycle in a few keys, you can extend the triads to four-note chords (seventh chords) by stacking another diatonic third on top of the fifth!

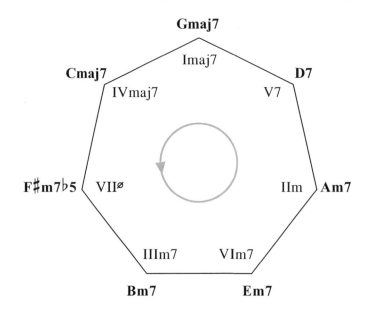

Work through them exactly like you did for the triads:

- Write out the four-note chord patterns within the major scale pattern.
- Practice these patterns.
- Practice seventh chord *Connection Exercises*.

- Improvise using only chord notes. Later on, add the remaining notes from the scale.

Diatonic Cycle in Minor

The diatonic cycle can occur in minor as well as major. **All chords stay the same**, but the reference point changes (the numbers now relate to the relative minor root as the I chord):

In this diagram, only the numbers inside changed compared to the major version (new reference point!):

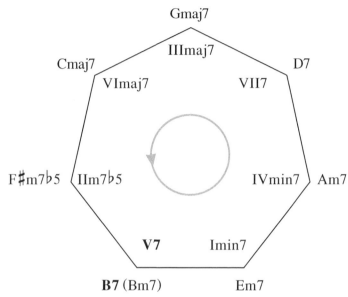

Or, with the minor tonic moved to the top:

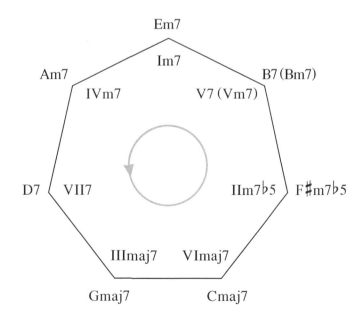

The Vmin7 chord in minor is often made dominant (V7) to create a leading tone and tritone resolution from the V to the I minor (which can also be a min-maj7 chord). Refer to my *Music Theory for the Bass Player* book for info on the minor dominant and melodic and harmonic minor scales.

Diatonic Cycle in Tunes

Most tunes feature snippets of the cycle, but some go (almost) all the way around:

Examples of tunes featuring the entire diatonic cycle in major:

- Fly Me to the Moon (Howard/Ballard, 1954)
- All the Things You Are (Kern/Hammerstein II, 1939)

And a few examples of the complete diatonic cycle in minor:

- Autumn Leaves (Kosma, 1945)
- Spain (Corea, 1971)
- Europa (Santana/Coster, 1976)
- I Will Survive (Perren/Fekaris, 1978)
- Still Got the Blues (Moore, 1990)

Which songs can you add to these lists? There are many more!

Some tunes go to the right (ascending fifths! — notice the sensation of "lifting" the energy), such as "Hotel California" by the Eagles (Felder/Henley/Frey 1978).

Remember that even tunes with just I – I – V – V – I essentially feature three slices out of the diatonic cycle. Find them! (Answer in appendix).

▌▌▌ TIP: There are three functions of chords in a diatonic context. All others are sub-functions of the main three.

FUNCTION	CHORD	SOUND (simplified)
TONIC	I (also IIIm, VIm)	Stable, "home"
SUBDOMINANT	IV (also IIm)	"Going somewhere"
DOMINANT	V (also VII°	Unstable, "want to go back home," bluesy

Listen to the tunes you play through the lens of the diatonic cycle as well as the table above. From now on, analyze the songs you learn and hunt for these progressions — with the patterns under your fingers, large portions of previously unknown songs are now at your fingertips, instantly!

Diatonic Cycle Practice

For this exercise, stay in one pattern!

Pick a key and an *Area*. This gives you a pattern.
Play it one time to calibrate yourself

No metronome (at first):

- Start with finding the roots only.
- Then play the triads starting from the roots at first.
- Also, play the triads from lowest to highest note and the reverse.

With metronome (or jam track*):

- Practice *Connection Exercises* through the entire diatonic cycle.
- Improvise using triads only.
- Improvise using triads and s calar runs.

Example: Diatonic Cycle in A Major (Pattern I, Area 2)

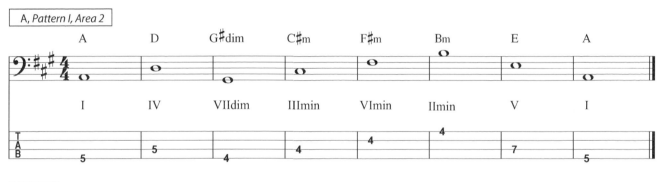

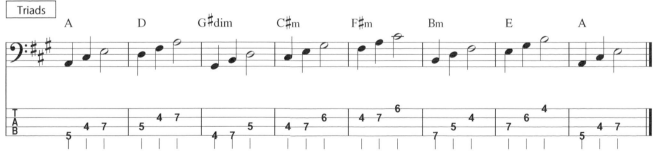

Connection Exercises: Diatonic Cycle in A Major (Pattern I, Area 2)

NOTE: In typical *Connection Exercises* fashion, you always do a defined number of beats per chord (below I use one bar of eighth notes) and keep going until you have reached the end of the pattern, then turn around. When you switch, you may land on the third, fifth or root. Just keep going. There is only one correct solution. Make sure not to skip any notes! Once you are beginning to get the hang of this, start switching your starting point and also use 5, 6 or 7 notes per chord! Contrary to the scalar *Connection Exercises*, those involving triads sound great with a jam track.

---

* Download various Cycle jam tracks from *ArisBassBlog.com/PatternSystem*

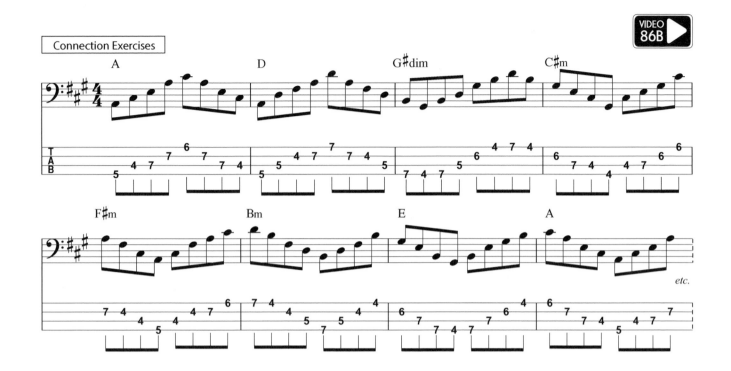

Connection Exercises

Improvised Explorations

Diatonic Cycle Exercise in A Major

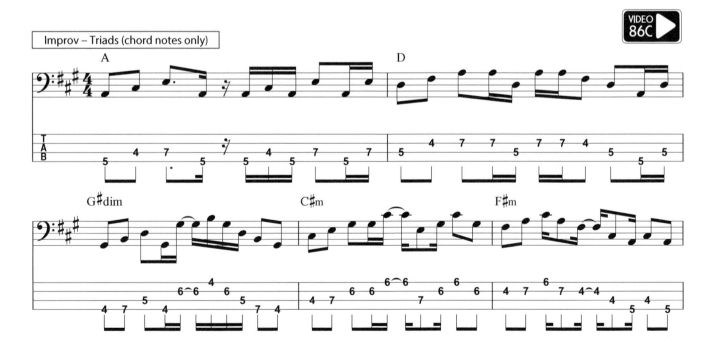

Improv – Triads (chord notes only)

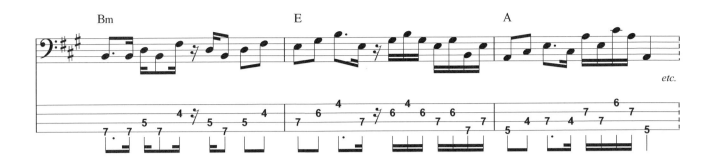

Improv – Triads and Scalar Runs

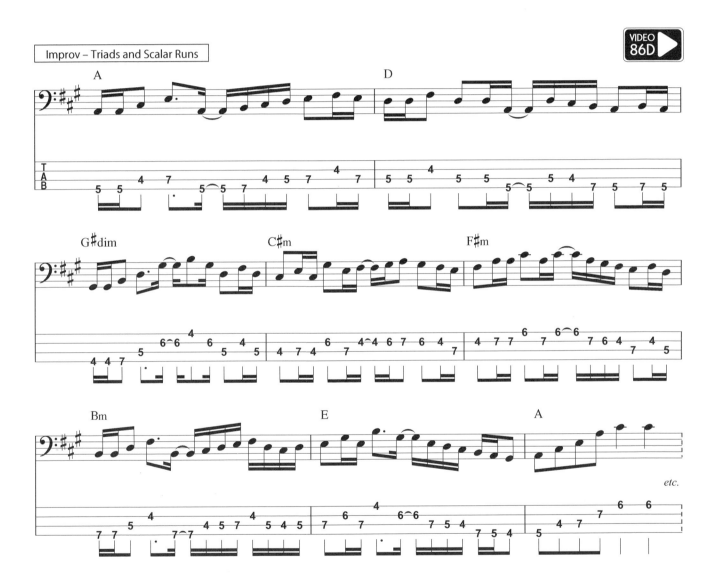

NOTE: These exercises help you get the notes under your fingers. They are like etudes (practice pieces) that you create on the spot. For a groove, the above examples will likely be too busy, but this approach can be great material for a "groove solo." Once you are more familiar with all the chords and the whole sequence, begin starting your lines on notes other than the root.

SIGHT-READING TIP: Knowing that all of these notes are within a pattern you firmly have under your fingers will help you to read the examples above. No need to look at the fretboard or to reinvent the wheel for each note. It all connects under your fingers. When learning to sight-read music, focus on the relationship of each note to the one before it and the general context each note is in, rather than spot placing each individual note. Recognizing common shapes such as triads also helps tremendously. Appreciate the existence of a general key signature — it tells you the pattern if you will! For more tips on reading, see our additional resources.

Example: Diatonic Cycle in A Minor (Pattern VI of C major, Area 2)

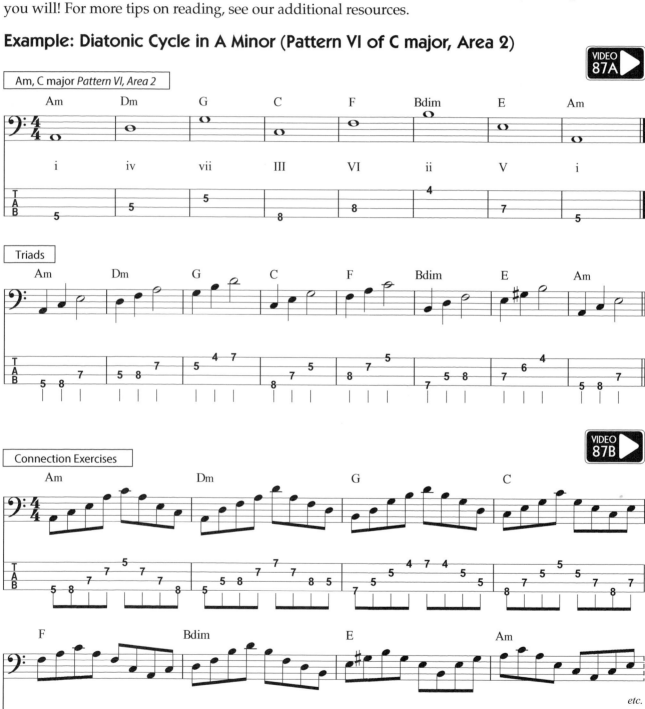

TIP: As a variation, play these improvisation exercises with shuffled sixteenth notes.

Diatonic Cycle Practice: Walking Explorations

In this exercise, you essentially play a walking bassline over a chord progression based on the diatonic cycle by using chord tones and scale notes.

The result is a highly educational concept that is very effective for creating beautiful walking basslines.

To deeper explore the creation of musical walking basslines:

- Add a variety of rhythmic embellishments.
- Include single or multiple chromatic approach notes* and "enclosures.*"
- Focus on the shape of the line (range, many jumps or fewer, amount of "inside" versus "outside" sounding notes, etc.).

Keep in mind that this exercise is a first step to outlining the chord changes; it will also help you come up with new ideas if you find yourself stuck in a rut on certain progressions.

This diatonic cycle snippet is the A section of the jazz standard "Autumn Leaves."

Key is G minor; the tune starts on the IVmin7.

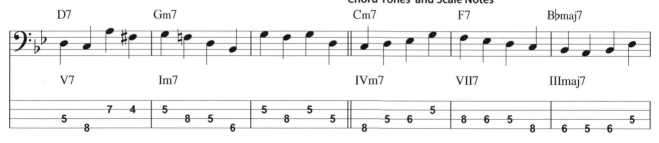

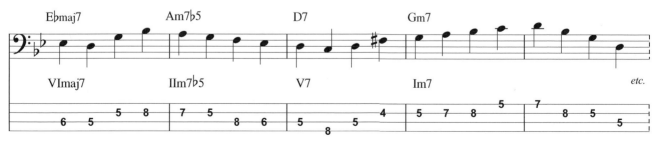

---

* Explained in *"Music Theory for the Bass Player"*

With all this emphasis on practicing patterns, won't I be compelled to only play patterns? And overplay? Will the patterns get in the way of my creativity?

No, they won't. Patterns are options and a field of possibilities. They are like a map. All the possible notes light up on the fretboard, or you can hear the notes before you play them. No need to poke around anymore, or chase what you are hearing inside your mind. If anything, being very familiar with the shapes and patterns frees your mind to make creative choices since it is less busy trying to find the right notes.

If you, in the beginning stages, get a bit carried away with your new-found technical skills and the security of knowing where all the notes are, remind yourself to use your powers to serve the music first. The most important skill we hope to give you is thinking ahead — thinking the music in your mind and facilitating its translation to the bass. When you find yourself overplaying — breathe, relax and let your focus zoom in on a musical detail — run the melody in your head, for example, or the lyrics; listen to what a bandmate plays, connect with the drummer. If you followed my system, your mind would be free to step back, relax, and join with the music rather than chasing after it.

Not learning something because you are afraid you might overuse it sounds like an excuse to not put in the effort. I have not once heard from my students that they wished they hadn't learned all the materials contained here. In fact, quite the opposite!

It's an amazing feeling to have the freedom to immerse yourself in the music rather than having to scramble to find the right notes. Remember my *Chapter 7* explorations on different learning channels, including the channels that are open questions and invite exploration? A solid understanding of the fretboard is an invaluable doorway to all of this. If you think about it, that's pretty deep…

 Pattern II starts with the second note, *Pattern III* with the third — so are the Patterns the modes?

Since the first note played in a scale has a big sonic impact, you might think — wait, *Pattern II* — that is Dorian! *III* — Phrygian! Well, yes — after all, *PII* starts with the second note of the scale, just like the Dorian mode does. But that would be a very limited way of using these shapes. You'd always have to jump to *Pattern II* for Dorian, *Pattern III* for Phrygian, and so forth. This rather myopic approach to scales does not grant you the freedom you are looking for.

In my experience, this misconception stems from students practicing too many scales only from root to root in one octave.

Stop thinking the lowest note must always be the starting note or the root of the scale.

What determines the mode is not the lowest note but the central reference note.

As you know and have studied by now, the *Five Patterns of the Major Scale* include all the notes of the scale within a given area. Within these patterns, many other structures exist — such as the modes. At first, you learn the major scale tonic as the primary reference point. When learning the modes, you can use any note of this pattern as the central reference point (or the new root). In essence, **every pattern contains every mode.**

A Great Practice Hack

Always be aware of the relation of the played triad note to the triad root, as well as to the tonic of the key. Saying scale degrees out loud definitely drills this relationship to the tonic. Feel free to slow it down or switch off the click when saying scale degrees.

So, for the IV chord, you would say "4 – 6 – 1" (or "4 – 6 – 8") and the V "5 – 7 – 2."

The power of practicing like this lies in the fact that you are now tracking more than one stream of information in your mind. Music requires the skill of multitasking very frequently, whether you are improvising over changes, following a conductor, or simply just listening to others while playing. Practicing any type of musical multitasking enhances your practice exponentially.

▌▌▌ TECHNIQUE TIP:

Want to switch up your *Pattern Practice*? — Change your right-hand technique! Use your thumb and give it some slap-thump-pop! Or use a pick! How about thumb-muting?

This provides not only a great way to double task on shedding your various playing styles, but it also shakes up the pattern practice a bit. You may feel like some of these patterns are not as ingrained as you once thought.

Here is a great way to use your thumb in triad *Pattern Practice*, for example. By repeating each note using a common funk rhythm figure — you practice the aim of your thumb while getting triads under your belt:

VIDEO
90 ▶

Come up with your own variations of pop, thumb, slap, thumb mute, pick playing! Tapping often invites a different fingering than the patterns provide, so hold off with that technique for now.

TEST YOUR UNDERSTANDING #10

1. Which finger plays the chord root in a diminished triad?

   ❑ a. The first finger or the third finger

   ❑ b. The second finger or the fourth finger

   ❑ c. It is best to use any random finger for maximum flexibility.

   ❑ d. The pinky should not work so hard. Avoid it.

2. You can build a chord from each scale degree of a scale. When you put the resulting chords in the order of ascending fourths (or descending fifths), you get…

   ❑ a. The modes

   ❑ b. The diatonic cycle

   ❑ c.   Major, minor and diminished chords

3. To improvise using the Dorian mode use (mark all that apply):

   ❑ a. *Pattern I*

   ❑ b. *Pattern II*

   ❑ c. *Pattern III*

   ❑ d. *Pattern V*

   ❑ e. *Pattern VI*

4. Within a major scale, the following triads occur (mark all that apply):

   ❑ a. Major triads (3)

   ❑ b. Minor triads (3)

   ❑ c. An augmented triad (1)

   ❑ d.   A diminished triad (1)

5. There are seven chords in a major scale but only how many functions?

   ❑ a. Four: major, augmented, diminished, minor

   ❑ b. Three: tonic, subdominant, dominant

   ❑ c.   Seven: Ionian, Dorian, Phrygian, Lydian, Mixolydian, Locrian

6. The Diatonic Cycle is important to know because:

   ❑ a. It occurs in music all the time, either in parts or in full.

   ❑ b. It is a fantastic practice tool.

   ❑ c. It drives understanding of frequent chord progressions.

   ❑ d. It sounds great to practice improvisation through the diatonic cycle.

   ❑ e. All of the above

TEST YOUR UNDERSTANDING #10

7. Mark chord progressions that are segments from the diatonic cycle (mark all that apply):

☐ a. ii – V – I

☐ b. IIImin – VImin – IImin – V

☐ c. V – I – IV

☐ d. iv – VII – III – VI – iidim – v – i

☐ e. I – IV – viidim – iii – vi – ii – V – I

10 WEEK PRACTICE GROUPS

Join a live
Pattern Practice Group!
Sign up at arisbassblog.com/practice

BLUEPRINT FOR PRACTICE #10

Written Assignment: Diminished triads in the *Open Area* **pp. 231–233**
Fill in the *Diminished Triad Map* in F♯ diminished   **pp. 234–235** • **Video 80**
Diminished triads *Area 1, 4* (or more) **pp. 236–241**
Various IIIm-VIm-IIm chord sequences **p. 223–226**

---

1. **SS:** Diminished triad arpeggios over two octaves **p. 242** • **Video 81**

---

2. **PP:** Diatonic Cycle practice, *up/down* variations, then *Connection Exercises*, in various keys
(major and minor) and areas;
major: **pp.247** • **Video 86A and 86B**
minor: **p. 250** • **Video 87 A and 87B**

---

3. **IE:** Diatonic Cycle Practice and Improvisation of this chapter; suggesting *Area 2*, keys of
C major and C minor;
major: **pp. 248–249** • **Videos 86C** and **p. 249** • **Video 86D**
minor: **p. 251** • **Video 87C and 87D**

---

4. **IE:** Walking Bass Improvisation of this chapter — Walking diatonic seventh chords; key of B♭,
do various areas; **p. 252** • **Video 89**

---

5. **Triad PP:** Diminished Triads as the seventh scale degree of the major scale through the cycle
(think the major scale) to the left and right, *Open Area; Up/down* variations, then *Connection Exercises*
(experiment with number of beats other than 8)

From Previous Chapters:

6. **PP:** *Up/down* variations, then *Connection Exercises*, 8 beats, *Areas 1* and *2*; sequence of minor seconds
to the right and left; say scale degrees/note names/nothing

---

7. **Triad PP:** Major Triads on tonic through the cycle to the left and right, *Area 3; Up/down* variations,
then *Connection Exercises* (experiment with number of beats other than 8) **p. 193** • **Video 59**

---

8. **Triad PP:** Minor Triads on the minor tonic through the cycle in minor to the left and right,
Area 1; Up/down variations, then *Connection Exercises* (experiment with number of beats other than 8)
p. 193 • **Video 59**

---

9. **SS:** Interval studies in fifths; various combinations as shown in *Chapter 6; Open Area;*
practice several keys (suggesting D and A♭) **pp. 142–148** • **Videos 47 to 52**

Pentatonics and Diagonals

MORE SHAPES WITHIN SHAPES: PENTATONICS

Introduction

Pentatonic scales are the source material for countless basslines, fills, melodies, and improvisations. Since both the major and minor pentatonic scales (the two most common ones) don't have any half steps, they have an open sound that also avoids any harsh dissonances.

Essentially, the major pentatonic is a major scale without the fourth and seventh scale degrees, leaving you with:

1 2 3 5 6 8

Those same notes re-arranged and started from the sixth — as any relative minor does — give you the minor pentatonic scale. Rearranging the scale degrees to account for the new minor root gives you:

1 ♭3 4 5 ♭7 8

The graph below shows the G major pentatonic scale over two entire octaves (spanning several areas), pointing out one octave of the E minor pentatonic scale within that G major scale.

The grey notes are the ones left out:

- as seen from the major scale: fourth and seventh
- seen from the minor scale: second and sixth

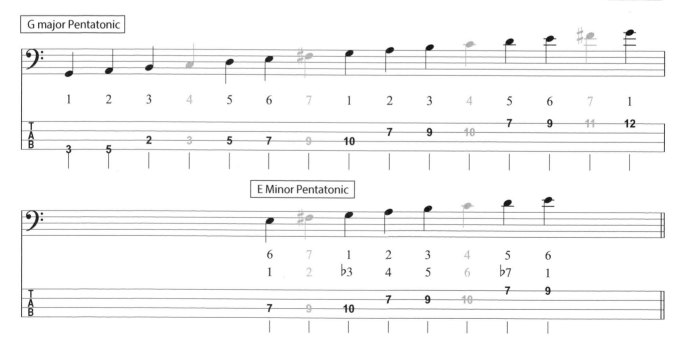

You can also create the pentatonic scale by stacking four fifths on top of each other. This means you could construct the major pentatonic from a slice out of the cycle of fifths (using the G major/E minor notes here as an example):

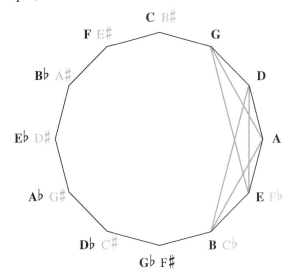

Notice how this forms a compressed pentagram — a magical symbol that points to the mystical origins of the pentatonic scale: 5 fingers, 5 Elements, the 5-point human (Vitruvian Skippy by Leonardo da Vinci):

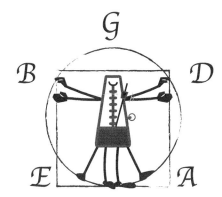

Five is a magical number!

If you have a five-string bass in standard fourth tuning, the open strings spell out the above scale: B E A D G

Rearranged in the order of the scale, with the major scale degrees in black outside and the minor scale degrees in grey inside, you get:

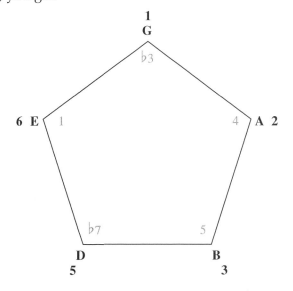

The Pentatonic Scales in The Pattern System

Since the bass strings themselves spell out the notes of a pentatonic scale, no wonder then that the pentatonic patterns form nice symmetrical shapes on the bass, especially once you leave the *Open Area*. Guitarists often refer to them as "box shapes." I like mnemonics, so I took it a step further and named the five pentatonic patterns up the neck by the shape they inscribe on the fretboard. In terms of *The Pattern System*, of course, the pentatonic shapes are shapes inside the five standard major scale patterns.

There are a few nice features about them:

- You consistently play two notes per string (exception: some pentatonic patterns in the *Open Area*).

- No shifts, no "crabs" — even *Patterns II* and *VI* sit nicely inside a four-fret span.

Pentatonic Scales in the Open Area

Since the shapes are the same for the relative major and minor pentatonic scales, feel free to fit both major and minor shapes into the same diagram in each area; just square the major tonic and make a diamond for the minor root.

If you like, you can fill in the major scale shape with grey at first and then find the shape within the shape. Or go straight to the pentatonic.

Here is an example in the key of G major/E minor in the open area:

VIDEO 92

G major
E minor

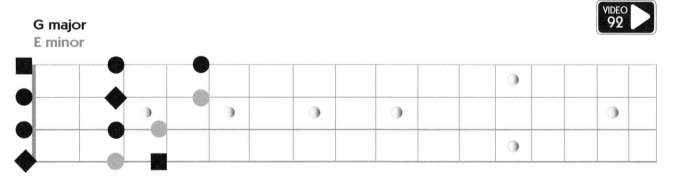

Open Area Pentatonic Scales Map

C • Amin

F • Dmin

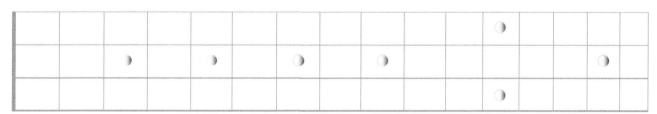

B♭ • Gmin

E♭ • Cmin

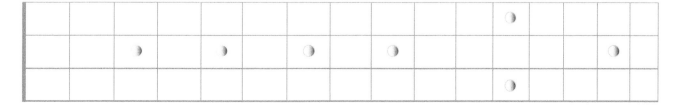

A♭ • Fmin

D♭ • B♭min

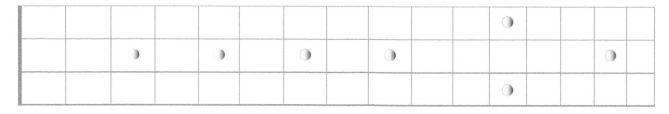

G♭ • E♭min

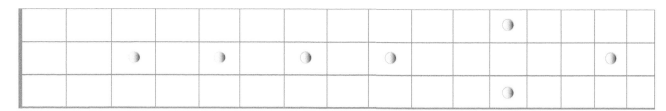

B • G♯min

E • C♯min

A • F♯min

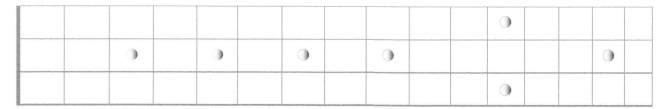

D • Bmin

G • Emin

F# • D#min

C# • A#min

Cb • Abmin

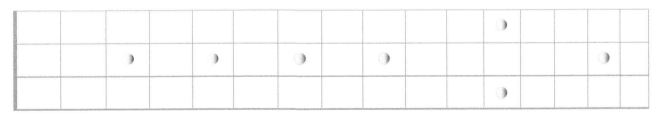

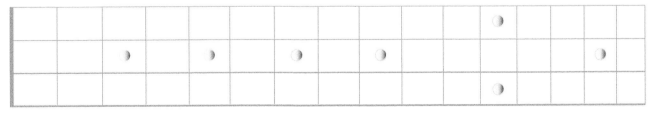

The Pentatonic Scales in the Five Areas

Similar to the Five Main Scale Shapes, seeing all five shapes up the neck is instructive. In these diagrams, I will introduce my box shape mnemonics and separate out the major and minor pentatonic scales. Make sure to learn the location of the squares and diamonds!

VIDEO 93 ▶

G major Pentatonic

Pattern I: "The Hexagon"

scale degrees

Pattern II: "The Boot"

Pattern III: "Big Box-Little Box"

Pattern V: Little Box-Big Box"

Pattern VI: "The Upside-Down Boot"

G major Pentatonic – Shapes Only

Pattern I: "The Hexagon"

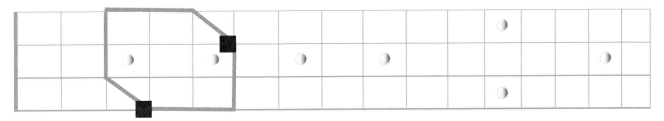

Pattern II: "The Boot"

Pattern III: "Big Box-Little Box"

Pattern V: Little Box-Big Box"

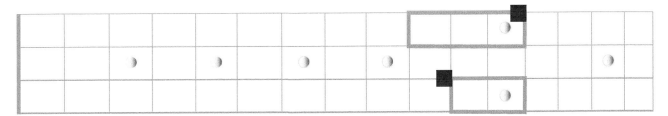

Pattern VI: "The Upside-Down Boot"

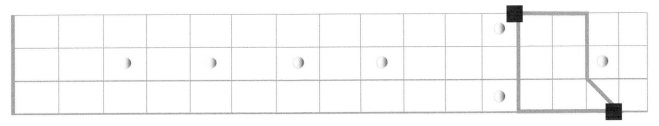

E minor Pentatonic

Pattern I: "The Hexagon"

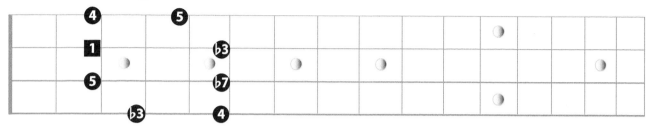

Pattern II: "The Boot"

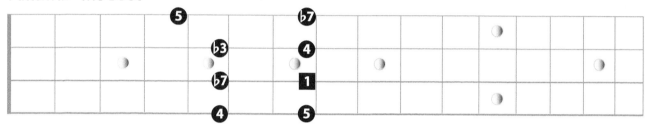

Pattern III: "Big Box-Little Box"

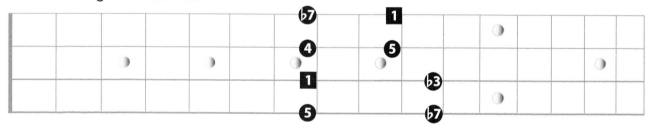

Pattern V: Little Box-Big Box"

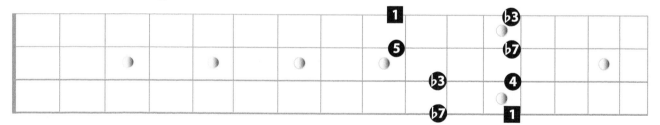

Pattern VI: "The Upside-Down Boot"

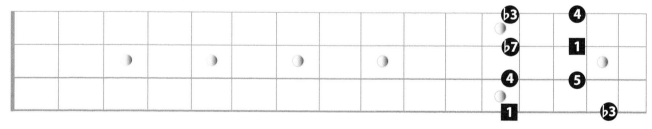

E minor Pentatonic – Shapes Only

Pattern I: "The Hexagon"

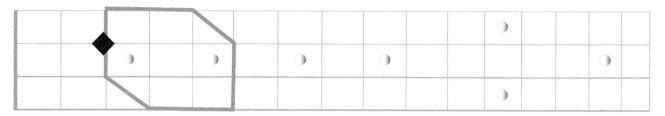

Pattern II: "The Boot"

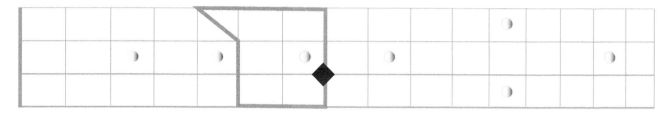

Pattern III: "Big Box-Little Box"

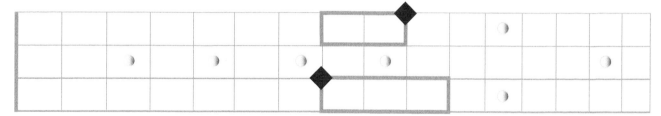

Pattern V: Little Box-Big Box"

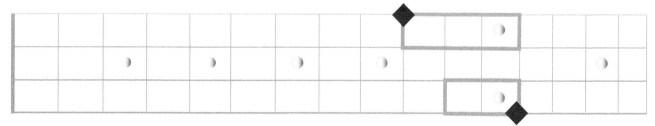

Pattern VI: "The Upside-Down Boot"

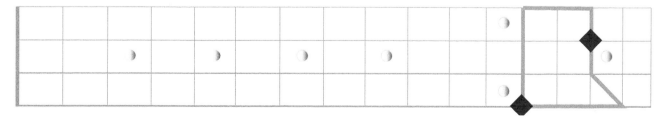

Pentatonic Area Maps

TIP: Rather than write in scale degrees, fingerings, and numbers, I recommend you just write the dots/squares/diamonds — but do it for each area. It serves as a great review besides being imminently practical!

Pentatonic Shapes in Area 1

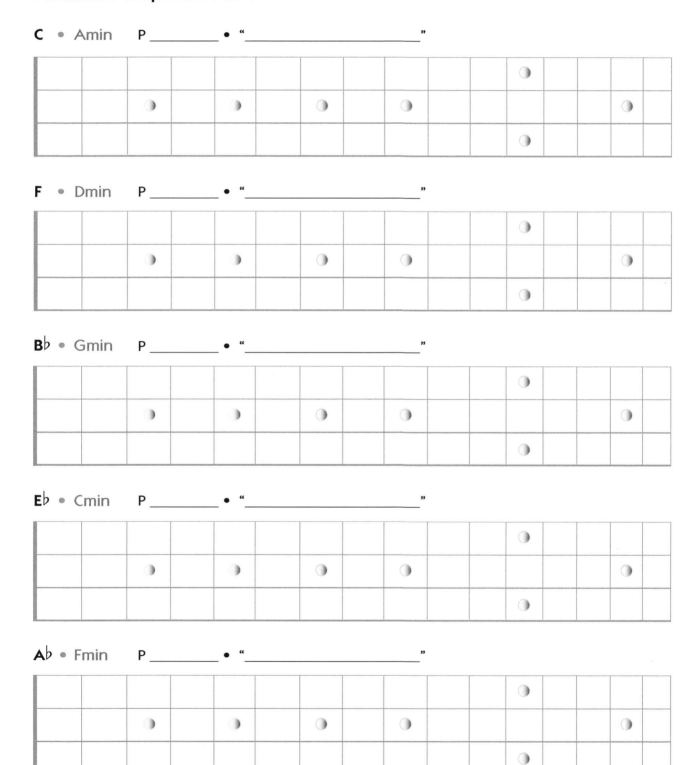

C • Amin   P _____ • "_____"

F • Dmin   P _____ • "_____"

B♭ • Gmin   P _____ • "_____"

E♭ • Cmin   P _____ • "_____"

A♭ • Fmin   P _____ • "_____"

D♭ • B♭min   P _____ • " _____ "

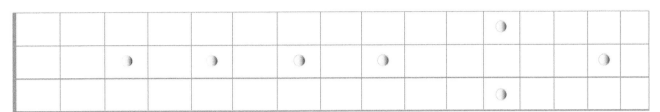

G♭ • E♭min   P _____ • " _____ "

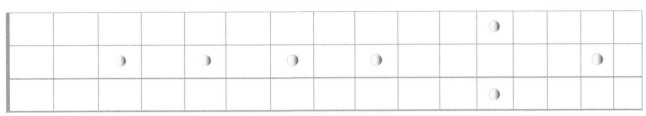

B • G♯min   P _____ • " _____ "

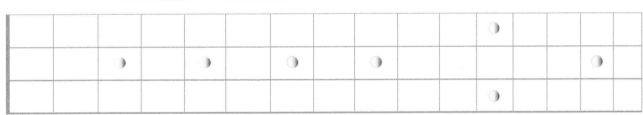

E • C♯min   P _____ • " _____ "

A • F♯min   P _____ • " _____ "

D • Bmin P_____ • "_____"

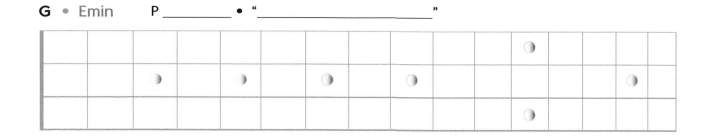

G • Emin P_____ • "_____"

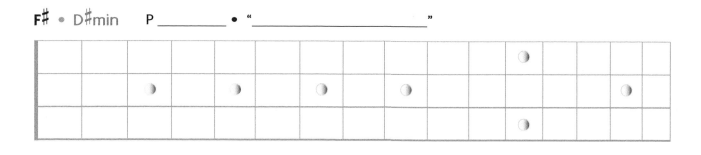

F# • D#min P_____ • "_____"

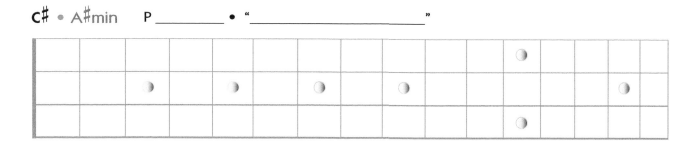

C# • A#min P_____ • "_____"

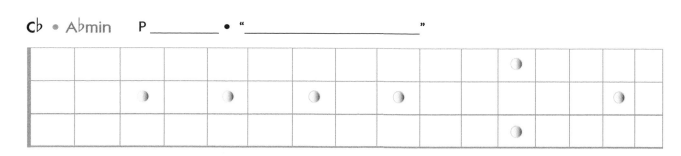

Cb • Abmin P_____ • "_____"

Pentatonic Shapes in Area ___

Pick one more area to write out in this book. If you feel you need to write out more, download pattern paper and go for it!

C • Amin   P _____ • "_____"

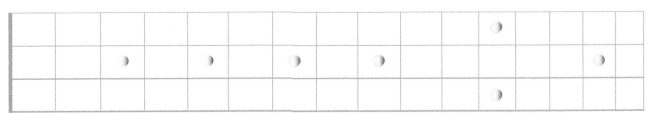

F • Dmin   P _____ • "_____"

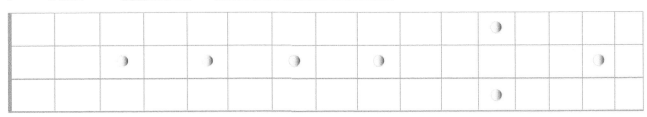

B♭ • Gmin   P _____ • "_____"

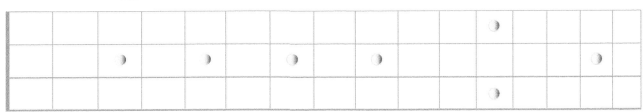

E♭ • Cmin   P _____ • "_____"

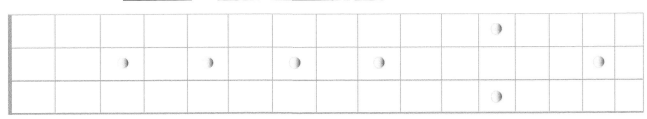

A♭ • Fmin   P _____ • "_____"

D♭ • B♭min   P_____ • "_____"

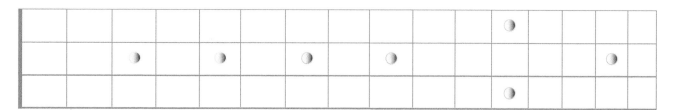

G♭ • E♭min   P_____ • "_____"

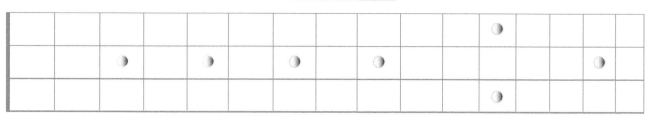

B • G♯min   P_____ • "_____"

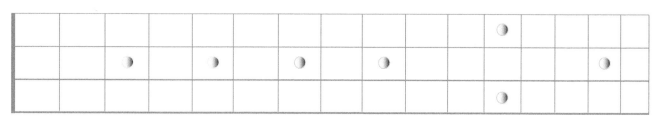

E • C♯min   P_____ • "_____"

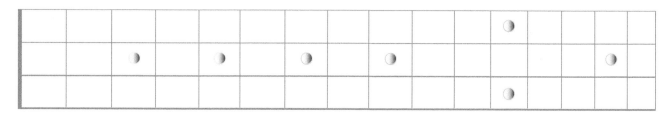

A • F♯min   P_____ • "_____"

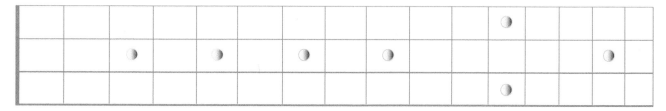

D • Bmin   P _____ • "_____"

G • Emin   P _____ • "_____"

F# • D#min   P _____ • "_____"

C# • A#min   P _____ • "_____"

C♭ • A♭min   P _____ • "_____"

Use the usual ways to familiarize yourself with the new area:

- Play each shape through the cycle to the left at first.

- Always think of these shapes as a *Shape Within the Major Scale Shape*. Be aware of the surrounding pattern.

- Make sure you know where the tonic of the major or root of the minor scale is. (Squares and diamonds, respectively)

- Use the metronome.

- Choose a few of the usual variations:

  - Say scale degrees, note names and fingerings.

  - Ascend and descend, descend and ascend.

  - Ascend all keys one after another, then descend all keys.

  - Do *Connection Exercises*.

  - Apply a variety of sequences: the cycle of fifths in both directions, whole steps, minor/major thirds, half steps.

  - No need to be comprehensive — Pick a few sample areas and sequences and keep changing things up.

Don't forget to bring in Skippy to have an accurate picture of how well you know your pentatonics!

A Highly Applicable Exercise: Diatonic Pentatonics

Just like practicing diatonic triads within each shape, it serves you very well to practice diatonic pentatonics within a key (i.e., pattern). However, while the triad shapes are different for major and minor varieties, the pentatonic major and relative minor shapes are the same, so you end up with only three shapes in total that cover all three major (I–IV–V) and minor (IIImin–VImin–IImin) pentatonic shapes:

Example in G:

The three majors:	G (I chord)	C (IV chord)	D (V chord)
The three minors:	Em (VIm)	Am (IIm)	Bm (IIIm)

Since G/Em, C/Am, D/Bm are the same pentatonic shapes (just with a different root location), you end up with only three shapes for six sounds.

First, start with the majors, then add the minors.

Pentatonics on the I, IV and V

Note that in the diagrams here as well as below (the minors), I kept the tonic of the overarching parent pattern — the G — as the square and placed a diamond for the root of the pentatonic of the scale degree because these two reference points are the pertinent sounds.

Pattern I, **Key of G**

I Chord (Hexagon) – G (*G/Area 1, Pattern I*)

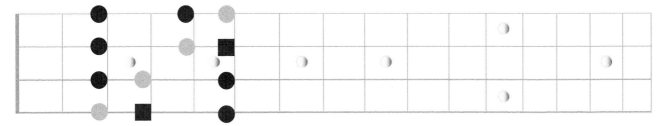

IV Chord (Little Box-Big Box) – C (*G/Area 1, Pattern I*)

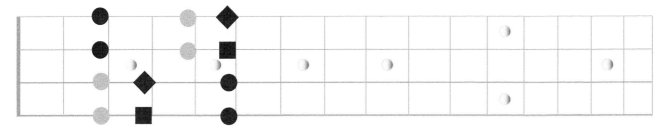

V Chord (Big Box-Little Box) – D (*G/Area 1, Pattern I*)

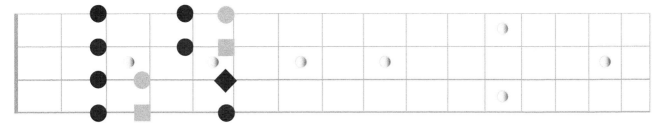

Pentatonics on the VIm, IIm and IIIm

Add the minor Pentatonics in G *(Pattern I, Area 1)*

VImin Chord (Hexagon) – Emin (G/*Area 1*, *Pattern I*)

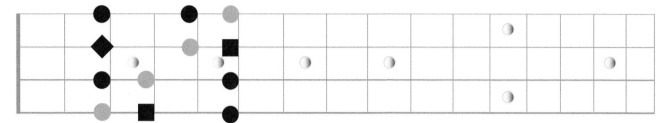

IImin Chord (Little Box-Big Box) – Amin (G/*Area 1*, *Pattern I*)

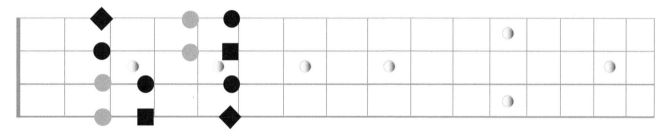

IIImin Chord (Big Box-Little Box) – Bmin (G/*Area 1*, *Pattern I*)

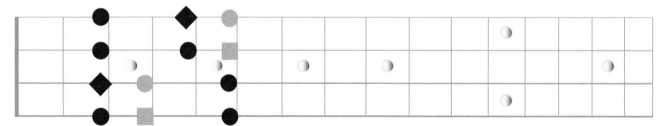

Pattern V, Key of C

I want you to stay in *Area 1* but hit all five patterns for practice. Here is *Pattern V*, Key of C in *Area 1*, with its pentatonics on the I, IV, and V chords. Please fill in the applicable pentatonics and name the shapes:

I–IV–V in C *(Area 1, Pattern V)*

I Chord "_____" – C (C/*Area 1*, *Pattern V*)

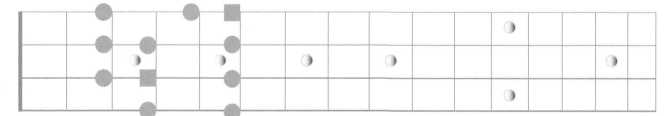

IV Chord "_____" – F (C/*Area 1, Pattern V*)

V Chord "_____" – G (C/*Area 1, Pattern V*)

VIm–IIm–IIIm in C (*Area 1, Pattern V*)

VIm Chord "_____" – Am (C/*Area 1, Pattern V*)

IIm Chord "_____" – ___m (C/*Area 1, Pattern V*)

IIIm Chord "_____" – ___m (C/*Area 1, Pattern V*)

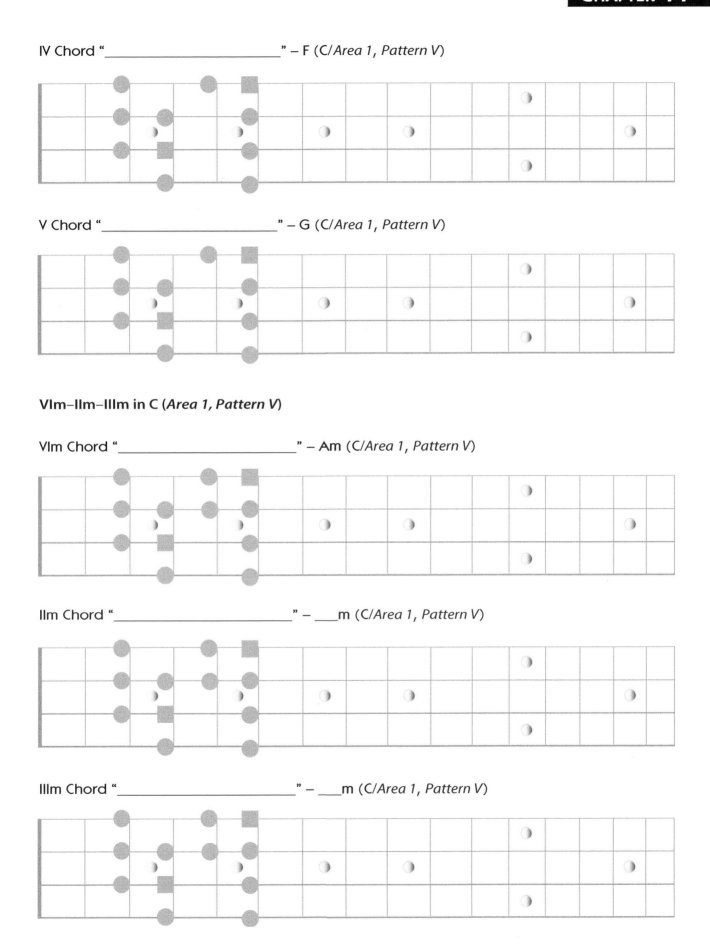

Pattern III, Key of D

I Chord "_____" – D (*D/Area 1, Pattern III*)

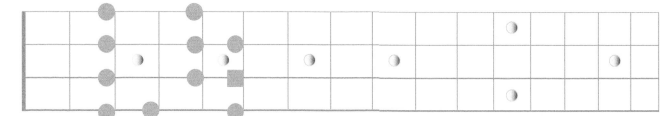

IV Chord "_____" – ___ (*D/Area 1, Pattern III*)

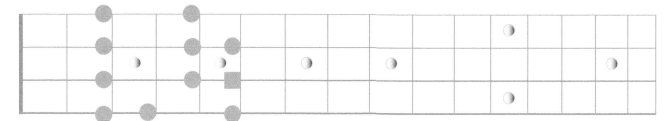

V Chord "_____" – ___ (*D/Area 1, Pattern III*)

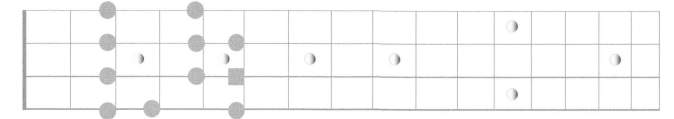

VIm Chord "_____" – Bm (*D/Area 1, Pattern III*)

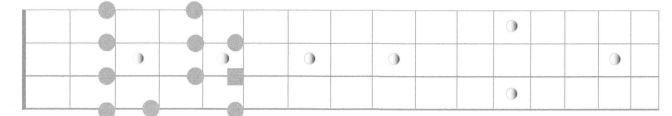

IIm Chord "_____" – ___m (*D/Area 1, Pattern III*)

IIIm Chord "_____" – ___m (D/*Area 1, Pattern III*)

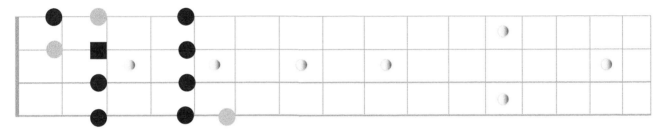

And the two tougher ones last —

Pattern II, Key of E

I Chord "The Boot" – E (E/*Area 1, Pattern II*)

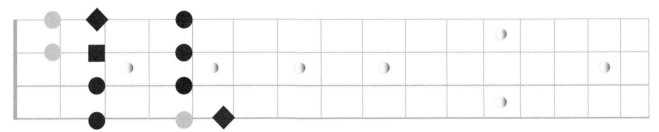

IV Chord "Upside-Down Boot" – A (E/*Area 1, Pattern II*)

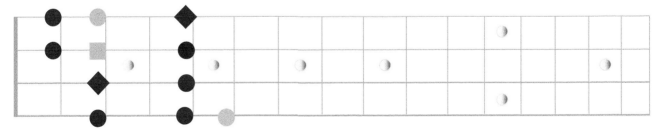

V Chord "Little Box-Big Box" – B (E/*Area 1, Pattern II*)

VIm Chord "_____" – _____m (E/*Area 1*, *Pattern II*)

IIm Chord "_____" – _____m (E/*Area 1*, *Pattern II*)

IIIm Chord "_____" – _____m (E/*Area 1*, *Pattern II*)

Pattern VI, **Key of A**

Now fill in the key of A, my example for *Pattern VI*:

I Chord "_____" – ____ (A/*Area 1*, *Pattern VI*)

IV Chord "_____" – ____ (A/*Area 1*, *Pattern VI*)

V Chord "_____" – ___ (A/*Area 1, Pattern VI*)

VIm Chord "_____" – ___m (A/*Area 1, Pattern VI*)

IIm Chord "_____" – ___ m(A/*Area 1, Pattern VI*)

IIIm Chord "_____" – ___ (A/*Area 1, Pattern VI*)

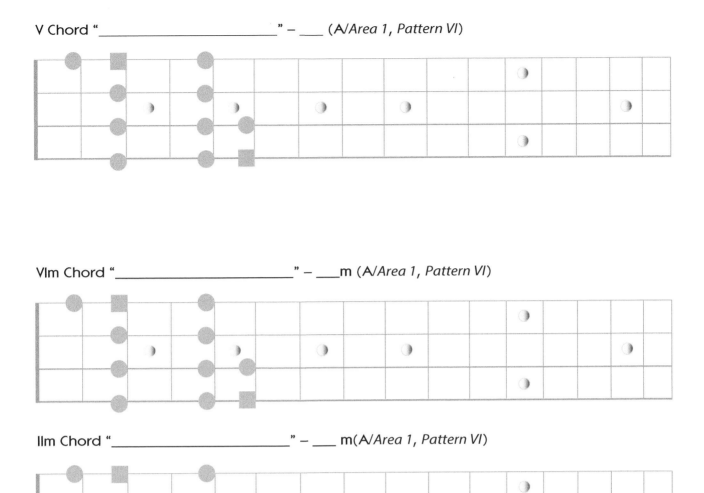

Practice **LIKE THIS**

Pick a key and improvise over I – IV – V.
The chord progression could be any of these:

VIDEO 97

① $\frac{4}{4}$ ‖: I | I | IV | IV |
| V | V | I | I :‖

② $\frac{4}{4}$ ‖: I | IV | V | I :‖

③ $\frac{4}{4}$ ‖: I | IV | I | V :‖

④ $\frac{4}{4}$ ‖: IV | V | I | V :‖

⑤ The 12-bar Blues:

$\frac{4}{4}$ ‖: I | IV | I | I |
| IV | IV | I | I |
| V | IV | I | V :‖

⑥ Now including the minors:

$\frac{4}{4}$ ‖: IIIm | VIm | IIm | V :‖

⑦ $\frac{4}{4}$ ‖: IIm | V | I | VIm |
| IIm | V | I | I :‖

⑧ $\frac{4}{4}$ ‖: IIm | V | IIIm | VIm |
| IIm | V | I | I :‖

⑨ The 12-bar Blues in minor — the V chord of this minor chord progression goes outside the pattern:

$\frac{4}{4}$ ‖: Im | IVm | Im | Im |
| IVm | IVm | Im | Im |
| ♭VI | V | Im | V :‖

Or, many other variations of the same ideas. Enjoy!

The Major and Minor Blues Scales

With the pentatonic scales under your fingers, the major and minor blues scales are just one note away:

- In the major pentatonic, add the flat 3
- In the minor pentatonic, the added note turns out to be the flat 5

And just like the major and minor pentatonic scales, these two scales have the same notes, only their root (and hence scale degree!) is different.

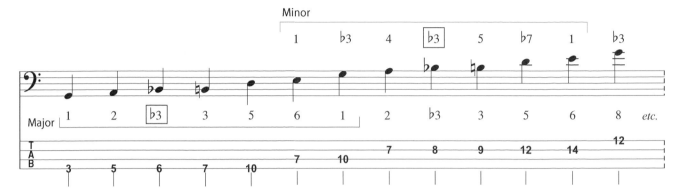

On the fretboard, the five shapes look like this:

I consolidated major and minor blues scales into one diagram below. The star signifies the "blue note" (♭3 or ♭5 respectively, depending on the point of view). Grey stars are alternate locations to finger these notes.

G Major Blues Scale and E Minor Blues Scale (or "E Blues Scale")

Pattern I: "The Hexagon"

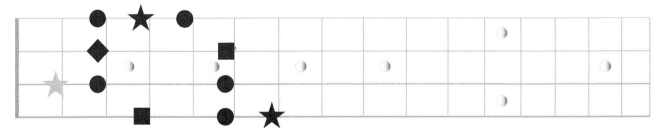

Pattern II: "The Boot"

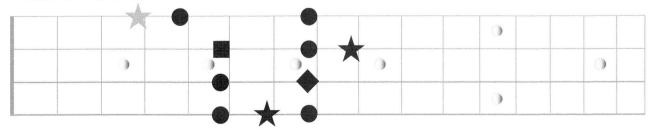

Pattern III: "Big Box-Little Box"

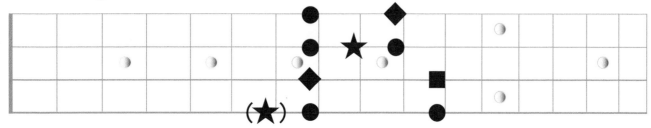

Pattern V: Little Box-Big Box"

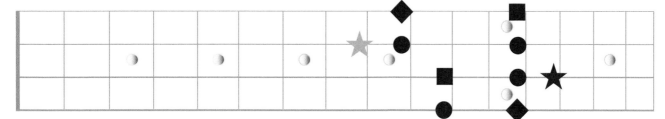

Pattern VI: "The Upside-Down Boot"

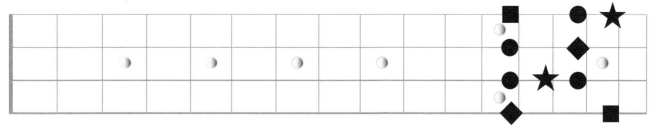

Notice that you need to shift in all of the patterns except for *Patterns III* and *VI*.

Regarding fingering:

> **Fingering option 1 (grey star)**

One option (grey star) is to reach for the note and then slide the first finger back into the position of the familiar pentatonic shape (see the stars in grey). This way keeps your fingers oriented toward the basic pentatonic scale shape and makes for a nice bluesy sounding slide/hammer-on.

Pattern V: Little Box-Big Box"

numbers = fingerings

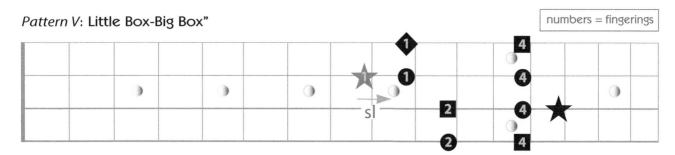

> **Fingering option 2: (black star)**

The other option is to do a one-fret shift for the spots where the chromatic note would lie outside of the pattern. For example, the fingering for *Pattern V* of the major blues scale is 1-3 (or 2-4), 1-3-4, shift 1-4, 1-4

Pattern V: **Little Box-Big Box"**

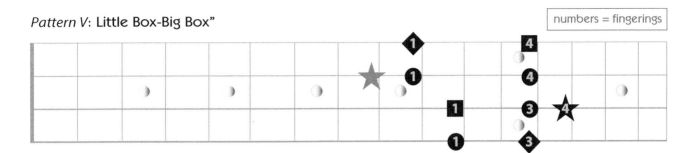

LIKE THIS Practice the above shapes in their major and minor versions. Start with the major root, play to the end of the shape, turn around, back to the lower end of the shape, then back to the root. Do this in all the major, as well as the minor versions.

Then apply the same practice routines as you did for the major scales, including practice in an area in each key up/down, each key down/up, all ascending only, all descending only and *Connection Exercises*. Work through various sequences (cycle in either direction, whole steps, etc.).

Play a blues grooving with the major versions of the scales.

$$\frac{4}{4} \| \colon \quad I7 \quad | \quad IV7 \quad | \quad I7 \quad | \quad I7 \quad |$$

$$| \quad IV7 \quad | \quad IV7 \quad | \quad I7 \quad | \quad I7 \quad |$$

$$| \quad V7 \quad | \quad IV7 \quad | \quad I7 \quad | \quad V7 \quad \colon \|$$

TIP: Try these various approaches to soloing over these chords:

- Use the major blues scales on the I, IV, V chords and switch to the corresponding scale for each chord. For example, in C, you'd play C major blues scale for the C chords, F major blues scale for the F chords, and G major blues scale for the G chords.
- Use the minor blues scales on the I, IV, V chords and similarly change scales with the changes (you will be playing the $\flat 3$ over the major third of the chords. This works because the $\flat 3$ — AKA $\sharp 9$ — is considered a "blue note."
- Use the minor blues scale of just the I chord over all the changes. This also works because of the "blue notes."
- You can also use a combination of blue notes from the major and minor blues scales, such as the $\flat 3$ and $\flat 5$ blue notes from the major and minor blues scales.

Remember that when you are tasked with grooving, you need to feature the major third. It is the major third in the chord in the lower range that makes the minor third (or $\sharp 9$!) shine when someone solos over it in a higher register. That bluesy rub between the major third of the chord and the minor third on top is one of the signature sounds of the blues. You can certainly incorporate the $\flat 3$ of the major blues scale for grooving as well, especially as accents, bends, slides and hammer-ons. Just make sure your groove sounds like a blues in major, not like a minor blues. When you solo, feel free to abandon that responsibility and use the minor blues scale (or scales!) throughout.

DIAGONAL PLAYING

What do you do if you need to cover more ground than one pattern allows for or have other reasons for wanting to move up the neck?

Combine various patterns as you go up the neck! This results in playing diagonally across the fretboard.

Essentially, you start with one pattern on the lowest two strings, then skip to another pattern (adjacent or not) and finish up higher on the neck. This affords you playing over a wide range of the fretboard.

There are many systematic ways to connect the patterns in this way. Experiment and find a few combinations that flow well. In our courses, we practice this systematically — here are two examples to get you started.

You already learned playing triads over two octaves, and you connected two different patterns diagonally that way. You can, of course, do this with any of the shapes — regular scales, triads, and pentatonic scales.

Looking at the C major or A minor pentatonic examples below, notice that I combine two adjacent shapes in the first example. In the second example, I skip a shape each time I move diagonally.

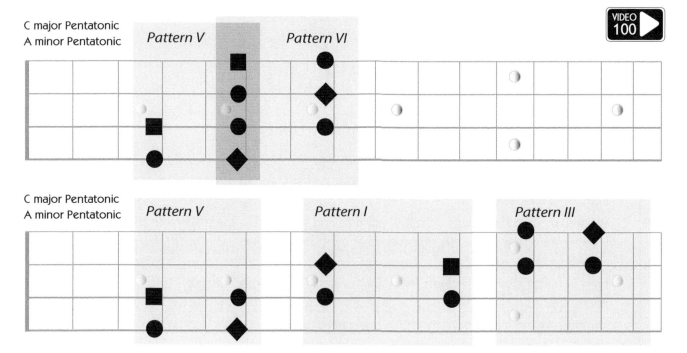

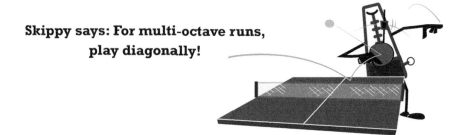

Skippy says: For multi-octave runs, play diagonally!

Here is one approach to playing an entire two-octave run of major pentatonics by starting with the tonic on the E-string (my sample below is in the key of C):

- Start in *Pattern I* (I am in the key of C, *Area 3*) and play the four notes of the major pentatonic on the E- and A-strings.

- Shift to *Pattern III* in *Area 5* (skipping *Pattern II* in *Area 4*) and play the next four notes on the A- and D-strings.

- Skip *Pattern V/Area 1* in the upper register and complete the scale in *Pattern VI* in *Area 2*.

This flows very well and is much easier to execute rather than describe in words. I recommend you practice this through the cycle. Since you start with the root on the E-string, the pattern sequence will be the same for all keys, and you will pick up on it quickly; starting on the root always makes it tempting to solely play by ear. Yes, always use your ears, but also keep awareness of which pattern you are in.

VIDEO
101

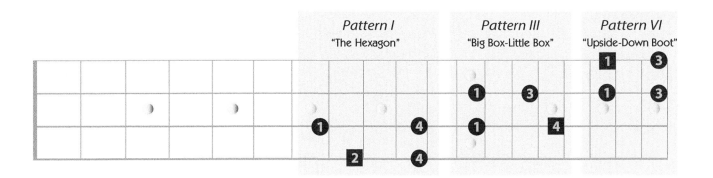

Another approach to playing pentatonics diagonally up the neck is to start in any given area and then use the same principle of skipping every other area. For example, start in *Area 1*, skip *Area 2*, proceed to *Area 3*, skip *Area 4* and then finish up in *Area 5*. As above, you play four notes in each area before switching. But unlike the above version, here you constantly change patterns (depending on what pattern you get in your given starting area) and are not necessarily starting on the root. This is much harder but highly beneficial! Always try to orient your ears toward the root as you play this (although most patterns won't start with the root). I wrote this out for the C major pentatonic again. For F, the patterns would be *Pattern II, V, I;* in B♭ *VI, II, V;* and so on.

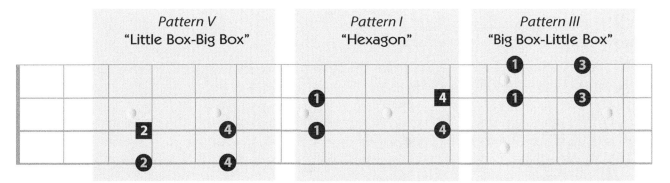

▌▌▌ TIP: Drills such as these in all major (and minor!) keys make for great warmup exercises. They warm up your mind, your fingers and your ears. Try them through the cycle. Just pick three areas (*1, 3* and *5* work great, for example).

A COOL PRACTICE HACK

Try this practice hack for a week. For best results, treat it as a playful experiment.

You need two ingredients:

1 – A short activity you do a few times a day. For example, taking a drink of water, flipping on a light switch, closing the kitchen door, operating the garbage disposal — a small, trivial activity that you do several times a day works best.

2 – One small assignment that only takes a few seconds to do — for example: imagining playing the D♭ major pentatonic in *Area 1* descending, or the B♭ major triad in *Area 3* ascending. A short, defined assignment works best.

Notice that you do *not* need your bass for this. This exercise takes place in your mind.

The Process:

Every time you do your chosen activity (flipping on the light switch, for example), visualize that pattern (B♭ major triad in *Area 3* ascending, for example). "Air-guitar it" (meaning finger it on an imaginary fretboard) and hear the quality of the sounds inside your mind (hum it if you like, no perfect pitch required, any key will do).

When you're done, do a short but meaningful celebration. This can be a happy smile, saying (internally or out loud) "Well done!" or "I did it!" and feel a positive emotion.

These mental exercises may seem trivial or unusual to you, but with my students, such short bursts of mental training have proven highly effective. They "restart the engine," keep your mind primed, and continually engage you with the material. These activities take less than a few seconds but can have more impact than a long, mindless practice session.

- If you think about these shapes several times during the day, the learning effect is multiplied, and you will commit the materials to long-term memory better and faster.

- Your mind, your whole being, gets the message that this is important to you and that you want to remember it.

- Mental practicing, in general, reinforces any physical practicing you do by focusing purely on the mental representation you have of the exercises.

- Celebrating (i.e., creating a good feeling*!) right after helps reinforce the activity and creates a habit. Don't skip it!

- For a week, keep the pattern and key the same. Change the direction, area, or the key once you get the hang of this exercise.

Think of transcending the bass fretboard like experiencing a hologram. It will reveal itself in fragments, from various angles — not consistently at first, but increasingly so — the more you practice. Eventually, all the pieces link together to form a cohesive internal map of every aspect of the fretboard.

---

* To learn more about the power of the celebration, see my recommendation for BJ Fogg's work in the appendix.

Scalar Studies

Pentatonic Scales — Groups of Threes and Fours

Pentatonic scales sound great played as groups of threes or fours. Essentially you follow the same prescription as the three and four-note groupings you did with the *five major scale patterns*, just that we have fewer notes here!

To get started, pick a few sample keys and practice them thoroughly, making sure you hit all five shapes! When you have made good progress, include more and more keys.

VIDEO 102

B♭ Major, G minor, Groups of Four

Area 1, Pattern VI, "Upside-Down Boot"

Area 2, Pattern I, "The Hexagon"

Area 3, Pattern II, "The Boot"

Area 4, Pattern III, "Big Box-Little Box"

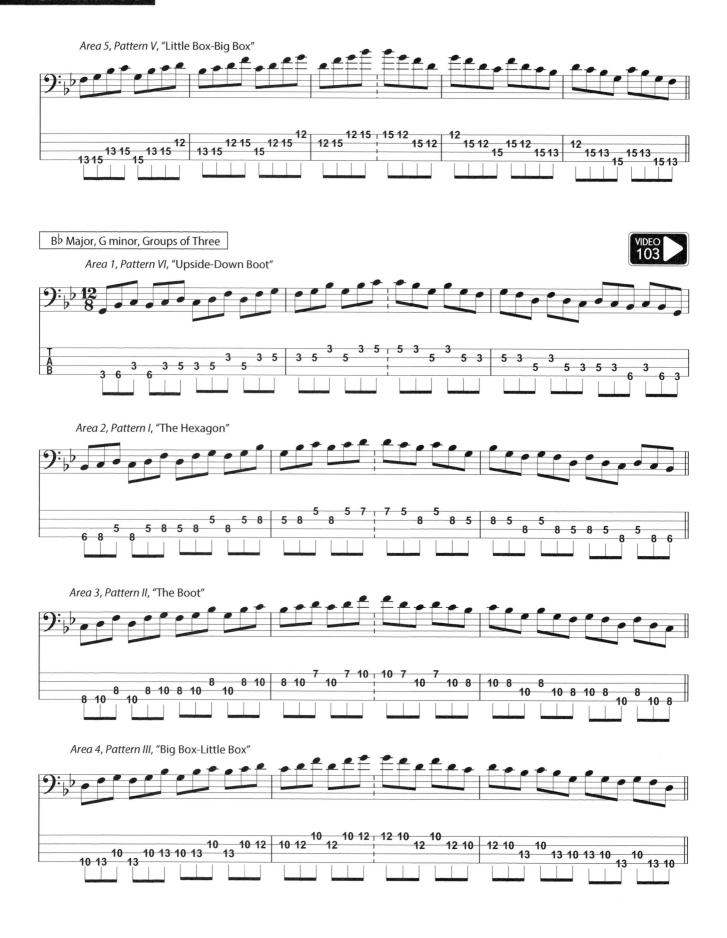

Area 5, Pattern V, "Little Box-Big Box"

Bb Major, G minor, Groups of Three

VIDEO 103

Area 1, Pattern VI, "Upside-Down Boot"

Area 2, Pattern I, "The Hexagon"

Area 3, Pattern II, "The Boot"

Area 4, Pattern III, "Big Box-Little Box"

Area 5, Pattern V, "Little Box-Big Box"

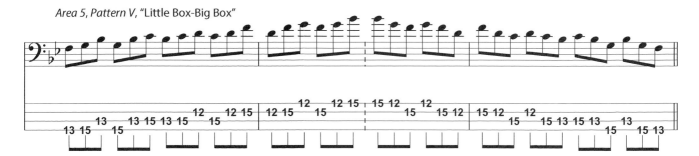

PRACTICE TIP: You can, of course, also turn the direction around — I wrote them out in the ascending/up and descending/down versions. And you could apply all the variations we applied to the scales. Some variations are more challenging to play, but all are equally musically valuable.

See the additional resources section for more info.

Make sure to stay cool and reward yourself when you have mastered the pentatonics in groups of threes.

**Hard to lick between the beats…
but well deserved, Skippy!**

Improvised Explorations

Groove and Fill Improvisation with Pentatonics

Let's again turn to the power of groove improvisation to make the shapes stick.

Two bar version:

One entire bar of *groove,* and an entire bar of *fill*.

One bar version:

The bar consists of a 2-beat groove *kernel* and a 2-beat *fill*.

Your assignment for the groove:

Keep a consistent rhythm. Start the groove with the root and then use notes from the pentatonic scale. Play the groove in the *Open Area*.

Your assignment for the fill:

Use notes of the pentatonic scale, *using a different area each time.*

This will make you move all over the fretboard and cement your knowledge of the patterns.

TIP: Before you start, map out (in your mind or on paper) — the five shapes all over the fretboard.

Ideally, you will see the shapes in your mind's eye. If not, map them out on pattern paper. Once you start moving all over the fretboard, aim for seeing the target notes of the next shape before you actually move your hand!

Example: D major pentatonic

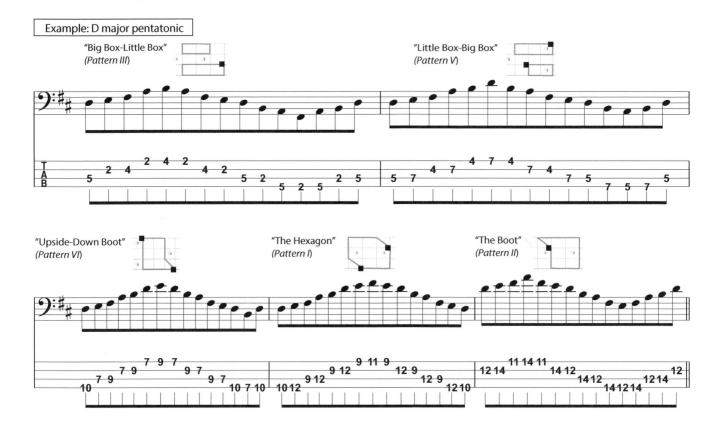

As step one, use a simple rhythm, play the groove, then the entire shape in order as a fill.

You can start the shape on its root, or on any other note. The groove must always be tonic-centered.

VIDEO 104

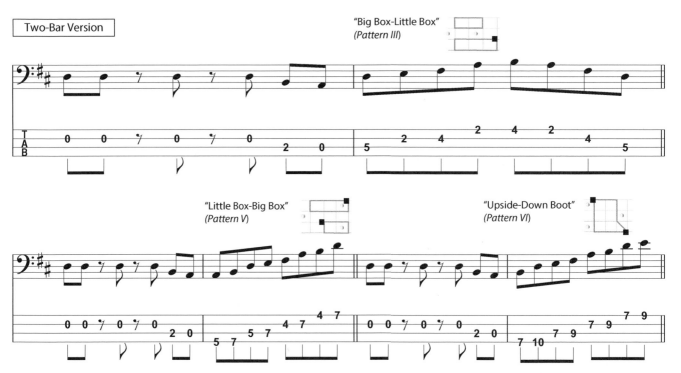

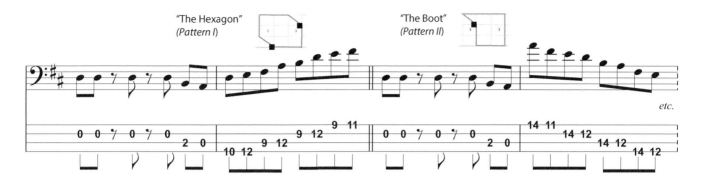

As you get more comfortable with the shapes and moving up and down the fretboard, aim to expand on your ideas. Use repetitions, only two strings at a time, scalar fragments, and jumps. Also, experiment with sliding into the shapes — it sounds very cool. Take note of the cool lines you discover. Write them out or record them and practice them in all the keys.

If you want to step it up a notch, try the one-bar version.

Here is an example using the one-bar "Groove and Fill" format.

VIDEO
105 ▶

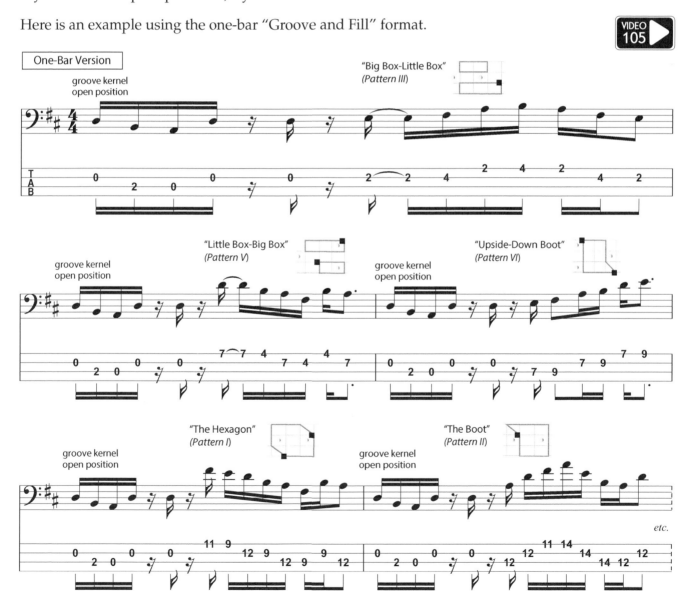

Enjoy the flexibility this exercise gives you.

TEST YOUR UNDERSTANDING #11

1. Which of the following statements are true? Pentatonic scales are *Shapes within Shapes* — they are essentially patterns located inside the five main scale patterns:

   ❏ a. This is true for only the major pentatonic scales since the scalar patterns are based on only the major scales.

   ❏ b. This is true for major and minor pentatonic scales.

2. True or False: The major and minor pentatonic scales contain the exact same notes but feature a different starting note.   ❏ True   ❏ False

3. True or False: The major and minor blues scales contain the exact same notes but feature a different starting note.   ❏ True   ❏ False

4. The major blues scale contains the following blue note(s):

   ❏ a. ♭3 and ♭5

   ❏ b. ♭5 and ♭7

   ❏ c. ♭3

   ❏ d. ♭5

5. The blues scale is…

   ❏ a. The minor pentatonic plus the ♭3

   ❏ b. The minor pentatonic plus the ♭5

   ❏ c. The minor pentatonic plus the ♭7

6. True or False: You can use the minor blues scale of the tonic (I chord) to improvise over an entire I7–IV7–V7 blues.   ❏ True   ❏ False

7. True or False. You can use the major blues scale to improvise over a I7, IV7, V7 blues, but you have to change the blues scale tonic with the changes.   ❏ True   ❏ False

8. Which of the following statements are correct?
   When…

   ❏ a. grooving on a major blues, it is a good starting point to play the major third over the chord changes.

   ❏ b. soloing you can just play the blues scale of the tonic over the entire 12-bar form.

   ❏ c. playing a fill during a major blues, using the minor blues scale sounds style appropriate.

   ❏ d. None of the above.

   ❏ e. All of the above.

9. True or False: It sounds good to play a ♭3 over a dominant 7 chord, but it does not generally sound good to play a major third over a minor 7 chord.   ❏ True   ❏ False

BLUEPRINT FOR PRACTICE #11

Written Assignment: Fill in the *Open Area Pentatonic Scales Map* **pp. 261–263**
Fill in the *Pentatonic Scales Area Maps* **pp. 268–273**
Various Pentatonic *Shapes Within Shapes* **pp. 276–281**

1. **Pentatonic PP:** Major Pentatonic scales through the cycle to the left, *Connection Exercises* 8 beats, *Areas 3* and *4* **p. 274** • **Video 95**

2. **Pentatonic PP:** Minor Pentatonic scales through the cycle to the left, *Connection Exercises* 8 beats, *Areas 1* and *2* **p. 274** • **Video 95**

3. **Pentatonic SS:** Pick a key and practice pentatonic scales in groups of threes and fours as described on **pp. 289–291** • **Videos 102 and 103**

4. **IE:** Groove over a blues using blues scales and pentatonics **p. 285** • **Video 99**

5. **IE:** Pick a key, a chord progression, and an area and improvise using pentatonics staying within a major scale shape **p. 282** • **Video 97**

6. **IE:** *Groove and Fill* Improvisation with pentatonics **pp. 291–294** • **Videos 104 and 105**

7. **Diagonal playing:** Pick a key and play pentatonics across the fret board **pp. 286–287** • **Video**

From Previous Chapters:

8. **PP:** *Up/down* variations, then *Connection Exercises*, 8 beats, *Area 3* and *4*, sequence of minor seconds to the right and left; say scale degrees/note names/nothing

9. **Triad PP:** Major Triads on tonic through the cycle to the left and right, *Area 4*; *Up/down* variations, then *Connection Exercises* (experiment with number of beats other than 8) **p. 193** • **Video 59**

10. **Triad PP:** Minor Triads on the minor tonic through the cycle in minor to the left and right, *Area 3*; *Up/down* variations, then *Connection Exercises* (experiment with number of beats other than 8) **p. 193** • **Video 59**

11. **Triad PP:** Diminished Triads as the seventh scale degree of the major scale through the cycle (think the major scale) to the left and right, *Area 2*; *Up/down* variations, then *Connection Exercises* (experiment with number of beats other than 8)

12. **SS:** Interval studies in fifths; various combinations as shown in *Chapter 6; Area 3*; practice several keys (suggesting G♭ and E) **pp. 142–148** • **Videos 47 to 52**

13. **IE:** Diatonic Cycle Practice and Improvisation of *Chapter 10*; suggesting *Area 1*, keys of F major and F minor; major: **pp. 248–249** • **Video 86C** and **pp. 249** • **Video 86D**
minor: **p. 251** • **Video 87C and 87D**

12 Beautiful Practice

INTRODUCTION

In this final chapter, you are rewarded for all your hard work with a particularly beautiful practice piece. I will show you one of my favorite exercises that combine the practice of:

- The diatonic cycle
- *The Pattern System*
- *Shapes Within Shapes*
- Open triad voicings
- Inversions of triads

I call it *"Beautiful Practice"* because it sounds like a sequence straight out of a piece by JS Bach.

Before we get there, here are a few more exercises to deepen your knowledge of the pentatonic scales from *Chapter 11*, as well as instruction for diagonal playing across the whole fretboard.

Scalar Studies

Pentatonic Scale Drills

First, let's start with a few scalar drills with pentatonics.

In this exercise, stick to only notes of the pentatonic scale, but do it in this fashion:

Play a note of the scale — skip one note — play next note — then return to the note you just skipped.

This is the equivalent of playing thirds through the major scale. With pentatonics, this turns out to be either thirds or fourths.

Here is an example in the D major/B minor Pentatonic. I wrote it out for you in all of its five shapes:

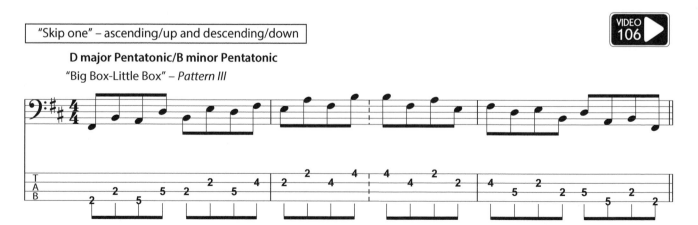

"Skip one" – ascending/up and descending/down

VIDEO 106

D major Pentatonic/B minor Pentatonic
"Big Box-Little Box" – Pattern III

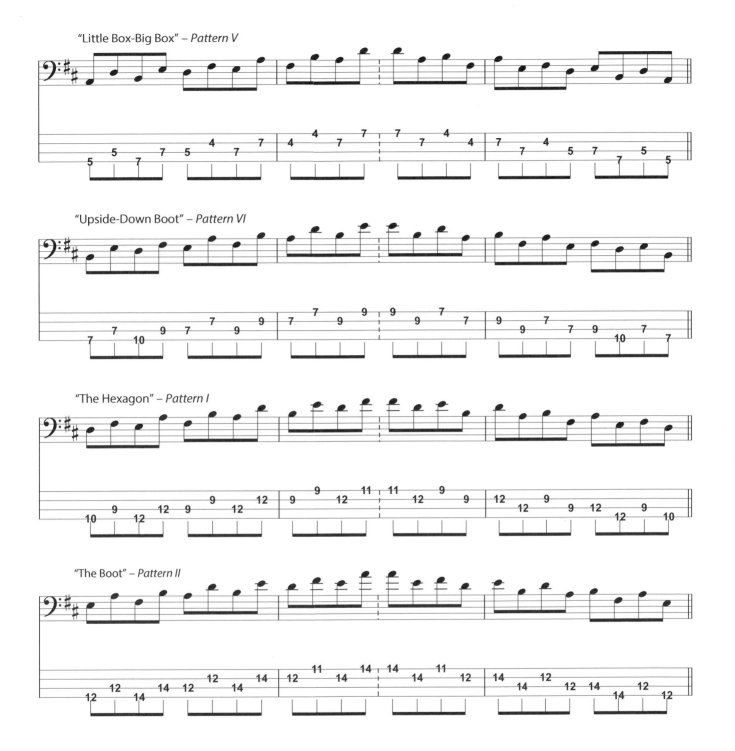

Practice LIKE THIS

Pick a key (major or minor) and find the five pentatonic shapes all across the fretboard.

Then play the above exercise in all areas.

As you are becoming more familiar with the pentatonic shapes, experiment with variations of the above, for example:

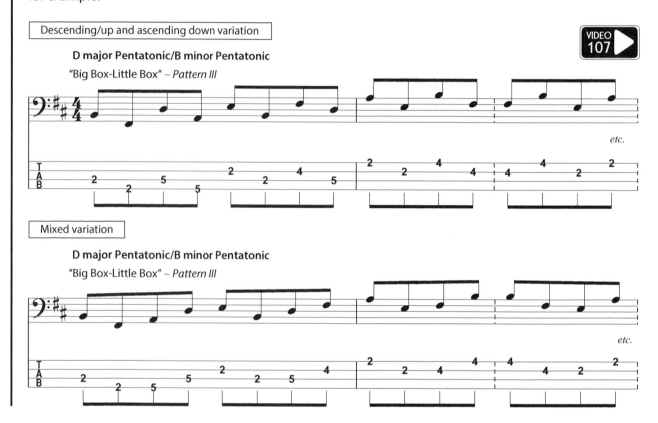

Descending/up and ascending down variation

D major Pentatonic/B minor Pentatonic

"Big Box-Little Box" – *Pattern III*

Mixed variation

D major Pentatonic/B minor Pentatonic

"Big Box-Little Box" – *Pattern III*

Creative Tip:

To make pentatonic scales sound smooth and driving, use sections out of the scale and avoid too many jumps in a row.

For a more angular effect, play lots of jumps and cross over strings.

This works for grooves, fills and solos.

MORE ON DIAGONAL PLAYING

To further develop covering a wide range of notes, I'd like to show you a few ways of connecting the five major scale shapes across the neck. Just like with the pentatonic scales, I refer to this as "playing diagonally."

You can be quite systematic about this project.

For starters, you can aim for shifting on each string between two patterns. In my examples below, I chose *Pattern I* and *Pattern III*. Then I make the shift on every single string. Make sure to visualize both the starting pattern and the one you are headed to and play the correct fingering for that pattern!

TIP: If you have practiced your *Pattern System* well, this is now very easy to do. Especially if you heeded my advice on visualizing the patterns on the fretboard, this will be very accessible.

My example is in the key of G. I am visualizing *Patterns I* and *III* on the fretboard, like this:

Starting point to connect Patterns I and III

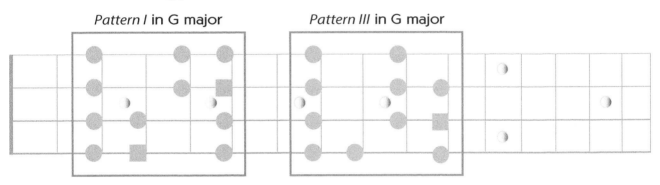

Pattern I in G major   *Pattern III* in G major

Now I combine the two patterns by starting with *Pattern I* and continuing on to *Pattern III* seamlessly. The switch from one pattern to the next can occur on any of the four strings. I demonstrate all four options below.

Switch on E-string

VIDEO 108

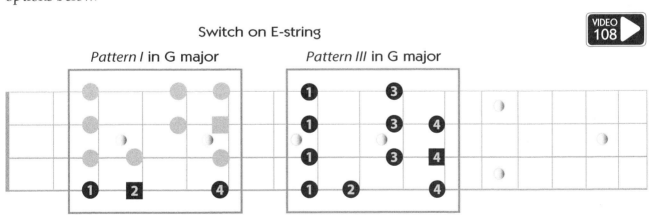

Pattern I in G major   *Pattern III* in G major

Switch on A-string

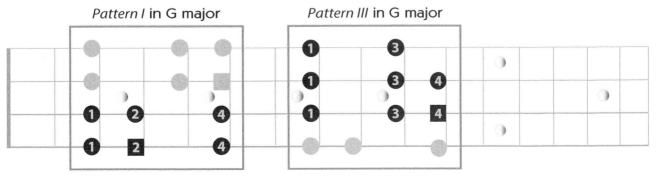

Pattern I in G major   *Pattern III* in G major

Switch on D-string

Pattern I in G major   *Pattern III* in G major

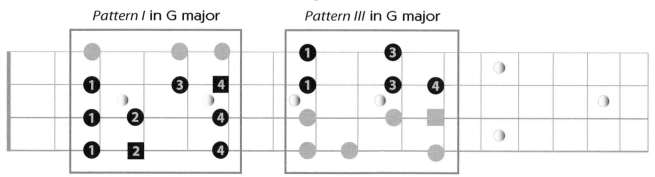

Switch on G-string

Pattern I in G major   *Pattern III* in G major

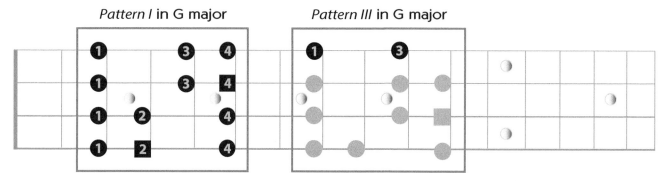

 **TIP:** Play the above examples ascending and descending. Descend the same way that you ascended.

As a variation, mix things up: ascend on the G-string and descend on the E-string, for example! Or ascend on the A-string and descend on the D-string. All work! Use the correct fingering of the pattern. These are excellent exercises to do without looking at the fretboard. While sight-reading music, having this skill allows you to keep your eyes on the score — not on the fretboard.

FAQ   When I groove, play basslines and improvise, do I need to be aware of which *Pattern* or *Area* I am in?

No! Absolutely not! Nobody will ever quiz you on the name of the pattern or area when you are on stage. In the heat of the moment — just play, relax into how all notes of a scale light up in your mind as you sense the repeating shapes under your fingers. What counts is that learning *The Pattern System* has placed all this information at your fingertips so that you can actually forget about all this and focus on the music. In other words, you know it all so well that recalling it is instantaneous and requires no mental effort. Unconscious Competence. That's true fretboard freedom!

Improvised Explorations
"Beautiful Practice" in Major

Congratulations! You have come to the grand finale! I call this exercise *"Beautiful Practice"* for a reason. Do it in major and minor (see further down) and in as many keys as possible. If you can do this on the fly in all keys — excellent work!

This is the premise:

1 → You step through the entire diatonic cycle in triads: (numbers are chords on scale degrees)
   1 4 7 3 6 2 5 1

2 → When playing chords, the way each individual note progresses to the next has distinct effects. This is generally called "voice leading."

If you always start the chord with the root, you create a lot of jumps, parallel fifths and octaves.

The example below demonstrating this sounds a bit disjointed and aimless:

A smoother way of connecting chords is to aim for smooth "voice leading."

In voice leading, the individual lines of the harmony move smoothly between the chords. One way to make the chord progression sound smoother is to use triad inversions so that voices don't jump too much and common notes can be held over or be represented in a different voice of the chord. This can be beautifully achieved by playing chord inversions:

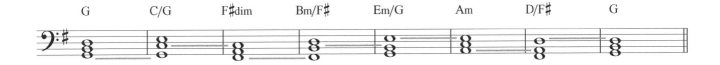

Holding over common tones makes for a smoother and more refined sound.

Above I marked out the notes that stay the same between the chords with a line. Voices that stay the same are not consistent between chords in my example, but for our specific purposes here, this will work just fine, and it's needed so I can fit the notes smoothly inside an area on the fretboard. In other scenarios – such as when arranging for a horn section where each individual horn carries a voice – you may have different priorities.

3 → On the bass, chords in closed voicings and in a low range, can sound very muddy. To avoid the mud, you can, of course, arpeggiate the notes, which is what bassists typically do when creating basslines from chord notes. I wrote 1, 3, 5 underneath the notes to show the root third and fifth of the triad:

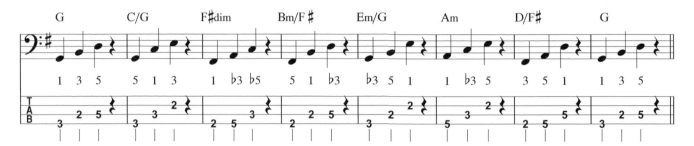

4 → To further add excitement to the sound, I will now use "open voicings." "Open voicing" means that a chord tone could fit between two of the chord tones. In other words, I **play a chord tone — then skip one — play the next chord tone — skip another — play the last one:**

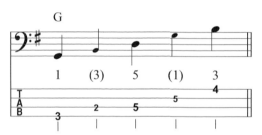

Practically speaking, I am taking the second note of each of the arpeggios above, place it up the octave and then move it in "third place" (on beat 3):

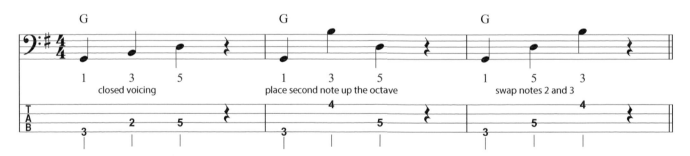

Doing this for the entire sequence, you get:

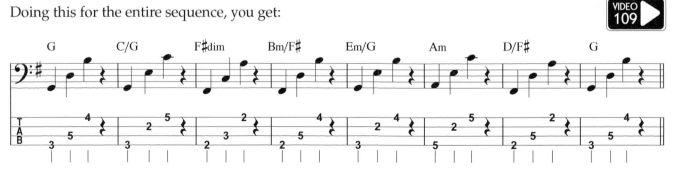

5 → The last step is to take this through all five shapes of the pattern system. The above sequence just so happened to fit beautifully into *Pattern I* in its entirety. This will not always be possible as these spread-out voicings reach across areas at times. When in doubt, go for the higher option. This is the result for all chords in all areas:

Wrap your mind around the sequence first. Once you have a handle on it, you can eliminate the rest on beat 4 and place a note there. A few great-sounding options:

1. **Repeat the first note of the measure:**

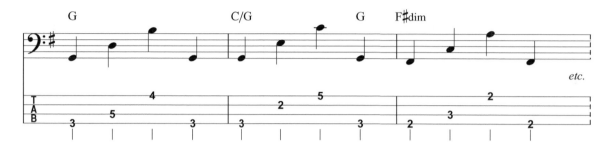

2. **Repeat the second note of the measure:**

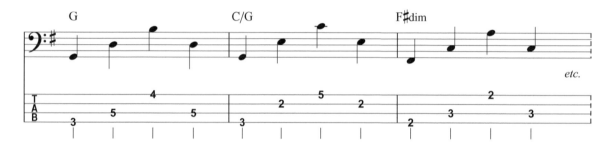

3. **Repeat the third note of the measure — sounds good when it has some tempo to it:**

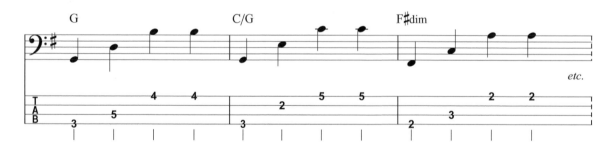

4. **Play the root of the chord (great thinking exercise!):**

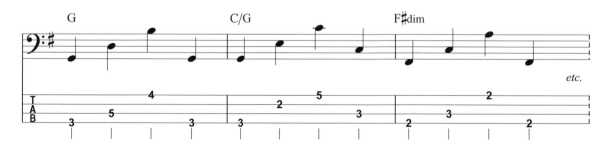

5. **Play a diatonic approach note to the next downbeat from above or below:**

On the topic of approach notes, you can also give chromatic approaches a try, but your mileage will vary as to how pleasing this sounds.

6. **Add the diatonic seventh somewhere inside the pattern (another great thinking exercise):**

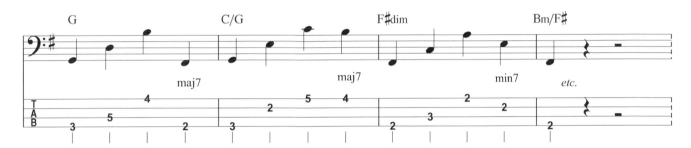

Doing this exercise with a delay pedal using the hocket delay setting is a great sounding variation. If you'd like to learn more on how to do this, request your free tutorial video on the hocket delay here: *ArisBassBlog.com/Hocket*

What other ideas can you come up with?

In our additional offerings, we do several more variations of this exercise, leading to beautiful and surprising results.

Practice
LIKE THIS

> The goal for this exercise is to first learn it in the key of G. Then see if you can recreate it — ideally on the fly — in other keys in all Areas. Remember to always skip a chord tone between notes, to go *Area* by *Area*, and to play only diatonic triad notes! It is a great exercise, not only musically, but also technically!

"Beautiful Practice" in Minor

Essentially the minor version of *Beautiful Practice* is identical to major, but now the central note is the root of the relative minor key — the sixth of the major scale. In addition — as often done in minor keys — the V chord is made major to account for the lack of a leading tone in minor (in the key of G minor, for example, you change the F in D minor to an F♯ to make it D major).

I have written out *Beautiful Practice* in G minor below.

As per *The Pattern System*, your guiding patterns come from the B♭ major scale (relative major of G minor).

Enjoy!

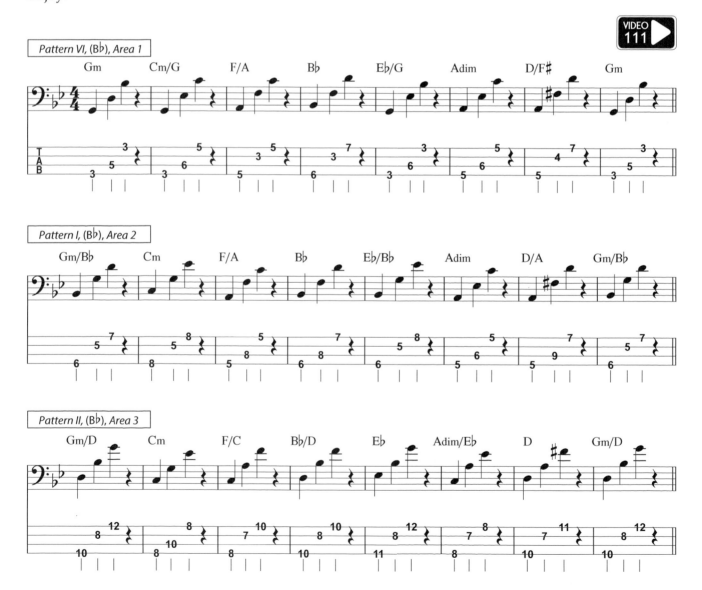

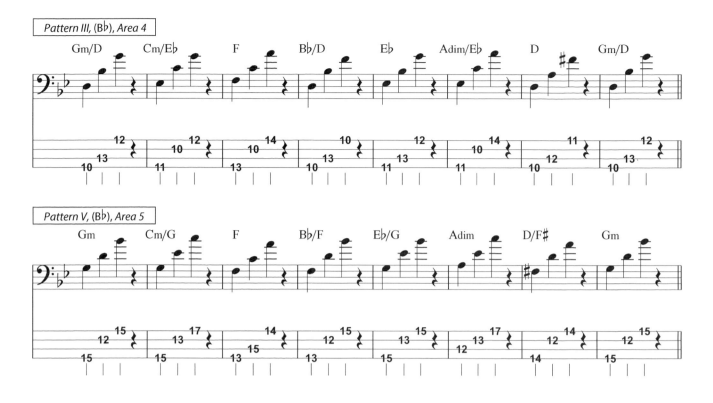

Pattern III, (B♭), Area 4

Pattern V, (B♭), Area 5

TEST YOUR UNDERSTANDING #12

1. True or false? When using pentatonics for fills and grooves, playing a lot of jumps is bad.

   ❑ True – Use them in order only   ❑ False – It depends on the situation

2. The idea of this system is that I should always be focused on the name of the pattern that I am playing.

   ❑ a. Yes, absolutely. Otherwise all this work here would be wasted.

   ❑ b. No. The goal of this method is to provide a systematic approach to learning this information so you know it so well that recalling the information becomes automatic.

   ❑ c. Yes, I think that's useful, and it also helps me to communicate with my bandmates.

3. How many major pentatonic scales are contained in each key?

   ❑ a. Is this a trick question? There is only one, starting on the tonic.

   ❑ b. Three, and they correspond with the three major triads.

   ❑ c. You can play a major pentatonic scale from each note of the key, except for the 7th scale degree because that is diminished.

4. Pentatonic scales are useful for:

□   a.   Grooves like the classic Rock'n Roll walking line only

□   b.   Fills only. Grooves are best based on triads.

□   c.   Solos, because it's easy to play fast licks using pentatonics

□   d.   They sound great for grooves, solos, fills, melodies and more.

5. When shifting between patterns:

□   a.   Always make sure to only shift to the adjacent pattern. It's the only way!

□   b.   It's often useful to skip one pattern because you can quickly extend the playing range with just one left-hand shift.

□   c.   Don't think about it too much, just do it.

6 Voice leading means:

□   a.   You are the leader of your section, like the rhythm section or the horn section

□   b.   That you are the one giving interviews for the band

□   c.   How the notes in a chord progression move from one chord to the next

7. Why is it useful to play open voicings on the bass?

□   a.   Because it opens your mind to new possibilities

□   b.   It sounds good because it avoids potential muddiness in the lower register.

□   c.   Because they involve open strings

8. Open voicing means:

□   a.   At least one note of the chord/triad can fit in the space between each note of the voicing

□   b.   A chord using an open string

□   c.   A voicing that is open to whether it's a major or minor chord

BLUEPRINT FOR PRACTICE #12

1. **Pentatonic SS:** Pick a key and practice pentatonic scale drills as described on
    pp. 298–300 · Videos 106 and 107

2. **Diagonal playing:** Pick a key and play pentatonics across the fretboard   **pp. 301–302 · Video 108**

3. **Beautiful Practice** in major and minor: start by reading the written out examples in G major and
    G minor respectively. Then, venture into other keys as described on **p. 307**

From Previous Chapters:

4. **PP:** *Up/down* variations, then *Connection Exercises*, 8 beats, *Open Area* and *Area 5*, sequence of tritones;
    say scale degrees/note names/nothing

5. **Pentatonic PP:** Major Pentatonic scales through the cycle of major seconds, *Connection Exercises*,
    8 beats, *Areas 1* and *2*   **p. 274 · Video 95**

6. **Pentatonic PP:** Minor Pentatonic scales through the cycle of major seconds, aeolian minor tonic,
    Connection Exercises, 8 beats, *Areas 4* and *5*   **p. 274 · Video 95**

7. **Triad PP:** Major Triads on the tonic through the cycle to the left and right, *Area 5; up/down* variations,
    then *Connection Exercises* (experiment with number of beats other than 8)   **p. 193 · Video 59**

8. **Triad PP:** Minor Triads on the minor tonic through the cycle in minor to the left and right,
    Area 5; up/down variations, then *Connection Exercises* (experiment with number of beats other than 8)
    p. 193 · Video 59

9. **Triad PP:** Diminished Triads as the seventh scale degree of the major scale through the cycle
    (think the major scale) to the left and right, *Area 5; up/down* variations, then *Connection Exercises*
    (experiment with number of beats other than 8)

10. **SS:** Interval studies in fifths; various combinations as shown in *Chapter 6; Areas 1* and *5*;
    practice several keys (suggesting G and D♭)   **pp. 142–148 · Videos 47 to 52**

11. **IE:** Diatonic Cycle Practice and Improvisation of *Chapter 10;* suggesting *Area 3*,
    keys of G major and G minor;
    major: **pp. 248–249 · Video 86C** and **p. 249 · Video 86D**
    minor: **p. 251 · Videos 87C** and **87D**

12. **Pentatonic PP:** Major Pentatonic scales through the cycle to the left, *Connection Exercises,* 8 beats,
    Area 1 and *5*   **p. 274 · Video 95**

13. **Pentatonic PP:** Minor Pentatonic scales through the cycle to the left, *Connection Exercises,* 8 beats,
    Open Area   **p. 274 · Video 95**

OUTRO

Congratulations!

Finishing a book is always a great feeling, and you deserve a big congrats! If you followed along as suggested, you are well on your way to reaping the rewards of your hard work. You have entered a new bigger world, and new musical adventures await. But for now — break out the champagne! Enjoy the moment!

What is next?

Would you like to go through this material and far beyond, with many musical applications and additional guidance? Check out our additional resources page to join our guided courses and practice groups, and find out about many more resources at *ArisBassBlog.com/PatternSystem*! I look forward to seeing you there!

Easy there, Skippy!
(Don't drink and groove!)

APPENDIX

RESOURCES AND LINKS

A Small Selection of My Favorite Books or Books Referenced in the Text

Indirect Procedures: A Musician's Guide to the Alexander Technique by Pedro de Alcantara

Ear Training: A Technique for Listening by Bruce Benward and Timothy Kolosick

Melodia – A Course in Sight Singing Composers by Samuel W. Cole and Leo R. Lewis

Flow: The Psychology of Optimal Experience by Mihaly Csikszentmihalyi

The Power of Habit by Charles Duhigg

Tiny Habits – The Small Changes that Change Everything by BJ Fogg

What Got You Here Won't Get You There: How Successful People Become Even More Successful by Marshall Goldsmith and Mark Reiter

The Inner Game of Music by Timothy Gallwey and Barry Green

ETunes by Rod Taylor

The Bassist's Guide to Injury Management, Prevention and Better Health Volume One

The Bassist's Guide to Injury Management, Prevention and Better Health Volume Two by Dr. Randy Kertz, DC

The Improvisor's Bass Method by Chuck Sher

The Music Lesson – A Spiritual Journey for Growth Through Music by Victor L. Wooten

Ear Training

Ear Confidence – Six Paths to Fearless Ears: *ArisBassBlog.com/EarTraining-Course*

EarMaster *www.earmaster.com*

Functional Ear Training *www.miles.be*

Meludia app for the smartphone

Transcribe! *ArisBassBlog.com/Transcribe/*

Notation Software

musescore.com (free)

Dorico by Steinberg

Further Resources

Dr. Noa Kageyama's excellent performance psychology courses (and newsletter!) *www.bulletproofmusician.com*

Bass Nature Camp with Victor Wooten and others *www.vixcamps.com*

Online bass instruction, including by the author *www.truefire.com*

List of song beginnings for interval recognition *www.earmasters.com/products/freetool/interval-song-chart-generator.html*

Courses in Jazz Orff (Orff Schulwerk)
Doug Goodkin
www.douggoodkin.com

Gear and Endorsements

Marleaux Bass Guitars*
www.marleaux-bass.de

Fibenare Basses Hungary*
www.fibenare-guitars.org

Accessories*
www.gruvgear.com

TC Electronic
www.tcelectronic.com

Dean Markley Strings
www.deanmarkley.com

BeatBuddy, Aeros Looper*
www.singularsound.com

Cables*
www.tsunamicables.com

Back Beat*
www.getbackbeat.com

Also by the Author

Music Theory Resources

The Book: *Music Theory for the Bass Player – A Comprehensive and Hands-on Guide to Playing with More Confidence and Freedom: www.ArisBassBlog.com/music-theory-for-the-bass-player/*

The Course: *www.ArisBassBlog.com/coaching-course*

The Cohort (Guided Version of the Course): *www.ArisBassBlog.com/cohort/*

The Music Theory Wallchart: *www.ArisBassBlog.com/music-theory-wall-chart/*

Core Principles — A Foundational Music Theory Course for Bass Players
www.ArisBassBlog.com/core-principles

Ear Confidence — Six Paths to Fearless Ears: *www.ArisBassBlog.com/eartraining-course*

Pattern System Resources

Please visit *www.ArisBassBlog.com/PatternSystem* to find resources for *The Pattern System:* courses, teacher resources and more

Skippy Swag, Stickers, T-Shirts and More

www.shop.arisbassblog.com/

---

* Author is official endorser

Other Topics

www.ArisBassBlog.com/truefire

- Pentatonic Playground for Bass
- Bass Thrills and Fills
- Bass Groove Creation Station

Contributor

notreble.com/lessons/talking-technique/
scottsbasslessons.com

Authors' Websites

ArianeCap.com
WolfTrackAudio.com

Author's Blog

ArisBassBlog.com

To access a multitude of additional resources to support you in the study of
The Pattern System, please scan the above code or go to:
ArisBassBlog.com/PatternSystem

ANSWERS TO QUESTIONS IN TEXT

Good Luck with your answers!

Answers to various Questions in the Chapters (For all area diagrams, please access the videos included with this book)

Chapter 7

Area 1	Area 2	Area 3	Area 4	Area 5
I	II	III	V	VI
II	III	V	VI	I
III	V	VI	I	II
V	VI	I	II	III
VI	I	II	III	V

Chapter 10

I–IV–V–I tunes – find the three slices out of the diatonic cycle:

1. I → IV
2. V → I
3. V → I → IV

ANSWERS TO THE TEST YOUR UNDERSTANDING QUESTIONS

TEST YOUR UNDERSTANDING #1

The Open Area

1. No. In *The Pattern System*, we always go from the lowest possible note to the highest possible note in the given area.
2. No. Same rationale as above —we always start from the lowest possible note and end on the highest possible note in an area.
3. The *Open Area* includes fret zero (the open strings) and the first four frets, so it encompasses frets 0 to 4
4. Because the scale lengths are different, the danger is that your intonation will suffer when you move from one bass to the other. I recommend reserving such bass switching for advanced players.
5. a. F major: Bb   (3rd finger – G-string 3rd fret)
   b. Bb major: Bb   (3rd finger – G-string 3rd fret)
   c. Eb major: Bb   (3rd finger – G-string 3rd fret)
   d. Ab major: Bb   (3rd finger – G-string 3rd fret)
   e. D major: B   (4th finger – G-string 4th fret)

TEST YOUR UNDERSTANDING #2

The Five Scale Patterns

1. Highest note: G (4th finger – G-string 12th fret) *Pattern V* always starts on the fifth note of the major scale, so the lowest note is D (2nd finger – E-string 10th fret)
2. Highest note: E (3rd finger – G-string 9th fret) Lowest: *Pattern III* always starts on the third of the major scale, so the lowest note is B (1st finger E-string 7th fret)
3. Lowest/Highest note: E /A. Fingers: 1st finger – E-string 12th fret /4th finger – G-string 14th fret
4. Highest/Lowest note: D/A. Fingers: 4th finger – G-string 7th fret / 1st finger – E-string 5th fret
5. Both are equally important. Knowing the shape will help you to instantly know all the notes of a key and to move effortlessly across the fretboard. Knowing where the tonic is will allow you to relate the pattern to any key you are playing in and will show you the relation of each note to the central note of the key.
6. False: *Patterns I, V,* and *VI* contain the tonic twice. *Patterns II* and *III* only have the tonic once.
7. Each pattern derives its name from their lowest note in relation to the tonic of the major scale. The one exception is *Pattern I*, which starts on the seventh note of the scale.
8. False: *Patterns II* and *VI* cover 5 frets and use a special shift called "the crab" to facilitate optimal fingerings for these patterns.
9. "The crab" is a one-fret shift of the left hand used in some of the scale patterns. The way the hand moves sideways reminds me of a "crab." It is a useful mnemonic and is an elegant way to shift by one fret without losing your place.
10. False: Each pattern goes from the lowest to the highest note of the key in a given area. Said differently, with one exception, there is always a lower or higher note than the tonic in any of the five patterns. The one exception is *Pattern V* where the highest note is also the tonic.
11. There are five major scale patterns (*Patterns I, II, III, V, VI*). Additionally, in the *Open Area*, every key has its own pattern (with Gb and Db already being covered by the major scale patterns, so ten more). However, in a different sense, there is a near-infinite number of patterns in music comprising many possible elements, not just scales.
12. Three (3)
13. True: There are six areas (*Open, 1-5*) and five patterns (*I, II, III, V, VI*), or counting the unique *Open Area* patterns, 10 additional *Open Area* patterns for 15 total.
14. False: The tonic of a major key is always played with either the 2nd (middle) finger or the 4th finger.
15. True: *Pattern I*, also known as the *Root Pattern*, does indeed start on the seventh degree. However, the name *Root Pattern* or *Pattern I* is what "stuck" over time.

TEST YOUR UNDERSTANDING #3

The Five Areas

1. Answer **c.** This is the safest method since it allows for only one solution. Remember, the lowest note will be the name of the pattern and will help you identify the pattern. A) works only if you already know the exact boundaries (lowest and highest fret) of that area, which is not something I think you should have to learn by heart. Therefore, I consider it a less reliable method. That said, in live playing situations, use whichever method is quicker in the moment. When performing, what counts is finding the notes in time, not whether you name the area or pattern correctly.
2. F#/Gb, Db/C# (B/Cb contains the open E/Fb, so technically, it does not belong in this group)
3. False: Minor seconds (or their inversion, major sevenths) also hit every single key.
4. Answer **e.** All of the above. The Cycle of Fifths contains every key, is sequential, and is a great way to name and organize the keys.
5. Answer **d.** All of the above.

6. An area is the smallest region on the fretboard that fits all keys represented by one of the five patterns. An area on the bass comprises the span of six or seven frets with the exception of the *Open Area,* which spans the open strings and 4 frets.

7. A "pattern" is a distinctive shape that outlines a common music theory shape on the fretboard, typically a scale, chord, or chord progression.

8. *Pattern IV* would be *Pattern III* minus one note, the third. This means it is contained in *Pattern III.*

TEST YOUR UNDERSTANDING #4

Area 2

1. *Pattern III*
2. *Pattern V*
3. *Pattern III*
4. *Pattern III*
5. *Pattern III*

6. *Pattern II*
7. *Pattern II*
8. *Pattern II*
9. *Pattern II*
10. *Pattern II*

11. *Pattern I*
12. *Pattern I*
13. *Pattern VI*

TEST YOUR UNDERSTANDING #5

Connection Exercises

1. Answer **a.** While the situation in actual music isn't typically exactly the same, the principle applies and being able to switch keys, scales, and chords anywhere on the fretboard is crucial to musical fluidity.

2. Answer **a.** It's a similar idea to the Solfeggio method — except that we spare you from having to learn yet another system of note naming.

3. *Pattern II*

4. *Pattern II*

5. *Pattern II*

6. B♭ G, C A♭, D♭ B♭, E♭ C, F D♭, G E♭, A♭ F, B♭ G… How to determine the correct key: Since the given sequence contains the notes B♭, A♭ and D♭, but not G♭, the resulting key has to be A♭.

7. F, F♯/G♭, G

8. A♭/G♯, A, B♭

9. False. When working something out without a steady tempo, turn the metronome off. Turn it back on at a slower tempo when you are ready to use it again.

TEST YOUR UNDERSTANDING #6

Connection Exercises

1. C D E F♯ **A♭ B♭ C**
2. A F D♭ **A**
3. D F A♭ **B D**
4. F♯ D B♭ **F♯**
5. Three (3) and each round starts a half note higher (or lower) than the previous one
6. Two (2) and each round starts a half note higher (or lower) than the previous one
7. Four (4) and each round starts a half note higher (or lower) than the previous one
8. F A, G B♭, **A C, B♭ D, C E♭, D F, E♭ G, F A, G B♭**—The key is B♭ major.
9. **E A, F♯ B, G♯ C♯, A D♯, B E, C♯ F♯, D♯ G♯, E A, F♯ B**—The key is E major.
10. E B, F♯ C♯, **G♯ D♯, A E, B F♯, C♯ G♯, D♯ A, E B**—The key is E major.

TEST YOUR UNDERSTANDING #7

Connection Exercises

1. False. You should take advantage of all of your learning channels. Use your favorite channels as a starting point and include the others from there.

2. Answer **d.** All of the above and more.

3. Answer **f.** Conceptual is the slowest. Auditory can be very fast too, but it requires the step of translating the information to the fretboard, so it isn't practical by itself when playing an instrument.

4. Answer **c.** All learning channels are important.

5. Which Pattern do you play for the following scales?
   a. G major – *Pattern III*
   b. D♭ major – *Pattern VI*
   c. F major – *Pattern V*
   d. C♯ major – *Pattern VI*
   e. E major – *Pattern V*
   f. A major – *Pattern II*

6. b) While many classical upright bass books teach scales very differently, the 5 patterns translate well and can be played easily by making small shifts where needed.

TEST YOUR UNDERSTANDING #8

Shapes within Shapes – The Major Triads

1. Five (5)
2. Answer **b.** The first, second or fourth finger. (First finger is in use for *Pattern VI* with the root on the top string! When fingering only the major triad, no crab shift is needed.)
3. Answer **d.** All of the above
4. Answer **a.** Either one or two
5. Answer **c.** I, IV, V

TEST YOUR UNDERSTANDING #9

Shapes within Shapes – The Minor Triads

1. Answer **a.** The first, third or fourth finger. (The third finger is in use for *Pattern VI*, with the root on the D string! When fingering only the minor triad, no crab shift is needed.)
2. Answer **b.** 1, 4, 5 (as seen from the minor root)
3. Answer **b.** Habits are formed by positive feelings associated with a task—not by sheer repetition.

TEST YOUR UNDERSTANDING #10

Shapes within Shapes – The Diminished Triad

1. Answer **a.** The first finger or the third finger. (The third finger is in use for *Pattern VI*, with the root on the D string! When fingering only the minor triad, no crab shift is needed.)
2. Answer **b.** The diatonic cycle
3. Any or all of the Patterns. Remember that each Pattern contains all 7 modes.
4. Answers: **a, b, d**
5. Answer **b.** Three: tonic, subdominant, dominant
6. Answer **e.** It really is this great and useful.
7. All progressions are derived from the diatonic cycle of fifths.

TEST YOUR UNDERSTANDING #11

The Pentatonic Scales

1. Answer **b.** This is true for major and minor pentatonic scales.
2. True. This is the same relationship as between a major and its relative minor scale.
3. True
4. Answer **c.** — the ♭3. The major blues scale is a major pentatonic scale with an added ♭3.
5. Answer **b.** The blues scale is the minor pentatonic plus the ♭5.
6. True. You still have to experiment with what sounds good over each chord, but it does work and has been done often.
7. True — but don't just believe it. Try it out.
8. Answer **e.** All of the above
9. True. This mostly has to do with the cultural development of blue notes and the resulting conventions of the style.

TEST YOUR UNDERSTANDING #12

1. False
2. Answer **c.**
3. Answer **b.** And their roots are on 1, 4 and 5.
4. Answer **d.** And they work in many styles. They are super useful to study deeply.
5. Answer **b.**
6. Answer **c.** While (a) can certainly happen as well, it is not the main driver.
7. Answer **a.** An open string (b) could be true, but not always. Do experiment with chords using open strings, though. This offers many possibilities. Answer (c) would be chords that do not contain a third such as sus4, sus2 or power chords.
8. Answer **a.**

Pattern System Terms

If you need a quick reference while reading

The Pattern System • In *The Pattern System*, we work with the core building blocks of music. In this volume, these include the major scales and the intervals, triads, pentatonics and chord progressions they contain. The goal is that you can execute these materials readily in every key and in every area on the bass — in short: to show you how you can achieve complete mastery of these elements. Beyond this, you will also learn how to think "music" and how the music in your mind is represented on the fretboard; you learn how to think ahead and simultaneously keep track of multiple streams of information (such as keys, chord progressions, notes of the individual chords and where to play them, all while keeping the groove steady).

Pattern/Shape • In *The Pattern System*, the term "Pattern" refers to two distinct aspects:

a) **In general terms: the patterns of music.** That can refer to any element of music that occurs as recognizable, repeating elements such as sequences of intervals (e.g., scales), chords forming chord progressions, rhythms, etc. There are a huge amount of patterns within music; therefore, we focus on a few select ones in this book.

b) **The repeated shapes that musical elements create on the fretboard.** We define a fretboard pattern — or shorter: "pattern" — as a distinctive shape that outlines a common music theory element on the fretboard, typically a scale, chord, chord progression or other sequence of notes. A (fretboard) pattern does not necessarily start and stop with the root. Rather, it is defined by the constraints of the bass, starting from the lowest possible note in that area and extending to the highest possible note in that area, hence creating a certain pattern or shape on the fretboard. Once you leave the open area, you encounter only five unique scale patterns that will deliver all scales in all areas of the bass. Within each pattern, you will find important diatonic structures (triads, pentatonics, modes). These are patterns within patterns. Learn these patterns and their inherent shapes, and you have all the core building blocks of music under your fingers.

This system narrows the fretboard possibilities of major scale patterns down to the most practical five that fit in a one-finger-per-fret shape. Extended fingering shapes are possible and applicable for speed licks and tapping applications. If you know *The Pattern System* as we teach it here, it will be easier for you to create the extended fingering patterns as well as move horizontally all over the fretboard.

A pattern is an entire scale pattern (major, minor, pentatonic) in an area. A shape can be the same, but also refer to excerpts of it, such as intervals, chords, or shapes the roots of chord progressions form within the pattern. The concept of *"Shapes within Shapes"* proves educational as well as a gigantic shortcut to allow you to perform equally well in all keys and all areas of the fretboard.

Order/Sequence • In the context of this book, the word order — AKA sequence — refers to the succession of keys or root notes that we will be practicing the patterns in. We start with the "Cycle" (or "Circle" when referring to the graphic representation) of "descending fifths" (AKA "The Circle to the left"). But we will expand this quickly and cover moving between keys by every single interval. Therefore, it is very important that you have a good handle on intervals as well as the Cycle of Fifths (to know keys and key signatures). Make sure to review these topics in *Music Theory for the Bass Player* (Chapters 3, 4 and 8).

Root/Tonic • In a diatonic context, the tonic is the central note. The note that ultimately all other notes of the piece of music relate and resolve to. Diatonic means using only notes out of a seven-note scale. In practical terms, nowadays, this also means functional-harmony-based tonal music (as opposed to atonal or modal music that does not really establish key centers). The tonic is also the first scale degree of the parent scale of a section or piece of music.

The root is the root note of a chord or a chord scale. It may or may not be the tonic (first scale degree in any given context). If we are playing a IImin–V–I, for example, each chord (IImin, V, I) has its own root. There is still only one tonic. If the tonic changes, this means that the music has modulated to a new key.

Area • The *Five Patterns* (*P I, II, III, V, VI*) naturally divide the bass into *Five Areas* on the bass. Together with the area involving the open strings — the *Open Area* — this makes for six areas total. By practicing the shapes, remember isolated pieces of information such as which key uses which pattern in a specific area. The context of the whole system will provide this information in an integrated way. The *Area Matrix* (see *Appendix*) you created in *Chapter 7* maps the patterns across the areas for each key.

Scale/Mode • In this book, we tackle the major scale and its modes. It is easy to play a scale from the root to the root because you can hear it! In this system, you learn to break free from this restrictive approach and use all the scale notes available in a given position.

Triad/Arpeggio/Chord • In the context of this system, think of them as *"Shapes within Shapes."* For music theory reference, please peruse *Music Theory for the Bass Player*.

Super short definitions:

- A chord means 3 or more notes sounding at the same time.
- Arpeggio: notes of a chord played in succession
- Triad: a chord consisting of 3 notes constructed by stacking successive thirds. In this book, we are using major, minor, and diminished triads.
- A pentatonic scale is a scale consisting of five notes. In this book, we work with major and their relative minor pentatonic scales.

Area Map • Each area has an *Area Map* — it lists the pattern for each key in that area. In this book, this typically comprises three pages of diagram paper that you fill in with the requested scales or chords.

Area Matrix • The *Area Matrix* is an overview table showing the pattern numbers for each area. Use it as a quick reference only when needed. There is no need to try to learn it by heart. You will integrate and absorb this knowledge as you go through the system. You'll find it in this book, as well as on our *Pattern System Wallchart*. Also, see "area" in this appendix.

Mental Practice • Mental practice is practice away from your instrument where you focus exclusively on the internal representations you generate. This involves all the senses — but using them internally rather than getting data from the outside world. In simpler terms: you hear, see, sense, and feel the music exclusively in your mind. This is as powerful as physical practice/music-making — and combining both modalities greatly enhances the effectiveness of each.

Musical Mind • The musical mind is how we process and invent music through the application of our mental faculties. It is also how we represent music internally, just like hearing a melody in our minds. This may sound purely intellectual, but by itself, that would be too limited. The mind is more than just intellect and includes every aspect of our being as it is linked to the physical world and (potentially) nonphysical realms. This is not at all spiritual woo-woo since one can argue every invention (including every piece of music) came about by the interaction of the mind with the physical. And, the realm of ideas, concepts, mathematics, or music theory directly interacts with the physical world and brings about inventions — music in our case — that we share with the world.

Reading the Diagrams • The lowest string on the diagram is the low E-string. Imagine you slide the diagram straight from the page under your bass. Do not reverse this (unless you are left-handed).

Legend:

- Grey numbers: fingerings
- White numbers: scale degrees relating to the square (root)
- Squares: tonic of the major scale
- Diamonds: roots of triads or modes
- Stars: blue notes in the blues scale

How did this system come about? What is its history?

The Pattern System is a combination of several distinct influences that Wolf – my husband, teacher and partner — and I explored over the years of our musical careers and that we enriched with several of our own unique contributions. All of the core materials used in this method have been well established for centuries: this includes intervals, major and minor scales, chords, diatonic harmony, note groupings, and the shapes these materials form on a fretboard tuned in perfect fourths.

What is unique about our method is how we bring these materials together and use them as the basic materials to train your musical mind. Some of the resources that inspired our learning process as it relates to *The Pattern System* are:

1 – Chuck Sher's book *The Improvisor's Bass Method*. This is where Wolf first encountered the concept of learning, practicing, and expressing musical concepts through improvisation. The book is filled with many great ideas for improvisation using all sorts of musical elements. At the time, he was overwhelmed with the possibilities and quickly noticed that he needed more basic knowledge of scales, chords, intervals, etc., in all keys and all over the fretboard.

2 – We found a very systematic approach for learning this core foundation in a system created by Peter Christel at the *Bass School Munich* where we both studied. Peter developed an excellent fretboard learning system that included the *Connection Exercises*. He is no longer teaching there, and to the best of our knowledge, the approach he used to teach it is no longer being utilized at this school (nor anywhere else we encountered).

3 – On the path of deeply learning and integrating these materials, we added further useful elements to the learning path:

- Mental practicing through visualization
- The systematic and creative use of associations and mnemonics
- Modeling skills and learning strategies from NLP (Neuro-Linguistic Programming)
- Functional Ear-training
- Behavior design and the study of habits
- Research on Sports Psychology and relating it to music
- Corporate coaching methods
- Qui Gong, meditation and yoga

We took the influences listed above, added much from our own experiences, reorganized and systematized everything quite a bit, and began sharing it with others.

Ever since I started to teach in the late '90s, I refined the approach to teaching this method with hundreds of my students. The results my students were getting were so impressive that in 2012 I decided to write a book about it to make it accessible to a wider audience. Because I wanted to be comprehensive, I wanted to include the basics of music theory as well as a concise introduction to good technique. It soon became clear that this section grew big enough to form a separate book, and I published *Music Theory for the Bass Player — A Comprehensive Guide to Playing with More Confidence and Freedom* in 2015. This book has enjoyed hundreds of positive reviews on Amazon and continues to sell thousands of copies worldwide.

The book you are holding in your hands continues where *Music Theory for the Bass Player* left off and describes *The Pattern System*. Wolf and I hope to give this fantastic method the strong attention and wide publication it deserves. We encourage every bass player with serious aspirations to go through this system. Professionals and hobbyists alike will be richly rewarded for practicing these exercises. Anyone will advance by even doing just bits and pieces of the method.

The effort you put into this system will pay off for you in multiple ways. We know this from our own experiences as well as from the hundreds of students we have taught it to. We wish you much success with *The Pattern System for the Bass Player!*

AUTHORS' BIOS

Ariane Cap is a bassist, passionate educator, self-published bestselling author, eclectic performer (electric bassist), a busy blogger and practice coach.

She is a prolific educator with a large online following. The bestselling author of *Music Theory for the Bass Player*, she created her own online teaching platform offering interactive and results-oriented courses of study that enjoy a high completion rate and a loyal following and community feel.

The founder and creator of Step Up Music Vallejo — a community music school — Ariane has taught droves of piano players and bassists as well as improvisers of a variety of instruments of all ages. Ariane has taught at Academy of Art University, the California Jazz Conservatory, the Golden Gate Bass Camp, was 10 years artist-in-residence teacher at the Wyoming Rock Camp Experience in Jackson Hole, co-taught masterclasses with Paul Hanson at the University of the Redlands, Colorado State, Montana State University and others. She was a featured performer at the London Bass and Guitar Show and has taught for Gerald Veasley's Online Bass Boot Camp.

Ariane runs popular seminars at *scottsbasslessons.com*, the web's largest music education website. She is a TrueFire educator, and her regular column on *notreble.com* called "Talking Technique" is a consistent favorite on the site.

In 2019 Ariane was one of four winners of an online *Bass Player Magazine* poll and was featured on the July 2019 cover of the magazine, dubbed "The Education Guru."

Ariane is a student of the Tiny Habits™ method, a member of Noa Kageyama's "The Bulletproof Musician," as well as an NLP Trainer with a keen interest in practicing habits and performance enhancement. She studied bass performance at The University of Vienna, Austria, the University of Miami, and the University of South Florida.

She attended several camps with Victor Wooten, Steve Bailey, and many prominent guest instructors at these camps. These mind-expanding and highly introspective experiences left a big impression on her as a musician and a person. Other seminal teachers include Wolf Wein, Kai Eckhardt, Jimmy Earl, as well as all her teachers at the University of Miami, especially Ron Miller and Gary Keller.

Highlights of her performance activities include recording with GRAMMY-winning producer Keith Olsen, touring with the Celtic rock band Tempest, the kindie-rockers "The Sippy Cups," Generation Esmeralda, Muriel Anderson, Tierra Negra, and many others.

Ariane co-leads the acclaimed duo "OoN — The bassoon-bass duo of Paul Hanson and Ariane Cap." and collaborates with Stuart Hamm as a bass duo. Ariane is the co-curator of *solobassnight.com*, a series dedicated to bass as a solo instrument.

Her blog and courses can be found at *arisbassblog.com*. Visit her artist page at *arianecap.com*.

Wolf Wein started playing bass at age 14 and became a professional player right after high school. While busy working in bands of many styles, from Heavy Metal to Jazz/Fusion, he studied classical upright and later Jazz Performance in the USA. Wolf holds a Masters of Music from the University of South Florida.

Wolf co-led and produced several bands and started writing and arranging for them. This inspired more and more composing activities, and he soon found himself in demand to create original music and sound design for video games, educational media and TV Shows. His clients include LeapFrog, Somatone, D-Sonic, PowerHouse Gaming, and others. His website is *WolfTrackAudio.com*.

Through his composing, Wolf gained valuable perspectives on the role of the bass within an arrangement and the great versatility inherent in the instrument. Wolf is also the producer of OoN, a Guitar Violist, and principal composer and contributor at *ArisBassBlog*.

When not deeply involved in music, Wolf is a student of The Dao.

Connect

Find us on Social:

https://www.facebook.com/groups/aribass

https://www.facebook.com/CapCatBass/

https://www.linkedin.com/in/arianecap/

@Arisbassblog on Instagram